AMERICAN CHILDHOODS

A Series Edited by James Marten

The Greatest Generation Grows Up

The
Greatest Generation
Grows Up

American Childhood in the 1930s

KRISTE LINDENMEYER

Ivan R. Dee

CHICAGO 2005

THE GREATEST GENERATION GROWS UP. Copyright © 2005 by
Kriste Lindenmeyer. All rights reserved, including the right to reproduce this
book or portions thereof in any form. For information, address: Ivan R. Dee,
Publisher, 1332 North Halsted Street, Chicago 60622. Manufactured in the
United States of America and printed on acid-free paper.

www.ivanrdee.com

Library of Congress Cataloging-in-Publication Data:

Lindenmeyer, Kriste, 1955–
  The greatest generation grows up / Kriste Lindenmeyer.
    p. cm.
  Includes bibliographical references and index.
  ISBN 1-56663-660-4 (cloth : alk. paper)
  1. Children—United States—Social conditions—20th century. 2. Teenagers—
United States—Social conditions—20th century. 3. Family—United States—
History—20th century. 4. Depressions—1929—United States. 5. New Deal,
1933–1939. 6. Teenagers—United States—Biography. 7. Children—United
States—Biography. 8. United States—Social conditions—1918–1932. 9. United
States—Social conditions—1933–1945. 10. United States—Biography. I. Title.
HQ792.U5L56 2005
973.91'6—dc22

                                                    2005017643

This book is lovingly dedicated to my parents and stepmother,
Rebecca Lynne, Wally Lindenmeyer, and Doris Lindenmeyer

Contents

Acknowledgments *xi*

Introduction *3*

1 Stable and Fragile Families in Hard Times *9*

2 Work, If You Could Find It *46*

3 Transient Youth: On the Road to Nowhere? *78*

4 The Importance of Being Educated *110*

5 Players and Consumers in Popular Culture *156*

6 Uncle Sam's Children *206*

7 Modern Childhood and the New Deal Generation *241*

Notes *247*

A Note on Sources *282*

Index *291*

Acknowledgments

ALMOST TEN YEARS AGO I shared a memorable dinner in a rural Mississippi catfish restaurant heavy with the smells and visual images that would have been familiar to many people who grew up in 1930s America. My dinner companions were a small group of scholars interested in the history of childhood. Philip Greven sparked an interesting discussion by remarking that despite our best efforts to be objective, we should be aware that in the end we were all writing about ourselves.

I have often thought about Philip's comment while working on this book. It seems especially significant since the work attempts to tell the story of the early experiences of a generation that guided me to adulthood. Recognizing this personal connection also emphasizes the fact that I did not complete this project alone. I owe an enormous debt to many people who helped to shape the ideas argued in this book. Of course, any errors and omissions are solely my own.

I want to begin by thanking the editor of the American Childhoods series, James Marten, for inviting me to write this book. His thoughtful suggestions improved the manuscript by sharpening the work's overall focus and chapter themes. Having worked with Jim on several projects, I am amazed at his professionalism, speed, and efficiency. The same is true of Ivan Dee, who patiently waited for me to finish this project, offered helpful suggestions for improving the text, and quickly but carefully guided the book to publication.

I gained insights about growing up during the 1930s by talking to many people who had lived through that experience. I especially want to thank the individuals who allowed me to quote them in this book: Mary Caliguri, Rebecca Lynne, Rueben Walter Lindenmeyer, Doris Lindenmeyer, Hiroko Kamikawa Omata, and Robert Omata. Special thanks also to Raymond F. Smith, who shared his own memories and loaned me a copy of his cousin John Smith Barney's privately published book about growing up in rural southeastern Ohio.

I also owe much to Sabine Schindler, who read early drafts of several chapters and offered useful comments based on her extensive expertise in modern American history, popular culture, and memory. Lengthy discussions about the book with Jeanette Keith also contributed important revisions to my analysis. My longtime mentor Roger Daniels went above and beyond the call of duty by quickly answering my questions and locating needed materials. Others who unselfishly replied to my calls for help include Vincent DiGiorlamo, Sharon Knecht, Donna Omata, Ed Orser, Shelley Sallee, Melissa Walker, and Errol Lincoln Uys.

Archivists and librarians are essential to every history project. The many professionals who have my gratitude include Janice Ruth and Bonnie Coles at the Library of Congress, Karen Klinkenberg at the University of Minnesota Archives, Thomas Hollowak at the University of Baltimore's Langsdale Library, and the Social Security Administration's historian, Larry DeWitt. I am also indebted to the staff at the University of Maryland, Baltimore County's Special Collections department: Drew Alfgren, John Beck, and Marcia Peri, who searched for and scanned many of the illustrations included in this book.

The University of Maryland, Baltimore County provided the supplementary funds and release time that made it possible for me to accept a Fulbright Senior Fellowship for 2004–2005. My colleagues in the history department at UMBC, especially John Jeffries and Joe

Tatarewicz, provided the collegial support necessary for a year that took me away from my usual administrative duties and commitments to students. In addition to Sabine Schindler, other colleagues at Martin-Luther-Universität, Halle-Wittenberg—Hans-Jürgen Grabbe, Christa Hartwig, and Anke Hildebrandt-Mirtschink—helped make my year in Germany an exceptional and productive experience.

Finally I wish to express my deep appreciation to my husband, Michael Dick. Besides offering unflinching emotional support, he read drafts of the manuscript and conducted library research. Above all, I thank him for his willingness to maintain our home in Baltimore while I completed this book more than four thousand miles away. I hope that seeing the final product helps to make up for that sacrifice.

K. L.

Halle, Germany
May 2005

The Greatest Generation Grows Up

Introduction

IN HIS 1998 book *The Greatest Generation*, Tom Brokaw provid[...] label for the group of young Americans who grew up during [...] Great Depression and entered adulthood in the war years. Whi[...] is fair to argue with Brokaw's sweeping premise claiming that [...] was "the greatest generation any society has ever produced," it is [...] the purpose of my book to refute or support that judgment.[1] [...] stead this synthesis concentrates on the important shifts in the c[...] tural and legal construction of childhood that shaped the lives [...] children and adolescents growing up during America's Great D[...] pression. It also tries to include some of the voices of young peop[...] born during the 1920s and 1930s.

Historians have generally overlooked children and adolescent[...] as active participants in the history of this seminal decade. Thi[...] book attempts to show how children both influenced and were th[...] targets of important social and political changes during the Great Depression years. At the time, many child-welfare advocates argued that the nation's economic crisis hit young Americans hardest. This was certainly the case for some children and their families, but others seemed untouched by the nation's economic turmoil. All, however, were witness to important shifts that embedded an ideal of modern American childhood in popular culture, law, and public policy. For the first time in U.S. history, the federal government provided a legal definition of childhood dependency extending

ıgh age seventeen. In addition, New Deal programs
ɔvernment intervention was necessary to help elim-
ities in opportunity among young citizens.

this shift failed to extend the ideal or even its basic
children and adolescents either during the Great
the decades that followed. Ambiguities in public
ɛd with a legacy of discriminatory social practices
inment of both the short- and long-term goals in
forts directed at children, adolescents, and youth.
nplementation of definitions of childhood, and
ɛral government as ultimate protector for Amer-
ɛed a significant shift from past ideas that had
dualism over commonality in the lives of the na-
ızens.

led a
the
le it
this
not
In-
ul-
of
e-
le

s
s

aintain that childhood is a social construction that
ɛr time. Many scholars have convincingly argued
ɔeen several American childhoods over the course of
.he 1930s marked an especially important one. It is
describe what life was like for every individual grow-
ɾica during this important decade. Even young people
ne family experienced the world in a unique way. The
perspectives of historical analyses that include race,
ıty, gender, age, and place also complicate the story.

pite the wide range of individual experiences, the major-
ng Americans growing up during the depression years
ne common themes. Overall public policy reinforced an
omoted in popular culture—of American childhood as a
ife protected from adult responsibilities. The model placed
l emphasis on an extended adolescence as a transitional
between childhood dependency and adult independence.
o, spending time in school rather than on the job became
ɾmative experience of childhood and adolescence. States en-
l compulsory school attendance laws more than ever before

and raised minimum-age-of-marriage requirements. Such laws varied somewhat by state because there was no federal regulation of these issues. But throughout the United States childhood dependency expanded. And for the first time in American history a federal law, the 1938 Fair Labor Standards Act, enforced restrictions on most children's wage work through age seventeen. This modern ideal of childhood as a separate, sheltered and protected stage of life had been around since at least the mid-nineteenth century, but it took the social and economic turmoil of the 1930s to stimulate the creation of a legal and cultural framework promoting the model as the normative experience for all Americans through age seventeen.

This does not mean that every young person growing up in the United States in the 1930s had an idyllic childhood or even one that simply matched the outer framework of the modern ideal. Quite to the contrary, a large proportion of young Americans struggled simply to survive the decade's hard times. Unemployment and economic loss among adults forced many children and teens to mature at an early age. At the same time other young Americans and their families escaped severe economic problems and lived lives that mirrored the modern ideal. But whatever their individual circumstances, those who grew up in the 1930s generation witnessed new public policies and a more universally accessible popular culture built on the modern ideal of childhood. New Deal programs promoted this definition by providing federal funding for needy families and communities, and through new regulations directed at children and teens. In other words, the 1930s established the legal and cultural infrastructure for the ideal of American childhood that proliferated in the postwar years.

Interestingly, this shift occurred at the same time children and adolescents made up a sharply smaller proportion of the total population than had been the case in the past. Rising life expectancy and lower birthrates contributed to a gradual rise in the median age in the United States, from twenty-three in 1900 to twenty-six in 1930.

An even lower birthrate and a continued rise in life expectancy caused a jump in the nation's median age to twenty-nine by 1940. During the Great Depression individuals under nineteen formed a smaller portion of the total population than any generation of younger Americans to that point in history. That trend temporarily reversed during the baby-boom years of the 1950s and 1960s, but it returned soon after, reflecting the smaller size of modern American families and the greying of the nation's population in the later decades of the twentieth century.[3]

In the 1930s policymakers generally used the term "children" to refer to all Americans under age eighteen. But the period also contained a trend defining adolescence—approximately the years between age thirteen and eighteen—as a period distinct from that of younger children and adults. "Youth" referred to individuals from eighteen to approximately age twenty-five. The term "teenager" did not become common until at least the 1940s, though some observers in the 1930s referred to "teens" and "teenaged" individuals. Many people at the time talked about "kids" and "youngsters" as interchangeable terms referring to anyone under eighteen. I have used the terms common to the Great Depression decade to refer to the generation that is the heart of this book (though to avoid tedious prose I sometimes use the term "youth" as a blanket description).

My interpretation has benefited greatly from the work of other historians and scholars. I have done some archival research and conducted several oral histories, but the book relies on extensive use of edited collections of letters and oral histories gathered by others, as well as memoirs written by individuals who grew up in the 1930s. Some of these works report unidentified voices of children and adolescents. I have followed the model of earlier scholars in these cases. For example, Robert Cohen's excellent edited collection of letters sent by children and adolescents to Eleanor Roosevelt identifies writers only by their initials and place of residence. I have respected Cohen's editorial decision in my citations referencing his book. In other cases I use the names of individuals whose identities have already been published or where I have received permission. I have also tried to identify the individuals mentioned in the text in the 1930 Census, though this was not possible in all cases. In quotations I have retained misspellings and grammatical mistakes. The life histories conducted by Glen Elder, Jr., and John Clausen with youth living in Oakland, California, during the 1930s are invaluable resources in my work and deserve more attention from historians.[4] Perhaps unfortunately I have few examples from immigrant children, but this decision reflects the limited number of immigrants who came to the United States in the 1930s.

Adults continue to argue about the proper role of government in the lives of young Americans and the parameters of childhood framed by public policy and popular culture. The modern ideals that no child should be hungry, suffer from abuse and neglect, or be denied access to education are goals that continue to elude the richest country in the world. The history of childhood during the 1930s provides some insights into the limitations of social policy to meet these goals. It also highlights the context of childhood as a flexible social construction that demands constant reevaluation, and rejects popular myths that idealize the past as a time of idyllic childhood.

CHAPTER ONE

Stable and Fragile Families in Hard Times

🌿 THE 1929 STOCK MARKET CRASH did not cause the Great Depression in the United States, but it certainly symbolized the economic crisis that touched the lives of many American children and their families over the next ten years. The approximately sixty-eight families living in Gee's Bend, Alabama, seemed to be far from the problems of Wall Street, but the repercussions from the nation's economic collapse in the fall of 1929 were also visible in this isolated rural community. Located in a U-shaped curve on the Alabama River, Gee's Bend was surrounded on three sides by water. A dirt road in and out of the area was impassable for much of the year. Even when conditions were good, traveling by land made the seven-mile as-the-crow-flies distance to the county seat of Camden a trip of more than forty miles. A rudimentary ferry provided an alternative route, but it operated only during good weather. Isolated and poor, the three hundred residents of Gee's Bend were the direct descendants of slaves who survived by sharecropping and a system of mutual support. Many residents had the last name Pettway, not necessarily because they were related but because their ancestors had been slaves on the plantation owned by a family with that name. In

1900 a Tuscaloosa attorney named Adrian Sebastian VandeGraaf had acquired all the land in the area, and his family became the region's absentee landlords.

A visitor to Gee's Bend in 1929 would have found children and adults living the same way that their ancestors had since the end of the Civil War: in simple shacks made of wood and mud, growing cotton and foodstuffs on small plots rented from the area's white landowner. There was only a rudimentary school. The area's residents were so isolated that other blacks in Alabama referred to the people in Gee's Bend as "Africans."

The lives of Gee's Bend residents had improved somewhat during World War I when cotton prices in New Orleans reached a high of $41.75 per pound. The end of the war, however, lowered demand, and by 1920 the price had fallen to 13.5 cents. That was enough to get by, but just barely. By the fall of 1929 things began to fall apart when the cotton market sank to 5 cents per pound. At that price families could not afford to pay the rents on their simple shacks, meet their tenancy payments, and pay off their debts to a local white merchant. Prices did not improve from 1929 to 1932, but families survived because the white merchant agreed to carry over their debts from year to year. This temporary solution collapsed when the merchant died during the summer of 1932. By that fall the merchant's widow demanded the immediate repayment of debts. Since Gee's Bend families had no cash or land, the widow's representatives confiscated anything of value, including wagons, chickens, household goods, oxen, and food. Threatened with violence if they did not cooperate, the Gee's Bend residents watched their meager but essential possessions carried away on a ferry.

Jennie Pettway was a young girl growing up in Gee's Bend during the 1930s. She remembers that the children and adults nearly starved to death that fall. The absentee landlord provided no help but did not force families off the land. Malnutrition and a lack of medical care encouraged the spread of tuberculosis and other op-

In the fall of 1932, visitors to rural Gee's Bend, Alabama, found a community of children and adults on the verge of starvation. Little had changed since the end of the Civil War, and the onset of the Great Depression only made conditions worse. *(Library of Congress)*

portunistic diseases. "Things were desperate," Jennie Pettway recalled. A Presbyterian minister from a nearby community visited Gee's Bend and was shocked at what he found. Children and adults were starving to death, illness was rampant, and there was no access to health care or basic education for children. He contacted the Red Cross, and with the help of the National Guard brought in emergency foodstuffs and shoes. The Red Cross administrator in the area remarked, "You can't imagine the horror of it. Starvation was terrific."[1] It was going to take more than traditional strategies of self-help, hard work, and charity to save the children and adults of Gee's Bend, much less bring them into the twentieth century's ideal of modern childhood.

The case of Gee's Bend is an extreme example of the deprivation brought to some Americans by the onset of the Great Depression.

But for most children and their families, cutting back, making do, and doubling up became common phrases that characterized their lives during the country's worst economic crisis. Most American households were touched in some way by the Great Depression's hard times. Yet not every young person's family suffered economic loss during the 1930s. For example, the affluent family of Henry Barr, who was born in 1928, seemed far removed from the nation's economic slide. Henry's father held degrees from a prestigious college and law school. In the early 1920s the elder Barr headed the San Francisco branch of a New York law firm. He left that position in 1926 to start his own business. Henry's mother had attended an elite women's college before marrying. At the time of Henry's birth the Barrs also had a four-year-old son and a two-year-old daughter. During the 1930s the family lived in what an interviewer from the University of California at Berkeley's "Oakland Growth Study" described as "a large, vine-covered, masonry house set on a terraced lot, with substantial lawn and garden." Full-time nannies tended to Henry and his siblings, and the children attended schools with youngsters from similar family circumstances. Once Henry reached the upper-level elementary grades, he spent his summers at camp and enjoyed a variety of recreational activities. He received a "moderate" allowance from his parents, and from the age of twelve earned money at part-time jobs such as "gardening for neighbors, working as a stock boy, selling mistletoe at Christmas." Henry did not need the money; the jobs were supposed to instill a strong "work ethic" in the growing boy. From an early age, Henry felt he was "destined for the law," and his pathway to social and economic success as an adult was not hampered by the fact that he grew up during the worse economic crisis in U.S. history.[2]

Henry Barr's childhood was very different from the lives of children in Gee's Bend and, in fact, from those of most Americans growing up during the Great Depression. Still, even children and adolescents like Barr, whose parents were able to shelter them from

Some affluent families were able to escape the decade's hard times and provide their children with the commercial pleasures of modern childhood. The boy is playing with an erector set, first sold in 1913. *(University of Maryland, Baltimore County)*

the major deprivations of hard times, witnessed the shifts in popular culture and public policy influenced by the depression. Children and adolescents living in families that Franklin Roosevelt identified as "ill-housed, ill-clothed, and ill-fed" became the focus of New Deal efforts to ease the depression's worst effects. Many children and adolescents growing up in families that lost income during the 1930s took part in their parents' efforts to maintain a "brave social front that local canon of respectable competence require a family to present to its neighbors." Some historians have speculated that such issues may not have been as important to children from families that were already poor or members of the working class before the onset of the depression. But it appears that during the 1930s, many children, especially adolescents and youth at the lower rungs of

American society, were unhappy about their families' circumstances and the inequities highlighted by the decade's economic challenges. Shifts in public policy and popular culture probably contributed to this trend.[3]

Despite the infinite possibilities in individual circumstances, the 1930s generation shared some common features. For one, the median age in the United States had risen gradually, from twenty-three in 1900 to twenty-six in 1930, and then climbed sharply to twenty-nine during the depression decade.[4] Adults simply chose to have fewer babies during hard economic times. This allowed them to focus their available family resources and energies on fewer children, thereby underscoring reformers' efforts to establish childhood and adolescence as a sheltered and protected stage of life for all American children. Life expectancy continued to rise, also contributing to the higher median age. During the depression, children under nineteen years of age formed a smaller portion of the total population than any generation to that date in U.S. history. As in the past, society depended on families to care for the economic security, psychological development, safety, and health of children. But the onset of the depression challenged the long-held belief that families could accomplish those tasks without help from the government. This shift occurred at the same time a growing number of Americans embraced a model of ideal American childhood as a period best spent in school and protected from adult responsibilities through age seventeen. By 1940 public policy and popular culture recognized this ideal as the sole model for modern American childhood.

Despite popular acceptance of the model, the decade's economic problems shook many stable families and completely toppled the most fragile ones. The same study that included Henry Barr also uncovered stories of other children in Oakland who lived in families directly affected by hard times. The mothers of children and adolescents in the study attributed "problems with offspring, kin, friends, and community roles . . . to lack of money and its side effects."[5] Many other families throughout the United States would have shared this circumstance. Seventy-seven percent of American households had incomes of less than $2,000 per year (the equivalent of $30,000 in 2000). Between 1929 and 1933 the national average household income fell from $2,300 to $1,500. New Deal programs aimed at providing work-relief pumped millions of federal dollars into the nation's infrastructure. Combined federal and state relief efforts kept the poorest American families from starving and also helped improve the lives of many children and adults who were not direct recipients of federal relief. But as late as 1940, 35 million American homes still had no running water, 32 percent continued to rely on outdoor privies, 39 percent did not have a bathtub or shower, and 27 percent contained no refrigeration device. From the perspective of a glass half full rather than half empty, these numbers also show that by the end of the depression decade most children did have access to at least the basic amenities associated with growing up in modern America. The years after Franklin Roosevelt's election in 1932 brought a new attitude to Washington that included the implementation of an alphabet soup of federal agencies and programs that helped ease the depression's worst effects for many children and their families. That shift was part of a new definition of modern American childhood that became embedded in law, public policy, and culture by the end of the decade. The trend continued through the 1940s, especially after World War II, making conveniences like electricity nearly universal for American families by 1950.[6]

When I Was Young

Many people who grew up during the Great Depression talk about how the nation's troubled economic times permanently influenced their attitudes toward money and security. Throughout their lives the 1930s generation tended to be more frugal than those who followed. They saved more and were less likely to go into debt since they held what the sociologist Glen Elder calls "a heightened belief in the power of money."[7] Memories of childhood in the 1930s expressed by Robert Hastings and Mary Caliguri are somewhat typical of those shared by many Americans who grew up in stable families but were still touched by the decade's hard times.

"I didn't go hungry during the Depression, but some things I did get hungry for. Milk, for instance. I never got enough," Robert Hastings wrote in his memoir about growing up during the 1930s. Robert was born in 1924 in Marion, Illinois, where his ancestors had lived for several generations. He was the youngest of four children and probably "a surprise" for his parents since nine years separated him and his next-oldest sibling. Even if unplanned, "Bobbie" was welcomed to the family. When Robert was small, the milkman delivered a fresh bottle of milk each morning. That ended when the Old West Side Mine closed in 1930 and Robert's father lost his job. "From 1930 on," Robert recalled, "it was a day's work here and a day's work there, a coal order from the welfare office, a relief check, a few days on WPA [Works Progress Administration], a garden in the back yard, and a few chickens and eggs." The family "cut back on everything possible. . . . We stopped the evening paper, turned off the city water and cleaned out our well, sold our four-door Model T touring car with the snap-on side curtains and isinglass, stopped ice and milk delivery, and disconnected our gas range for all but the three hot summer months," chopping wood for the stove the rest of the year.[8]

Like many families, the Hastingses cut back and made do, but also like most households in small towns and the rural countryside they had no telephone to disconnect. Their everyday lives were absent many of the conveniences available to urban Americans. Marion did attract a small for-profit utility company that provided gas and electricity, but the Hastingses had only a few electric lights in their house and one electrical appliance, an iron. The monthly bill for electricity had to stay under one dollar so they could afford even these minimal conveniences. The family spent only three dollars a year on natural gas fuel. Robert Hastings remembered the amounts because he rode his bicycle to town each month with the money to pay the utilities. Even from a young age, Robert remembers being very aware of family expenses and the best ways to save money. For example, the Hastingses used baking soda instead of toothpaste, pages from mail-order catalogues for toilet paper, and had no water or sewer bill since they relied on well water and had an outhouse. Reflecting his rural way of life, Robert had simple tastes. His favorite meal was milk and cornbread. Nonetheless he was bothered by his family's lack of money. He remembered being embarrassed about the lunches his mother made for him to take to school because they included sandwiches made with homemade biscuits rather than the store-bought white bread carried by some of his more affluent friends. Like the Hastingses, most families tried to save on food expenses, spending an average of 24 percent of their disposable income on food and rarely eating in restaurants. A single person could do well surviving on ten-to-fifteen-cent blue-plate specials in local diners, but even such inexpensive restaurant meals were out of reach for many families.[9]

The Hastingses had it better than some but did not do as well as others. They had some good luck when the local bank offered to settle the outstanding debt on every mortgage in the community for ten cents on the dollar. Hundreds of banks closed after the 1929 crash when they were unable to collect on outstanding debts, mostly consisting of home mortgages. For the Hastingses, the bank's offer meant a single payment of $125—a bargain, but still more money than the family had on hand. An aunt who received a small pension for her late husband's military service during the Spanish-American War loaned them the money. Hastings recalled, "I knew my father for forty-four years, but I never remember a day when he showed more elation" than the day he came "home to tell us the house was saved—it was ours!"[10]

There had never been much to do in small towns like Marion, Illinois. Children entertained themselves by playing games with friends, riding bicycles, and listening to the radio. Some older adolescents and youths in small towns often had access to cars and trucks since there was no public transportation and families depended on private vehicles as part of their survival. The onset of the depression, however, forced many families like the Hastingses to sell their cars. Living in town helped the Hastingses since stores, the local school, and other public buildings were within walking distance of their home. In communities like Marion, schools and churches served as centers of social activities. But especially in the early 1930s schools struggled to stay open due to a crippling loss of tax revenue, and many families quit going to church in order to avoid having to put money in the collection plate. Robert attended the local public school but noted that in the early 1930s the term was cut from nine to eight months in order to save money.

Going to school beyond the elementary grades became more common in the 1930s, despite the decade's hard times. Robert's older brothers had dropped out of school even before the worst days of the depression, and his mother and father had completed only the fifth and eighth grades, respectively. Unlike the older sons who had come of age during the 1920s, both of Robert's parents encouraged their youngest boy to continue his studies. As his parents had hoped, Robert earned a high school diploma and also went on to college. Even with the problems that faced many children and their families in the late 1930s, for the first time in American history most seventeen-year-olds attended high school and more went on to college than ever before.

The Hastings family experienced hardships as the depression hit their community and the nation, but things got better by the end of the 1930s. On May 22, 1939, the Hastingses paid a four-dollar deposit to the local water department and installed an indoor bathroom. Cutting back and making do were part of everyday life, but hard times did not keep Robert Hastings from holding fond memories of growing up in a small town supported by a poor but stable family.[11]

Mary Caliguri also has fond memories of her childhood, but like Robert Hastings she still recalls the effects of the depression on her family. Caliguri and Hastings shared a similar socioeconomic status, but their family backgrounds and the neighborhoods where they grew up were very different. Both had fathers who had worked as miners before the depression, but Mary's parents moved from their small hometown of Barnesboro, Pennsylvania, to Brooklyn, New York, in 1930, when she was about six months old. Her parents, who were both born in the United States to Italian-American parents, wanted a life "away from the coal mines." Her father found a job as a truck driver for a lumber company, but the work was not steady. Her grandfather worked for the WPA, but Mary is not sure if her father ever held a work-relief job. Some men and women were embarrassed to accept WPA employment. Others claimed they felt frustrated when treated with disrespect by higher-paid supervisors. A few also wrote letters to President Roosevelt and other government officials complaining that the relief payments were too low to help families survive. Overwhelmingly, however, Americans employed by the WPA welcomed the small paychecks as better than nothing. And even WPA jobs were scarce. The New Deal program provided only a small proportion of jobs to the millions who applied. Even if the Caliguris did not receive work-relief through the WPA or other federal programs, their neighborhood housed exactly the kinds of families that benefited from New Deal funding.[12]

The uncertain employment situation meant that families in Mary's neighborhood watched their pennies carefully. They often found ways to bring income into the household that did not rely solely on a father's employment. For example, when Americans "doubled up," they moved in with extended family or close friends

"We'd starve without WPA," explained this young mother whose husband held a federal relief job in Carbon Hill, Alabama. *(National Archives)*

in order to cut living expenses. Mary remembers that "a lot of family came to live with us off and on." Living conditions were crowded since both of the Caliguris' New York apartments had only four rooms: a living room, kitchen, and two bedrooms. Bathrooms were in the hall and shared by at least one other family. Some families also took in boarders, a common practice used by many people trying to make ends meet.

Another strategy was to send mothers into the paid labor force. When Mary was eight years old, her mother, like a growing number of women throughout the United States, got a job. Approximately 25 percent of American women worked for wages in 1930, and the rate rose only 1 percent by 1940. But the composition of the female labor force changed. In 1930 just under 12 percent of married women worked outside the home. By 1940 the rate had risen to just under 16 percent. A higher proportion of married black women had always worked outside their homes, but the practice became more common among all racial and ethnic groups during the 1930s.

Mary remembers that other mothers in her Brooklyn neighborhood also held jobs. In most of these families older siblings (usually girls) or female relatives living in the neighborhood cared for the young children of working mothers. That was not the case for Mary Caliguri and her sister since they had no older siblings or other extended family permanently living in Brooklyn. Mary resented having to go to a neighbor's apartment for lunch during school days, and she hated the fact that her mother was not home when she returned from school each weekday afternoon. As they grew older, girls like Mary took on domestic tasks such as cooking, cleaning, doing laundry, and caring for younger brothers and sisters. Boys from poor families also had additional responsibilities as they matured, but sons generally contributed to their families by earning money rather than taking on the domestic duties assumed by daughters. And boys also had the advantage of freedom to spend some of the money they earned. In general, boys had greater autonomy and independence from parental authority than their sisters.[13]

Even when beyond the watchful eyes of their parents, children and adolescents in Mary's neighborhood found themselves overseen by other adults. Families and friends lived within close quarters in the multi-unit housing. Mary remembers that she liked growing up in the "strictly Italian neighborhood" where she knew most of the families. During good weather, Friday night block parties drew people of all ages into the streets where they "danced, talked, listened to phonographs, and let the kids run rampant." On hot summer days "someone always opened the fire hydrant, which was great fun for the kids until the cops came by and turned them off." Mary recalled that the children also liked to fill balloons with water and launched them at one another like bombs. Her mother sometimes joined in the fun. Living in the city also gave Mary the opportunity to visit the Statue of Liberty, various municipal parks, the Bronx Zoo, and other New York sites with her family, friends, and as part of school field trips. Christmas and other holidays were important to Mary's Roman Catholic community, but parents limited holiday gifts to children to two or three practical items like "clothing or a sewing set."[14]

During many "three-day holidays" the Caliguris drove to Pennsylvania to spend time with grandparents. Mary remembered that "the roads were treacherous they were so bad." Trucks put wood and coal ashes on snow- and ice-covered roads to improve traction, but still the trips were frightening: "I sat on the floor in the backseat to avoid seeing the road." At the end of each school year Mary's father took the family south to Pennsylvania again, but he and his wife returned to Brooklyn alone, leaving Mary and her sister behind to spend the summer with their grandmother. With few other options for child care, the Caliguri girls spent their summer vacations in Barnesboro. It was fun to be in the countryside, but Mary also missed her parents. She spent every summer at her grandmother's house until age thirteen, the same year Mary's grandmother died. She remembers not wanting to go back after her grandmother's death because the house seemed empty. Losing a grandparent was a common experience for children in the 1930s. The average life expectancy in the United States rose from 63.5 in 1930 to 66.6 in 1940, but that meant that many children and adolescents still suffered the loss of at least one grandparent.[15]

Robert Hastings and Mary Caliguri lived in stable families touched by the decade's hard times but not crushed by them. Economic difficulties and growing cynicism led some adults, though, to turn to criminal behavior. Bootlegging was a common way to make money during Prohibition and beyond. A widowed mother of six children in Bridgeport, Connecticut, sold homemade wine to make money. Other parents engaged in more serious criminal behavior that ruined families. Rhuel James Dalhover teamed up with Alfred Brady to form the infamous Brady Gang. They and their associates began robbing jewelry stores and over the course of the next two years held up hundreds of businesses from Wisconsin to Maine. In the course of their criminal activities they murdered several people, including a teenaged store clerk in Ohio and at least one police officer. In 1937 Dalhover and Brady married two teenage sisters in Baltimore, Maryland. Dalhover's wife became pregnant, but his luck had run out. On October 12, 1937, Brady died in a shootout with FBI agents. Dalhover was captured at the scene and later convicted of murder. The State of Indiana executed him by electrocution on November 18, 1938. His widow gave birth to a daughter one month later. Dalhover had ruined his own life, harmed others, and made life terribly difficult for his new daughter.[16]

Obviously most parents did not turn to criminal behavior, but the death of a parent under any circumstances was usually a devastating emotional and economic blow to children, especially during the depression. In 1931 Russell, Doris, and Audrey Baker's thirty-three-year-old father died suddenly in Morrisonville, Virginia. Their mother, Lucy Elisabeth Baker, felt she could not raise three children on her own. She decided it was in the best interest of her family to split up the children. She took five-year-old Russell and two-year-old Doris with her to New Jersey where they moved in with relatives. Ten-month-old daughter Audrey went to a childless aunt and uncle. The separation was permanent, not temporary. The sudden death of the children's father would have been difficult anytime, but the onset of the depression made things worse. Jobs were hard to find, and the entire Baker family had been hurt by the worsening economy. As an adult, Russell Baker wrote that his mother's decision to give up his youngest sister had haunted him throughout his lifetime.[17]

Even the expected death of a parent did not make it easier to deal with the loss. Jane McMahon's father was ill for several months before he died in 1932. His long illness made it impossible for him to plant a crop that year on the family's farm in southern Colorado, so his surviving widow and children had little food to hold them over the winter. Completely out of supplies during a terrible snow-storm, Jane's mother rode a horse in search of a neighbor willing to sell the family food. After several refusals she finally found a neigh-bor who gave her enough beans to feed the family. Things did not get much better over the next four years. Jane remembered that her mother "tried to hang on as long as she could." Since there was no man in the household, other ranchers in the area tried to take ad-vantage of the family by placing livestock on the McMahons' prop-erty. Jane and her siblings chased the animals from their land, but other problems remained. Water was a huge challenge because Jane's mother did not have enough money to drill a well. "So we'd take a wagon to the river and back it right into the water to fill up our barrels," Jane recalled. "We only had enough water for the house and the stock—not much for baths." Then the drought and winds arrived in what became known as the Dust Bowl. "There was nothing to stop them, so they just ripped the topsoil up and sent it flyin'," Jane lamented. "Finally in 1937, there was nothing left, so we walked away. We just walked away from it; sold the animals and left. By that time my oldest brother was on WPA. . . . My mother and I went into town looking for housecleaning jobs."[18]

Illness and death devastated families even before the Great De-pression, but the decade's hard times presented added challenges. Stuart Campbell was born in 1920. His parents, who had immi-grated to the United States from Scotland, had two children after Stuart—Barbara born in 1922 and James born in 1924. The children's mother died of tuberculosis in 1926 and their father, devastated by his wife's death, soon abandoned his children. He died in Canada in 1933. The Campbell children's widowed maternal grandmother became their primary caretaker and guardian. She had come from Scotland to Oakland, California, to care for them after her daughter's death. The Campbells survived on a pension from a small trust fund left by their late grandfather, but money was always tight. While growing up, Stuart Campbell confessed that he always carried with him the fear that someone in his small family might die. Having lost both his parents when he was young, and growing up during the uncertain years of the depression, made it difficult for him to feel a sense of security about his family or the future. Providing security for children like Stuart Campbell who had lost a parent, or even both parents, became a major goal for a growing number of reformers and politicians during the 1930s.[19]

The Federal Government and America's Families

By 1930 it was obvious that something was terribly wrong with an American economy that threatened even the most stable families and devastated those that were more fragile. For several decades politicians and child-welfare advocates had been working to improve the lives of America's youngest citizens. Theodore Roosevelt had sponsored the first White House Conference on children in 1909. Agreeing with the Swedish reformer Ellen Key, participants at that meeting had argued that the next hundred years would be "the century of the child." Partly in response to demands from conference participants and their supporters who continued to lobby federal authorities, three years later Congress established the U.S. Children's Bureau. President Woodrow Wilson called the second White House Conference on children in 1919. One outcome of that meeting was passage of the 1921 Sheppard-Towner Maternity and

Infancy Act, the first federal legislation directed at reducing infant and maternal mortality in the United States through education, public nurses, and diagnostic clinics.[20]

By the time delegates met for President Herbert Hoover's 1930 White House Conference on Child Health and Protection, the Sheppard-Towner Act had been allowed to expire and the United States had slipped into depression. The troubled economic times and Herbert Hoover's own interest in children's issues, especially child health, seemed to suggest that the time had come for the federal government to address the needs of children and families aggressively. In his opening remarks welcoming conference participants to Washington, Hoover explained that "the fundamental purpose of this conference is to set forth an understanding of those safeguards which will assure to them health in mind and body." He maintained that "there are safeguards and services to childhood which can be provided by the community, the State, or the Nation—all of which are beyond the reach of the individual parent. . . . If we could have one generation of properly born, trained, educated, and healthy children, a thousand other problems of government would vanish."[21] Most adults probably agreed with the president that children had a right to protection, but there was little national consensus on how that should be accomplished, or even exactly what years of life encompassed childhood for America's youngest citizens.

The outcome of the 1930 conference mirrored this ambiguity. In hindsight the conference did little to help America's children, and the president did not call for federal action on their behalf. Conference reports even avoided a clear definition of childhood dependency. The nineteen-point Children's Charter was the only major outcome of the conference. Replete with romantic and optimistic phrases, the document described guidelines "recognizing the rights of the child as the rights of citizenship." As an editorial in the *Nation* concluded, the meeting resulted in "little tangible achievement." It is unfair to say that Herbert Hoover did nothing to try to soften the blows of the Great Depression for America's children and adults. Nonetheless the Hoover administration did too little too late and did not initiate a single program specifically directed at helping children.[22]

Hoover's disinterest in acting to protect the rights of America's youngest citizens through government action could not have occurred at a worse time. The president distrusted reports from the U.S. Children's Bureau and his own Emergency Committee on Employment showing a direct relationship between high unemployment rates and rising evidence of malnutrition and poor health among America's children. When disastrous floods struck parts of Arkansas, Kentucky, and Tennessee in 1931, Hoover announced that the Army Corps of Engineers confirmed that relief services in the area were "adequately meeting the existing need." Children's Bureau reports that same year came to a very different conclusion. Other evidence of the declining quality of life for young Americans was the rise in relief expenditures to urban families of almost 90 percent in only the first year after the stock market crash. Worsening conditions were visible to many Americans. Homeless families and individuals built makeshift shelters out of cardboard and scrap metal in squatter settlements that the public disparagingly called "Hoovervilles." Long lines for free soup and bread distributed by private charities and local governments were obvious testaments to hard times. A growing army of transients wandered the nation looking for work. The commissioner of relief services in Salt Lake City claimed that hundreds of children in his city were slowly starving to death and being kept home from school because they had nothing to wear. A social worker in West Virginia reported that a man found cremating his dead infant explained that he did not have money to pay for a funeral. National suicide rates rose from 14 per 100,000 in 1929 to 17.4 in 1932.

Adults able to hold on to jobs had their wages cut and hours reduced; almost three-quarters of the nation's workers were employed only part-time. Unemployment reached almost 13 million, translating to the reality that 28 percent of American households did not contain a single wage earner. For older teens and youth, it was twice as hard to find employment as it was for adults. On average, black Americans experienced unemployment rates as much as three times those of whites. In Chicago the typical black family earned an income half that of native-born whites in the same city. Mexican-American families also suffered at disproportional levels, and some became scapegoats targeted for deportation. More than 300,000 Mexican Americans, some of them U.S. citizens, were forcibly deported in the 1930s. Bad times "encouraged" another 82,000 people of Mexican ancestry to leave the United States. In Los Angeles County in 1931, welfare rolls rose from 3,500 to 35,000. More than half of American Indian families living on reservations had incomes of less than $200 per year. Many farmers had not benefited from the nation's overall prosperity during the 1920s and fell into even more dire circumstances after 1929. Some who had owned their land before 1930 lost it as banks failed and farm prices collapsed. Environmental catastrophes—drought in the Midwest, flooding in the central South—added to the problems of rural children and their families.[23]

Despite this deepening pool of evidence, the Hoover administration continued to maintain that the economic crisis was only temporary and not as serious for children as it might appear. At the height of the nation's unemployment crisis, Hoover's close adviser and secretary of the interior, Ray Lyman Wilbur, told Americans, "unless we descend to a level far beyond anything that we at present have known, our children are apt to profit, rather than suffer, from what is going on." Although wrongheaded, Wilbur was not alone. An editorial in a Muncie, Indiana, newspaper claimed, "Many a family that has lost its car has found its soul."[24]

While some people may have agreed with such remarks, government agencies, private charities, and average Americans understood the accumulating evidence. The individual choices being made by many Americans showed that they were trying to adapt to hard times. Marriage rates dropped during the early years of the depression, and, as noted, birthrates declined to the lowest levels up to that point in American history. The divorce rate also declined, but the rising frequency of husbands deserting their wives and children showed that marital harmony was not a positive consequence of rising unemployment and lost wages.[25] The psychological effects on families are difficult to measure, but anecdotal as well as statistical data support the idea that tensions rose within many households, especially among those stressed by unemployment, underemployment, and the accompanying loss of social and economic status.

The Health of Families

While the loss of a breadwinner could devastate a family, poverty also contributed to rising ill health. And illness forced many families into poverty. Studies conducted in the 1930s suggested that families on relief were twice as likely to include someone with a chronic disease as those who had moderate incomes of at least $3,000 per year. The Farm Security Administration found that illness was the major contributing factor in half the agency's loan defaults. Many people who had slipped out of the middle class into poverty suffered the most severe health problems because embarrassment and pride kept them from taking advantage of government programs or private charities that might have helped. In other words, adolescents and children from families with the steepest decline in status were the most likely to suffer from malnutrition, disease, and even death due to insufficient medical care.

This does not mean that most parents intentionally neglected their children's health. Caregivers did what they believed to be appropriate when children or other relatives fell ill. Every family

carried a heritage of home remedies transferred from one generation to the next, and many people turned a suspicious eye toward
doctors and hospitals. Whiskey, Epsom salts, and cod liver oil
served as common medicines in most families' arsenals against illness. Some caregivers used goose grease and turpentine, rubbed
into the chest and back and covered with warm flannel, as a standard remedy for colds and chills. Teas made from various roots
and herbs might ease a loved one's suffering. Other remedies
could be potentially harmful. A man from Oregon remembered
that sick children were given tea made from dried animal dung.
"In the case of my grandmother," he explained, "the most effica-
ciously medicinal dung is that of the swine, the common sty-pig,
which, when dried and baked in an oven and made into a tea is
said to cure evils of all sorts, from the slightest indisposition to
measles and smallpox." Children drank the stuff, "being too
young to know what the concoction was."[26] Science and medical
care had made significant advances by the 1930s, but doctors and
hospitals cost money, and health insurance was rare. The limited
health insurance plans that did exist were generally linked to full-
time employment, a problem for most Americans during the
1930s. Even if people trusted hospitals and could afford care,
many were too far away to do much good.

The heartbreaking situation that arose for Robert Hastings's
family in the spring of 1936 was shared by many people living outside the nation's cities. When Robert's twenty-year-old brother,
LaVerne, arrived at the family's home for a visit, he felt ill. He had
recently been diagnosed with diabetes and thought that eating
something and getting some rest would take care of things. After
eating, spending a day trying to relax, and getting a footbath from
his mother, LaVerne did not improve. In the middle of the night he
awakened his family complaining of severe nausea and a high fever.
His parents considered their options: the nearest hospital was ten
miles away, and most townsfolk viewed it only as a place where peo-

ple went "to die." The best hospital in the area was seventeen miles away in Carbondale, Illinois, but the family had sold their car when Robert's father lost his job. The family also had no telephone, so they could not even call the local doctor for help. When the sun came up, they sent for him. He suggested larger doses of insulin, but "with every shot LaVerne grew weaker." A product of his local community, even the doctor did not suggest hospitalization. Two days later LaVerne died in his parents' home. The Great Depression did not cause his death, but the family's isolation and poor circumstances contributed to the sad outcome.[27]

Caring for the sick and the chronically ill had always been one of the primary functions of American families. During the 1930s, illness added strains to families already stressed by hard times. In 1934 a fourteen-year-old girl from the Bronx, New York, wrote to Eleanor Roosevelt to ask the first lady for a bicycle. Thousands of children wrote begging letters to Eleanor and Franklin Roosevelt during the 1930s asking for everything from bicycles to clothing, money, and even cars, but this girl's request was slightly different. "I have diabetes," she explained. "You might not know much about this disease but it is most unpleasant and painful. I take needles twice a day which hurt extremely. As you can see I haven't gotten much fun out of life. I also cannot eat a bit of sweets. . . . I have thought several times of committing suicide." The depression did not cause the girl's diabetes, but her family's economic circumstances made life more difficult. "I received nothing for Christmas because my father makes $18 a week. . . . My medicines cost $3 a week. This . . . takes up a lot of money." If she and her sister could have "a model 18 bicycle blue in color," the girl told Mrs. Roosevelt, things would be better. Having a bicycle offered more than fun. "If I had a bike I could ride to school and save carfare. If my sister had a bike she could run errands. . . . And if I ride to school it will use up some of the excess sugar in my blood. Please regard my request carefully."[28]

Taking care of the needs of ill children and those stricken with chronic health conditions or disabilities presented special challenges for families during the Great Depression. Even simple treatments could stretch family resources during good times, and, as with the girl from the Bronx, bad times only made things more difficult. Many doctors charged as little as possible or even offered free consultations in the 1930s. But many families still found it tough to pay for medical care. Clyde Edwards learned he had juvenile diabetes in 1930, when he was sixteen. His younger brother, Duval, remembers that the diagnosis placed another burden on the family even though Clyde was not seriously ill. The boys' father barely made enough money to keep the family fed and a roof over their heads. Keeping Clyde healthy required "a considerable, continuous cash outlay for the special medications and foods then in vogue for victims of this life-threatening disease."[29]

Injuries were another threat. By the 1930s medical science had discovered new treatments, but hospitals were still rare in many parts of the United States. Thirteen-year-old Katharine Cochrane fell one day while playing baseball. That night at dinner she told her parents about the incident but only laughed when her father suggested she see a doctor. At thirteen Katherine probably understood that her father's job at a local North Carolina textile mill provided little money to spend on medical care. Two months later, however, she began to complain of aches and pains. She was diagnosed with a spinal injury and had an expensive operation that her parents could barely afford. After the surgery everything seemed to have been worth the sacrifice, but the Cochranes' problems with their daughter's health were not over.

About six months later, Katharine had an accident while driving the family car. At the time she did not seem seriously injured, but soon it became clear that she had lost her memory. Brent Cochrane took his daughter to a hospital in Queenstown, "but the doctor there didn't know what was wrong," Cochrane remembered. He pleaded "with them to do something and they told me to try Kings Hospital. She stayed there for weeks but her mental condition showed no improvement." Katharine's father then "begged the doctors to send him to another hospital" that might offer a different treatment, "but they said it was no use." Instead they suggested that Katharine enter the State Hospital for the Insane in Overton. Over the next few months Brent Cochrane took his daughter in and out of the state hospital, but she did not improve. "I am going to take her to Johns Hopkins soon," he told a Federal Writers' Project worker in 1938. "Maybe it won't do any good but I just got to keep on trying."[30] In the 1930s, many children with disabilities ended up in institutions.

Other parents were able to keep their disabled children at home. John D. McKee was born on December 22, 1919, after his mother experienced a bad fall while walking over some ice. John arrived two months premature and weighed only two and a half pounds. Like most births before the 1940s, John's mother delivered her son at home. John later wrote what he had been told about his delivery: "There was no incubator available; so I was bundled into a clothes-basket and surrounded by hot water bottles and hot bricks wrapped in flannel." He survived but had cerebral palsy. Doctors could do little for children like John McKee during the 1920s and 1930s, and most suggested institutional care. "Treatment was by trial and error if there was any treatment at all," John explained. Through perseverance, he learned to walk and tried to live as normal a life as possible. During the depression, his parents were able to maintain a comfortable middle-class existence, but medical science could do little to help John control his spastic muscles. In high school, his disability presented special challenges, but his family's more comfortable financial circumstances helped ease some of John's difficulties.[31]

Childbirth and infant care had made tremendous progress during the early twentieth century, but monetary concerns affected this aspect of family health, especially during the depression. From 1921 to 1929 the Sheppard-Towner Maternity and Infancy Act had contributed to a reduction in preventable deaths among infants and mothers. The nation's infant mortality rate of 64 deaths per 1,000 births in 1930 was approximately half what it had been in 1900 but still ranked poorly among industrialized nations. Maternal mortality was also lower, but only slightly. Approximately 67 women died for every 10,000 births. The U.S. Children's Bureau concluded that illegal and botched abortions contributed to high maternal mortality rates. Improvements in public sanitation and access to medical care helped overcome consequences associated with economic deprivation in the 1930s. Infant and maternal mortality rates continued to decline during the decade (to 47.0 and 38.0 respectively in 1940). This was an obvious improvement, but there was still a long way to go to reach the levels of the late twentieth century (6.8 for infants and 0.1 per 10,000 live births among mothers). The greatest progress in reducing death rates among mothers and babies began during the 1940s when for the first time in American history a majority of women delivered their babies in hospitals. And birth-control information became more accessible and reliable.[32]

In the 1930s home delivery was the most common birthing experience, especially for families with limited economic resources or those living outside cities. Having a baby at home could be perfectly safe with the help of an experienced midwife, nurse, or physician and a situation free of complications. By the 1930s a growing number of Americans understood that healthy babies and mothers needed at least the help of a trained nurse or doctor at the time of delivery, but access to good care could still be difficult. Mildred Kine safely had her first child at home in Boulder City, Nevada, in January 1933. Kine was part of the wave of more than five thousand workers and their families who had moved to the area when the federal government began construction on what eventually became Hoover Dam. "I had a nurse come in and help," Kine recalled. "It was either that or go to Las Vegas, because the hospital up here was only for workmen and they didn't want to have maternity cases up there." Lillian Whalen, another Boulder City resident, remembered that a local doctor also supervised many births in the town. A lot of local deliveries occurred "on the screen porches of the little houses, with the fans drifting around. . . . evidently it was a healthy thing, because [the doctor] never lost a mother or a baby."[33]

Despite the success of the nurse and doctor in Boulder City, ill health and a lack of prenatal care among many poor mothers, exacerbated by the depression's economic conditions, raised the risks of pregnancy and threatened infant health. The example of a woman living in Carbon Hill, Alabama, who was unable to breast feed her newborn baby because she had "kidney trouble" was all too typical. Her first baby had died, and a doctor told her not to try again. But she and her husband wanted children, so they took the risk. The couple spent "$4.68 per month" on milk. "We'd starve without WPA," the young mother maintained, but even this help was barely enough to ensure good nutrition for her child.[34]

Health advocates had long known that small children and pregnant women were especially susceptible to malnutrition and its associated illnesses. The Great Depression threatened to reverse progress that had been made before 1929. A woman with seven children told a Federal Writers' Project interviewer that her family's struggle with illness had been made worse by conditions common to the depression that often separated families. The mother and six children were living alone in Maine. There were few jobs in the area, so the children's father had moved to Connecticut in search of work. Before she and the children could join him, they all fell sick with influenza. And the mother was pregnant at the time with the couple's seventh child. "There was no one to take care of us," the woman recalled. "One of the boys . . . I almost lost. He had convulsions; then when he got over that . . . [caught] Pneumonia. . . . We got by as best we could. I was so sick I had to go to bed. I felt like a pig, depriving them of care. They used to come crying to the bed saying, 'Mama, I'm sick, I'm sick.'"

The woman's multiple pregnancies had been hard on her health, and the infants had often been born in poor condition. After she gave birth to her fourth child, a doctor had told her not to have any more children because she probably would "not live through it." Information about birth control was not readily available to most poor women like this mother. Only physicians could legally distribute birth-control information in the 1930s, and most poor families did not have a private physician. What's more, this woman was a Roman Catholic, and the church prohibited the use of any birth control other than the rhythm method, though it was a church directive that couples often ignored. Nonetheless, in the 1930s, with little money to spend on doctors, many poor women relied on birth-control information passed from mother to daughter or on methods sold in pharmacies.

After giving birth to her seventh child, the mother explained, "I had hemorrhages for twenty-one days. I guess that was because I was so undernourished. Well, I didn't intend to have any more. . . . You're married, aren't you?" she asked the interviewer. "Well you know how husbands are, they don't think of your health. I guess Birth Control doesn't work with me because I'm weak. I get those— what do you call them?—suppositories from the drug store—they cost seventy-five cents a box." The Writers' Project interviewer told the mother that the suppositories were probably just a waste of money. "I wish I knew what to do," the woman sighed. She had a Polish neighbor who also needed advice. "She's having such a hard time—she's got six children, and just lost one."[35] The interviewer advised the mother to go to her local maternal health clinic. Privately funded maternal health clinics, staffed with a physician, opened in several cities in the 1930s.

Failed contraception or a lack of good information about birth control led some women to choose abortion. The procedure was illegal but was used nonetheless. Some abortionists were highly skilled, but poor and unmarried women were particularly vulnerable to less qualified practitioners, and some desperate women died after self-induced abortions.[36]

Many of the health problems faced by low-income families in the 1930s would have been familiar during any period of American history. But the recording of such problems by the federal government drew new attention to illness in America's most vulnerable families. A woman recorded by a Federal Writers' Project worker as "Mrs. A, a French Canadian," had four children, three boys and a girl. At the time of the interview in 1939, the youngest boy and the three-year-old girl had "colds." The little girl had been sick for about three weeks but had not yet seen a doctor. "She has a fever one day, and the next day it goes, and then comes back again," Mrs. A recounted. "If she don't get better soon, I'll have to call the doctor." Mrs. A hesitated because the family could not afford doctors.

Mr. A had what his wife described as "a brain clot." He had worked for the WPA for a while, but the job had been too physically demanding. He had frequent and incapacitating headaches. The family survived on charity, disability relief, and two dollars a week Mr. A. earned cleaning a neighborhood restaurant. "He can't do much cause he's sick," Mrs. A told the interviewer. "It started six years ago with headaches. . . . When he gets sick, I pour cold water on his head so the blood will go down." Things seemed to be getting worse. "The last time my husband got sick, he was so bad I called the doctor—my parish priest paid for it. I didn't have no money to pay for a doctor.[37]

By the early 1930s most private charities and local governments had run out of money to help in cases like that of the French Canadian family. The federal government stepped in after Franklin Roosevelt's election by providing some health and nutrition services through the Federal Emergency Relief Administration (1933–1935), the New Deal's Resettlement Administration (1935–1937), and the

The Great Depression severely damaged children like these who lived in a camp for migrant farm workers in El Rio, California. It would take more than traditional charity and self-help strategies to lift them from desperate poverty into the model of modern American childhood. *(Library of Congress)*

Farm Security Administration (1937–1946). The FSA's health efforts were the most extensive. The agency provided basic medical care, prenatal and maternity care, and emergency hospitalization and surgery for children and adults in families that were part of the farm federal loan program. In addition the FERA funded the construction of hospitals and public health clinics in some areas where none existed. The Office of Indian Affairs worked with county health departments to send public health nurses to Indian reservations. By the mid-1930s the program had helped to dramatically lower rates of communicable disease among American Indians, especially children.[38]

The example of Carbon Hill, Alabama, shows the web of public health efforts implemented by the federal government as part of the New Deal. Federal dollars paid for the construction of sewers in Carbon Hill, which prevented the spread of typhoid and diarrhea. The federal program also funded the construction of 120 outhouses near homes without access to the town's new sewer lines. Before the federal government moved in, "the vicinity was almost surrounded by mosquito breeding pools of water . . . as the result . . . Carbon Hill had lots of malaria." Government funding paid for the draining of swamps and standing pools of water. The local county health officer later reported that the "incidence of Malaria has been greatly decreased and there has also been an almost complete eradication of the pest mosquito as well as the malaria breeding mosquito." Children were especially susceptible to health problems, so these public sanitation efforts directly benefited youngsters in the community.[39]

The federal government's support for schools during the 1930s, which will be discussed later in more detail, also aided public health work among children and adolescents. Schools became the focus of diagnostic programs aimed at children's preventive health care. Efforts to eliminate pellagra are a good example of what could be done. Pellagra is a nutritional deficiency common among people with diets high in corn and low in niacin. It had been a persistent problem among poor Southerners for decades. Youngsters suffering from pellagra manifested scaly skin patches, diarrhea, and dementia. Schools, public health officials, and federal agencies worked together to identify children and adolescents with the disease, and by the 1940s it was almost unheard-of.[40]

On the other hand, schools could also help spread contagious diseases such as measles (rubella), whooping cough (pertussis), scarlet fever, mumps, and chicken pox. Such illnesses could be life threatening in malnourished children and those unable to access proper medical care. Schools closed and children infected with contagious disease were quarantined. Headlines like the one in a Milwaukee newspaper on May 16, 1936, announcing reported cases of measles in a local school, "STUDENTS SUSPENDED AS HEALTH MEASURE," sent pangs of fear through families. Severe outbreaks of measles in the United States in 1934, 1935, and 1938 doubled the incidence of the disease from an average of approximately 300 cases per 100,000 population to 600. Whooping cough also remained one of the most serious illnesses among children in the 1930s with an average of 140 cases per 100,000 reported each year.[41]

Less contagious infections could also be deadly serious. Richard Waskins was eleven years old when he developed an infection in the bony prominence behind his ear called the mastoid. The area, composed of tiny air cells which communicate with the middle ear, is susceptible to infection in children. Before the advent of antibiotics, mastoid surgery was a common operation. Waskins's family lived in Detroit and, like many of their neighbors, struggled to make ends meet in the early thirties as the city's unemployment rate climbed. The Waskinses had no money to pay for the operation necessary to eliminate Richard's painful and massive growth, so they did what they could for him at home and hoped the problem would go away. By the time they called in a doctor, the side of Richard's head was swollen to twice its normal size. Waskins remembered that on the day the doctor arrived, "he took one look at my head and . . . called the ambulance immediately. . . . They took me to Children's Hospital . . . operated on me that night and I must assume that that saved my life." Government funding paid for the surgery.[42]

Even with the help of government and charities, paying for medical care remained a problem for many American families that went unsolved during the Great Depression. The New Deal's limited emergency medical programs were not made permanent, but medical advances and a new commitment to public health by state and local authorities helped eliminate some of the worst scourges of childhood. Expanded public health efforts after 1933 helped reduce the incidence of diphtheria in the United States. Although an anti-toxin had been developed in 1890, the immunization of children did not become common until the 1930s. In 1930 diphtheria occurred at a rate of 54.1 cases per 100,000 population. The rate had been reduced to 11.8 in 1940.[43] During the 1940s and 1950s polio became the more important threat to children, and lessons learned during the 1930s helped to eventually curb the disease.

America's Dependent Children

Families that failed to care for their children left behind what government officials called youngsters with special needs. These were mostly young Americans who depended on the state for their support. In 1933 the U.S. Children's Bureau counted an estimated 120,000 children in foster care and an additional 144,000 in orphanages. In the 1930s the humorist Art Buchwald spent much of his childhood in foster homes. He recalled that during the depression many foster families were happy to get the twenty-five dollars each month that the state paid for taking in dependent children—but still there were not enough foster homes to accommodate the growing number of children whose families were unable to care for them. "Thousands of children are being refused care," the Child Welfare League warned in 1933, "because neither public nor private agencies in their respective communities are in a position to provide such care." Many institutions, like one in Chicago, had experienced a drop in population during the 1920s as foster care became a more common strategy and economic prosperity helped curb demand. The onset of the depression, however, brought a new wave of neglected children to the doorsteps of institutions and foster-care programs. State foster-care programs begged for placement homes but also found coffers running out of money. Overcrowded orphanages boarded out children they could not house. In Ohio 56 county orphan homes housed more than 8,000 children in 1933 and sent some to foster homes. Other states reported similar conditions. In Waco, Texas, the State Home for Dependent and Neglected Children had housed 42 children in 1923; ten years later 307 children lived there.[44]

Art Buchwald, like most dependent children, was not technically an orphan. His mother was institutionalized, and his unemployed father found it impossible to care for Buchwald and his three sisters. The local orphanage, however, had no room for Buchwald, so he spent the next eleven years in a series of foster homes. Most orphanages accepted children whose parents or guardian "died, divorced, had a mental or physical disability, suffered an accident, [was] a drug addict," or if a child was "impoverished, abused, or abandoned." Many then farmed out children to foster homes.

Others remained in the orphanage for years. Samuel Prince entered the Israel Orphan Home in New York in 1924 when he was three years old. He remained there until 1928 and over the next three years lived with his father, stepmother, sister Sylvia, and two brothers, Nathan and Harry. When his stepmother's baby died, Prince remembers that she "stopped taking care of us," yelling to his father, "Why didn't one of your four children die instead of my one?" Besides the verbal abuse and neglect, Samuel's stepmother beat her stepchildren. In 1931 his father divorced his stepmother, and the children went to different homes: Nathan stayed with the children's father, Sylvia lived with an uncle, and Harry and Samuel entered the Hebrew National Orphan Home (HNOH) where they stayed until 1940. Sam George Arcus entered the HNOH in 1928 soon after his thirty-eight-year-old mother committed suicide. Some children did well under such circumstances, but others found the loss of family too much to overcome. Care could be good, but state care did not necessarily protect children from abuse. In addition, most states separated black children from whites, and "colored orphan asylums" received even less funding than institutions housing white children.[45]

Interestingly, a rise in the number of dependent children paralleled the growing popularity of adoption. The legal claims retained by biological parents made most dependent children ineligible for adoption, and most adopting couples wanted infants or very young children, not the older children in orphanages and foster care. Blonde girls were also preferred. The economic threat to families seemed to place a renewed focus on the nuclear family model as the normative ideal. In addition, the celebration of middle-class motherhood created an aura of suspicion about childless couples. In other words, social norms called for couples to have at least one child.[46]

Since there were no federal laws governing the practice, the Child Welfare League of America lobbied Congress to provide standards for adoption. Between 1925 and 1935, 39 states enacted or reformed their adoption laws. Tennessee was not one of them. The problem with a rising demand for young adoptees and shrinking institutional budgets combined to seed a major adoption scandal at the Tennessee Children's Home in Memphis that continued over the next 20 years. Georgia Tann became supervisor at the home in the 1920s. Beginning in December 1929 she organized a campaign with the *Memphis Press Scimitar* to attract a pool of adoptive parents. As part of Tann's scheme, each day the Memphis newspaper featured a photograph of an attractive potential adoptee. By 1934, 150 couples from several states had contacted the home about adoption. The campaign continued through the 1930s and drew more public interest each year. At the same time demand was rising, Tann's agency faced budget cuts. Sometime during the 1930s she began to "sell" adoptees to couples outside Tennessee. Most of the "buyers" were affluent couples living in California. Most of the biological mothers and fathers who "gave up" the babies were poor unmarried whites residing in Tennessee and surrounding states. In 1950 information about the Tennessee black-market baby scandal finally surfaced in the press, revealing that Tann had engaged in improper adoption placements and the removal of several hundred children from vulnerable biological mothers for approximately twenty years. The story showed the growing emotional value placed on children by the 1930s. It also revealed the vulnerability of poor children and their parents at a time when the middle-class ideal of childhood became the only acceptable model.[47]

Families and America's Greatest Generation

The Great Depression placed added strain on families at the same time reformers and government policies emphasized the middle-class family ideal. According to this model, fathers acted as sole breadwinners, mothers were full-time housewives, and children did household chores and attended school through adolescence. The model had been around for several decades, but the New Deal aggressively promoted it as possible for all American children and their families regardless of race, class, or ethnicity. Tann's method of selling babies to parents who she believed would provide an ideal childhood experience was unacceptable, but in the 1930s government policies and popular culture combined to build a framework for the middle-class model of American childhood.

Even isolated communities like Gee's Bend, Alabama, were touched by such efforts. Eleanor Roosevelt became interested in the children and families of Gee's Bend in the spring of 1933. With the Red Cross running out of supplies and money, over the next two years the first lady encouraged the transfer of federal and state aid to the community as part of early Roosevelt administration relief efforts. In 1935 the New Deal's Resettlement Administration began buying the area's sharecropping plots from the local white landowner and instituted modest modernization strategies for the families living in Gee's Bend. During the next several years the children there witnessed the construction of their community's first school, store, new houses, a cooperative cotton gin, and better community sanitation. One girl who grew up in Gee's Bend remembers that she and other children were fascinated by the school's new flush toilets. They had never seen flush toilets before the federally funded school was built. In 1937 the Resettlement Administration completed purchase of the sharecropping plots from the VandeGraaf family. The agency also opened a health clinic, providing the first modern medical care many people in the community had ever received. An article in the *New York Times* that year praised the citizens of Gee's Bend for their fortitude and unique culture. By 1939 there were visible improvements in the community, and the children of Gee's Bend were regularly attending school. In the 1940s many families in the area had done well enough to buy their farms from the federal government for an average of $1,400 each. This meant that for each of the eighty-seven plots it had originally purchased, the Resettlement Administration paid a subsidy of about $2,600, an amount typical of most Farm Security Administration projects.[48]

The story of Gee's Bend emphasizes the new role of the federal government in the lives of children and families in the 1930s. It also highlights the vast differences that existed among Americans. There was no "typical" American family in the 1930s. The government's experimental programs did not benefit all families equally and did not even reach many who most needed help. Nonetheless the 1930s saw a growing emphasis on childhood as a special time of life protected by the combined efforts of families and government, part of an overall plan to secure a more stable future for all young Americans.

CHAPTER TWO

Work, If You Could Find It

🖋 IN 1938 fourteen-year-old Slim Collier lived on his family's 160-acre farm in rural Iowa. From a distance it may have seemed that Slim was living the modern childhood ideal. When he was a preschooler his father had a good job as a tool-and-die maker at the nearby John Deere tractor plant in Waterloo. Because the family did not have to depend on income from the farm, young Slim was freed from the long hours of labor that had been common for most farm children during much of America's history. In 1931, however, things changed for the Colliers, and especially for Slim. He later remembered that he "had just barely started school" when his father lost his factory job as part of a massive layoff at John Deere. Factories across America were laying off workers in the worst years of the Great Depression. The Colliers were certainly not alone in their situation, but Slim remembered that his father's personality and indebtedness made the job loss in his family especially difficult.

Slim Collier described his father as an overbearing man, "sort of a fancy Dan" with lots of "pretensions." He had a mortgage to pay and increasingly took his frustrations out on the family. "All of a sudden my father, who I saw only rarely, was around all the time. That was quite a shock. I [was] disciplined by him instead of my mother," Slim recalled. Things got a little better in 1933 when John

Deere called Slim's father back to work part-time. He was not around as much, and the local bank canceled its foreclosure order when the Colliers were able make up overdue mortgage payments on the farm. Daily life improved again in 1935 when Slim's father installed running water in the house, but like most farm families the Colliers continued to live without electricity. Overall, times remained tough, and Slim found himself working harder and harder on the family farm. Although Iowa had enacted a child labor law in 1906, the legislation did not cover the work of children on family farms, or any form of agricultural labor.[1]

Slim had to balance his home and school responsibilities since Iowa law required all children to attend school full-time through age fourteen.[2] At the same time tensions heightened between father and son as Slim matured and the depression dragged on. Slim described his father as "a stubborn old cuss" who freely used "the old woodshed" to impose discipline on his children. Slim increasingly resented his father's attitude and harsh treatment. The two had heated arguments, especially about the farm work Slim had to do without the aid of a tractor. In 1938 Slim decided he wanted out. "My last day's work . . . for the old man was taking logs out of the woods with oxen," he recalled. Slim Collier ran away from home. His decision to go off on his own was not unique in American history. From colonial times, adolescents like Slim had been leaving home in search of work, land, or better opportunities. The trend increased with the onset of the Great Depression, but the decade's high unemployment rates made it difficult for adolescent boys like Slim who had to compete for wage work with older jobseekers. And the days of free land had disappeared.

Slim Collier also had to deal with the fact that Iowa's child labor law required fourteen- and fifteen-year-olds to obtain a permit for work outside of agriculture. Earning a work permit required the signature of a parent. Despite his distaste for farm work, Slim sought employment as a hired hand because Iowa law did not include restrictions on agricultural employment. He found a job paying sixteen dollars a month plus room and board. At least he had a warm place to stay and food to eat. The farmer's "wife washed [his] clothes and saw [that he] had a clean shirt on Sunday for church." Not a terrible situation for a fourteen-year-old runaway, but Slim hated farm work and resented the class bias associated with his new status. Hired hands had little power or status, especially during the depression when all jobs were scarce. On Sundays he was expected to sit in the back of the church during worship services, not in the front with the family he lived and worked with during the week.

Slim eventually left the farm but discovered that getting a better job was not easy. Employers continued to treat him with little respect, and available work was low-paid and temporary. While harvesting asparagus for fifteen cents an hour in 1940, he stood up to rub his "aching back." The boss yelled at him, "See those men standing by the road? They're just waiting to get you fired. If I catch you straightening up once more, one of them will be working and you won't." By age sixteen Slim had had enough of farm work and was finally old enough to qualify for other employment. He was lucky to find work as "a theater usher, bellhop, truck helper, and coal loader," but none of the jobs offered stability. When he turned seventeen in 1941, Slim Collier joined the army. He discovered that in his entire company, only he and one other recruit had completed the eighth grade. Slim's education, though limited, qualified him to train as a medic, his first good job.[3]

Children like Slim Collier had always worked in America, so it should not be surprising that he began his lifetime of paid employment at only fourteen years of age. For most of the nation's history, adolescents had worked instead of attending school. But by the 1930s the nation's long transition from a rural to an urban economy had redefined the meaning of labor for both children and adults. During the nineteenth and early twentieth centuries, the economy's increasing reliance on wage labor equated "work" with "employment." For the country's youngest workers, this new context equated paid work with "child labor," a term that took on negative connotations as one state legislature after another passed laws regulating children's employment.

By 1930 every state had enacted some form of anti–child labor law, and related public policies promoted the idea that children under fourteen years of age—and even those under sixteen in a few states—should spend the majority of their time in school, doing chores at home, or engaged in recreation and play, not as part of the paid labor force. In 1910 more than 2 million children 10 through 14 years of age had worked for wages. Very few children under 14 worked for pay by 1930, but as the United States entered its worst economic depression the government still counted more than 650,000 young people under 16 on the job. Anti–child labor reformers lamented the fact that unlike many other Western nations, the United States had no federal regulation of the employment of children and adolescents. And the shortage of jobs led a growing number of Americans to criticize the employment of adolescents as a practice that took wage work away from unemployed adults. In response to shifting public opinion, a new federal law, the 1938 Fair Labor Standards Act, for the first time prohibited most wage work for anyone under 14 years of age and regulated the wage work of 15-, 16-, and 17-year-olds at the national level. The New Deal thus set a fresh standard for the relationship between wage work and modern American childhood.[4]

Child Labor and the Onset of the Depression

The early years of the Great Depression resulted in two contrasting trends in the history of paid work among young Americans. On the one hand, the poor economy led some children and adolescents to seek ways to earn money as the adults in their families became unemployed or lost income. Reformers argued that the trend reversed the progress that had been made in eliminating child labor through state regulation. They also noted that many youngsters forced into the job market by desperate family circumstances found themselves vulnerable to exploitation and abuse by unscrupulous employers who circumvented existing laws. During the depression a growing number of adults agreed with reformers and joined with groups such as the National Child Labor Committee to pressure government officials for legislation that would remove all children, including most adolescents, from the wage-labor force.[5]

Many children and adolescents made important contributions to their own economic survival and that of their families. A study of approximately six hundred teens conducted in Oakland, California, in the 1930s found that two-fifths worked at part-time jobs. The rate was higher among boys than girls, with over half the males and one-fourth of the females holding some form of paid employment. Those from families that had experienced at least a 40 percent drop in income were most likely to work. Even though girls held fewer jobs than boys, 82 percent of the females in the study contributed to their family's domestic economy by performing unpaid chores at home or caring for younger siblings. Fifty-six percent of the boys made similar contributions.[6]

The Federal Government and Young Workers

Since the nineteenth century, child-welfare reformers and educators had discussed the links between compulsory school attendance laws and prohibitions against child labor. After the 1929 stock market crash, child-welfare advocates worried that the depression might produce a growing number of adolescents like Slim Collier who would leave school to seek paid employment. Slim was somewhat unusual among his Iowa peers since his home state had one of the highest school attendance rates for 14- through 17-year-olds in the United States. But his experience was more typical when compared with national averages for adolescents. Of every 1,000 students who entered the fifth grade along with Slim in 1935, only 842 stayed in school long enough to complete the eighth grade. Only 467 out of 1,000 in this age group would remain in the classroom long enough to earn a high school diploma by 1942. Urban teens were more likely to stay in school than those living in rural areas, and whites were more likely to stay in school than blacks.[7]

In the spring of 1932 the U.S. Children's Bureau called a conference in Washington, D.C., to review "the whole question of child labor." As family incomes fell throughout the United States, the agency pointed to what appeared to be a growing number of adolescents roaming the country looking for work. Conference attendees also maintained that "new sweat shop industries had sprung up during the depression." Surprisingly, they concluded that even in light of such problems the time was not right for ratification of the federal child labor amendment that had passed Congress in 1923 but was not yet ratified by the states.

Since its passage, the child labor amendment had faced powerful and vocal opposition in several states, especially among Southern textile mill owners. In many mill towns more than half of all fourteen- and fifteen-year-olds worked in factories. Conference participants decided that rather than support ratification of the amendment, their time would be better spent lobbying for the adoption of state-based child labor restrictions that would eliminate the employment of fourteen- and fifteen-year-olds in all states.[8] This conclusion proved to be "a gross misjudgment of public opinion." The 1930s drew new public attention to the issue of child labor and increased pressure on federal politicians to end the employment of children and adolescents in the interest of protecting adult jobs. In addition, state legislatures raised the age for compulsory school attendance to sixteen.[9]

The 1930 Census reported that 20 percent of 14-through-17-year-olds were "gainfully employed" in the United States, a decline from 31 percent just ten years earlier. But, as the U.S. Children's Bureau warned in a 1936 press release, the bare numbers did not reveal the entire picture. The bureau's 1935 study of 2,019 working children found that working 14- and 15-year-olds seemed to be taking jobs—in retail and "personal services"—that 16- and 17-year-olds had held in 1930. Meanwhile the older children had moved more strongly into manufacturing jobs.[10]

Apparently some employers were hiring young workers believing they would be willing to work for lower wages and under poorer conditions than many adults. The bureau's 1935 study pointed out that having an unemployed adult in the household was the major factor shared by wage-earning teens, especially among young workers under sixteen years of age. Of those, only 45 percent lived in a family with "a father present or employed." The situation suggested that some adolescents were dropping out of school to replace the lost wages of unemployed adults. A majority of these young workers spent more than forty hours per week on the job, and a higher proportion of those under sixteen spent more time on the job than their older peers. Among children under sixteen, 23 percent worked sixty or more hours per week, and 5 percent more than eighty hours in a single week. Among sixteen- and seventeen-year-olds, the respective numbers were 13 percent and 2 percent. Spending more time at work, however, did not mean higher earnings: "Half of the children under sixteen years of age made less than $4.15 a week and only 1 out of 12 made as much as $10." Among the older boys and girls, wages were slightly better, but the median still was only $7.40 per week. Workers in the South had the lowest incomes: whites averaged $6.60 and blacks only $3.40 per week.[11]

Region and race also made a difference when it came to the educational levels attained by young workers. Only 3 percent of the children who lived in New England and only 8 percent of those in the

Midwest had left school before age fourteen. In the South, however, the majority had left the classroom before reaching fourteen. Within the South, race was a major predictor. Among whites, 31 percent had left school before age fourteen, but 60 percent of blacks had done so.

The Children's Bureau noted that its findings reflected only part of the story of children, schooling, and employment since the study was limited to employed teens. It ignored those who had already quit school, or were thinking about quitting, and could not find paid work. Because government policy encouraged fourteen- and fifteen-year-olds to stay in school the Department of Labor did not calculate unemployment rates for Americans less than sixteen years of age. So at least in theory there was no unemployment among Americans under sixteen. The Children's Bureau noted that compulsory school attendance laws existed in every state and that "the trend [in public opinion] is toward 16 years as the minimum age for leaving school." It was clear, however, at least in the six states included in the Children's Bureau's study, that many fourteen- and fifteen-year-olds worked, and even some children under fourteen were able to circumvent existing laws.[12]

The Department of Labor's unemployment calculations for sixteen- and seventeen-year-olds presented problems. In 1930 the official unemployment rate for this group was 8.7 percent. That estimate seems very low since less than half of the same age cohort would eventually graduate from high school, and the adult unemployment rate in the same year was twice as high. The overall unemployment rate in the United States hit its highest point of 24.9 percent in 1933. It stalled near 20 percent for the balance of the 1930s and finally fell to 14.9 percent in 1940 as the nation prepared for war. It seems reasonable to speculate that in the 1930s the actual unemployment rate for sixteen- and seventeen-year-olds was much higher than official government estimates.[13]

As Slim Collier's story testifies, during the 1930s many teens resisted laws designed to keep them out of the paid labor force and in school. Some struck out on their own while others quit school and simply remained at home. As the following letter from a seventeen-year-old boy in Cleveland testifies, many found themselves unable to find a job even if that had been their main reason for leaving school.

Cleveland, Ohio
November 10, 1940

Dear Mrs. Roosevelt:

I am a boy of 17, I quit school 2 years ago in order to find a job. Since my dad died 3 years ago we haven't been able to do so good. We stretched his insurance money so far as it would go, but now we have to face it.

We are behind 2 months in our rent and the 3rd falling due this Wednesday, the 13th. We pay $15 a month for 4 rooms. There are 5 of us, mother, 3 boys and myself. I really wouldn't be writing this, but I can't see ourselves evicted from our house. We've got till Wednesday to get either all or at least half of our rent paid up. It would be all right if it was only me because I could take care of myself one way or another. My mother can't get work because she is recovered from tuberculosis and must rest. I am afraid that if nothing comes up I will turn to crime as a means of getting financial help.

My little brothers are shoeshiners. They go out at night and shine shoes. They mostly go in beer gardens. Their little money even helps. You might say, why don't we go on relief, well you just can't convince my mother on that. She said she would rather starve than get relief.

I am working as a grocery store clerk at $8.00 a week. We could get along on this in summer but not in winter on account of the coal problem.

I was wondering that maybe you could loan us about $35.00 or more, we could get on our feet again and once again hold up our heads. We will greatly appreciate this second start in life with all our hearts.

Will you please be so kind as to answer this letter in some way. And will you please congratulate your husband for us for winning the election. I read all about how angry Hoover and all the rest were about not letting your husband have a third term. The reason for that is because they weren't good enough to be re-elected for a second term and are angry. We all have faith in our president.

Thanks Ever So Much

V. B. F.

P.S. Please, again I say, try to answer this letter before Wednesday somehow. I'll be praying every night for your loan. I'll give you $1.00 a month with interest until it is all paid up.

P.S., The reason I marked it personal is that I was afraid it might be thrown out by your secretaries before you even read it.[14]

High unemployment rates among teens and the wide variance in circumstances make broad generalizations about the paid work of children and adolescents during the depression difficult. Age, race, ethnicity, gender, class, and hometown all influenced individual experience. Yet it is possible to provide some insights into the most likely areas of paid employment held by America's youngest wage workers in the 1930s: agriculture, the street trades and service work, and industrial labor.

Agricultural Workers

Thanks to New Deal agency photographs and John Steinbeck's popular 1939 novel *The Grapes of Wrath*, the struggling farm family during the Great Depression is an image familiar to many Americans.[15] In the 1930s thousands of families looked for work as they were forced off their farms or lost jobs and businesses in towns devastated by the nation's failing agricultural economy. Many such families ended up working as migrant farm laborers in the growing number of consolidated agribusiness farms during the depression years.

Cesar Chavez was born on March 31, 1927, in Yuma, Arizona, a Mexican-American community where Spanish was more common than English. During his early childhood, Chavez's parents worked on his grandfather's ranch and in the family's small store in Yuma. The depression eventually crushed the family's businesses, and by the early 1930s the Chavez family headed to California in hopes of finding work. Like most migrant farm families, everyone, even young Chavez, was expected to work in the fields. State child labor laws did not forbid the employment of entire families in agricultural piecework, even including young children like Cesar. Lobbying by the owners of large farms and outdated cultural assumptions about children's farm labor being restricted to family chores contributed to the absence of child labor regulations in agriculture. His family's constant moves and young Cesar's responsibilities in contributing to the family's income greatly hindered his education. By the time he entered the eighth grade, he had attended thirty different schools. At fourteen he spoke little English and quit school altogether before entering high school.[16]

A study of sugar-beet workers by the U.S. Children's Bureau in 1935 showed that there were many young migrant farm workers like Cesar Chavez in the United States. The 946 families interviewed for the study included 670 children between the ages of six and sixteen who reported that they had worked for wages in the beet fields sometime during the past year. Among the youngest workers, 280 were under age fourteen and only two-thirds had enrolled for any schooling in 1935. Workdays could be as long as twelve hours, and pay was low. Families earned a median income of only $340 for the entire year. Government officials judged that poor living conditions resulted in an "inadequate diet, insufficient clothing, poor housing, and [a] lack of needed medical service" for all workers. Some 67 percent of the families in the study were of Mexican or Spanish-American heritage. Families identified as "Russian-Germans" comprised the second-most-frequent ethnic group at 22 percent. Profits drove landowners to hire entire families "due in part," investigators concluded, "to the fact that men with families are considered more reliable and more likely to see work through to completion than solo workers." Officials estimated that more than 15,000 children worked in the sugar beet fields each year.[17]

Working the beet fields involved two infamous tools despised by migrants and especially dangerous for children: the short-handled hoe and the machete. The short hoe had a twelve- to eighteen-inch handle; the machete was kept very sharp. Workers used the hoe to remove weeds from between young beet plants. The tool's short handle forced workers to stoop over. Employers believed this stance made it less likely workers would damage the beet plants, but the tool caused aching backs, and the stooped posture could cause permanent spinal deformities in children. The machete's razor-sharp, semi-curved blade was used to pick up beets off the ground and cut off their green tops. Many beet workers, both children and adults, lost fingers to the sharp machete.[18]

The sugar beet industry was only one of many cash crops that involved child agricultural workers. In the West and Midwest, individual family-owned farms still dominated, but migrant farm families served as a common source of seasonal labor, even on relatively small farms. In the South, blacks and poor whites living as sharecroppers or tenant farmers made up the largest share of the region's agricultural labor force. Migrant workers were not as common in the South, but child farm workers were an everyday fact of life, especially when many poor families "hired out" during the harvest or planting season. Throughout the United States in the 1930s, agricultural labor was the most common type of wage work engaged in by children and adolescents. But images of children working in the fields did not stir the same public outrage as the photographs and stories of youngsters laboring in the nation's factories, mines, or streets. Many Americans continued to hold romantic notions about the nation's agrarian heritage, though each decade the country was moving farther away from its rural origins. The 1930 Census reported that less than half the nation's population lived in the rural countryside (43.9 percent) while 56.1 resided in urban areas (defined as towns of at least 2,500 people).[19]

Many children who lived on the nation's farms in the 1930s could identify with the experiences of Virginia and Dorothy Skinner, who grew up in rural Lee County, South Carolina. The depressed cotton market and lasting effects of the boll weevil made life hard for the Skinners and other farm families in Lee County. Most of them lived on plots of fewer than 50 acres, much smaller than the national average of 151.[20] At that size the average Lee County farm could barely grow enough food and a small cotton crop for a family's survival. Approximately 80 percent of the county's farmers were tenants or sharecroppers, and African Americans made up about 75 percent of the latter group. The Skinners were luckier than most of their neighbors because the family owned a large cotton farm. Dropping prices hurt, but the Skinners remained a step ahead of their neighbors. Virginia's and Dorothy's father hired some of the other farm families in the area to help with planting and harvesting. The girls and their six siblings were expected to do "chores"—laundry, kitchen work, gardening, milking, and churning butter around the family home. They also picked cotton for pay at harvest time and used their earnings as personal spending money.[21] Of course the work done by the Skinner sisters did not show up in government employment statistics. In general the labor that children and adolescents did on the nation's farms was not viewed as paid employment, despite the important contribution these youngsters made to the American economy. Many Americans did not view children's labor on farms as "work," either for its monetary value or its relationship to adult employment.

By the 1930s, romantic notions about the healthy and benign conditions for children working on family farms ignored the plight of a growing number of youngsters who labored with their families as migrant farm workers. *(University of Maryland, Baltimore County)*

The Street Trades

Unlike agricultural labor, the street trades were clearly identified by the government and most Americans as children's paid employment. The street trades had long been one of the first places where young people, especially boys under sixteen, looked for a way to earn money. Despite their popularity among young workers, the street trades were also one of the most controversial employment opportunities for children and adolescents. In the first two decades of the twentieth century several states passed legislation regulating the employment of children and teens in the street trades. For example, New York had required the licensing of newsies (newspaper sellers) since 1903 and bootblacks (shoeshiners) since 1928. Critics

The number of children working in the street trades had declined during the 1920s, but the depression seemed to bring more children back
onto the streets to earn money. This young bootblack shined shoes in
Connecticut in 1931. *(University of Maryland, Baltimore County)*

claimed that street work took children out of school and placed
them amidst inappropriate temptations such as gambling, alcohol
consumption, criminal activities, and prostitution. Employers argued that, to the contrary, children employed in the street trades
could still attend school and that in their work they learned important values associated with entrepreneurship and capitalism.

This debate continued as the Great Depression hit America's
cities. Rochester, New York's street trades enforcement officer, George
W. Zorsch, warned in 1932 that "the depression . . . had a considerable
effect" on children trying to make money on the city's streets. He
claimed to see more youngsters than ever working as "shoeshine boys
and selling newspapers." Zorsch's observations were likely true since

many officials hinted that during tough times they ignored laws against children working in the street trades. Asked if the police chased bootblacks from street corners, one boy replied, "Chase us? Ha: Ha: We shine their shoes." Zorsch observed that law enforcement authorities and the children felt justified in skirting the law since in many cases the "boy is and has been the main support of his family."[22]

In 1928 the International Circulation Managers Association counted 100,000 newsies in the United States selling 7.5 million newspapers a day. The same association dramatically increased its estimate in 1934, counting 174,000 newsies and another 415,000 newspaper carriers operating on designated residential routes. More boys than girls worked as newsies and carriers, and most were immigrants or the children of immigrants. In Omaha in the 1930s, 64 of the city's 119 downtown newsies were Italian or Jewish. The remainder included "11 white Americans, 10 Irish, 6 Negroes, 4 Bohemians, 3 Germans, and miscellaneous others."[23]

Selling newspapers could be exciting and profitable for young entrepreneurs, but incomes were vulnerable to the ups and downs of the retail marketplace. Dempsey Travis was nine years old when he sold the *Chicago Defender*, a black newspaper. His business had been growing until the stock market crash, but "Before the year's end," Dempsey remembered, "my customers were more concerned about feeding their stomachs than feeding their minds." Other newsies faced similar circumstances. Black newsies like Dempsey also encountered the added burden of racism. White-owned and -controlled newspapers generally refused to hire blacks, so boys like Dempsey sold newspapers like the *Chicago Defender*, the *Indianapolis Recorder*, the *Philadelphia Tribune*, and the *Baltimore Afro-American*. Dempsey's business suffered even more quickly than that of his white peers since unemployment hit African Americans first and at higher rates than among whites.[24]

Despite the difficulties, selling on the street was one of the easier and more readily available ways for children and adolescents to make money in the nation's larger towns and cities. Earnings could be used to help young workers' families or solely to fulfill childhood needs and desires. As a boy growing up in New York City, Frank DeMarco sold newspapers with his brother outside the Waldorf restaurant in Manhattan. He made fifteen cents profit on his first day and turned the money over to his mother who bought a loaf of bread and a quart of milk "with pennies to spare." Frank sold two to three hundred papers on days when big news events grabbed headlines. He recalled that headlines announcing Franklin Roosevelt's defeat of Herbert Hoover in 1932, the repeal of Prohibition, the Lindbergh baby kidnapping and murder, the deaths of Will Rogers and Wiley Post in a plane crash, coverage of World Series baseball, and the results of the Joe Louis–Max Schmeling boxing matches were especially good for sales.[25] The exploits of criminals like John Dillinger, Al Capone, Baby Face Nelson, Bonnie and Clyde, and the Brady Gang also grabbed headlines and customers. Newspaper comics gave many parents an inexpensive entertainment to share with their children. Retailers' advertisements attracted bargain hunters, and a young salesman's own pitch could also boost income.

Such incentives helped to sell papers, but overall the poor economy and competition with radio and magazines diminished newspaper sales in the 1930s. Of the 2,086 U.S. dailies operating in 1929, 400 failed or consolidated by 1940. Daily circulation grew from 40 million in 1930 to 41 million in 1940, but over the same decade the nation's population had expanded by 10 million.[26] As part of strategies to stay in business, publishers required newsies and carriers to buy more newspapers than they could realistically sell and to purchase their own rubber bands and account books. Newspapers also tried to turn their young workers into super salespeople by offering training classes and encouraging the government to advocate that Americans buy newspapers. In 1932 the Newspaper Boys of America trade organization published a handbook of sales tips. The Department of Commerce encouraged Americans to purchase newspapers

As newspapers shifted their marketing attention to suburban subscribers and adult-owned newsstands, the number of newsies who hawked newspapers on the nation's streets diminished by the close of the 1930s. *(University of Maryland, Baltimore County)*

by pointing out that a family could save more than $50 per year by buying the sale items advertised in local papers. Several publishers also tried to foster goodwill and increased sales by advertising the soup kitchens and other services they established for their young newsies.[27]

These kinds of public relations campaigns suggest that the companies were facing growing problems with their pool of young workers. In June 1933, for example, a group of carriers from the *Bronx Home News* went on strike over working conditions. The *News* had been able to hire older newsies because of the poor job market, but these workers could also be more demanding. Most of the boys, all aged sixteen and over, earned about four dollars in an average week during the summer and five dollars during the winter, working a total of at least twenty-five hours over a seven-day week. This was not bad money compared with many jobs available during the depression, but the boys complained that their earnings were actually much less because the paper continually levied fines against them for breaking "the rules." Charges that a boy arrived late, made too much noise, or was caught smoking could result in a fine of fifty cents for each infraction. Like other papers, the *Bronx Home News* also required its newsies to buy more papers than they needed, and to seek new subscribers. The newsies eventually won the labor dispute, but two months later the publisher fired the union's leaders and one hundred of the union's members, most of whom were Jewish. The paper justified the firings by claiming that the boys were "instigating revolt" and "spreading communism." Seventeen-year-old Leon Felderman, a union leader, "was beaten up and hospitalized with a concussion." Another activist, Benjamin Gura, testified that he had been told to quit his job by "a bunch of thugs" who threatened to beat him up after arriving at his house in his boss's car.[28]

The Bronx strike points to another factor complicating the lives of young newsies during the depression. Since the Progressive Era, many publishers had been among the strongest opponents of efforts to regulate child labor. The debate was an old one, but child labor reformers of the National Child Labor Committee (NCLC) added a new twist to their objections during the depression. In 1931 a representative of the New York branch of the NCLC warned that "the use of child labor in the sale and distribution of newspapers is indefensible during normal times, and is doubly so during periods of economic depression and widespread unemployment." In other words, selling newspapers was no job for children amidst rising unemployment for adults.

On another level, changes in the newspaper business also made the newsies' job more demanding. Publishers began to shift their major form of distribution from street sales to adult-owned news-stands and neighborhood carriers who worked designated routes. As part of the trend, the International Circulation Managers Association headed an effort to replace the terms "newsie" and "newsboy" with "newspaper boy." The move revealed a feeling among association leaders that the old labels called to mind ragged, neglected street urchins of the past, "a picture not helping the newspaper business in any way." The group also intensified efforts to expand membership in the Newspaper Boys of America. Unlike the boys who wandered the street selling newspapers, NBA members had to have a regular designated route or specific spot to ply their trade.[29]

This may not seem like an important change since the earnings of individual newsies were low in any case, but the shift marked an important change in the availability of paid street work for children and adolescents. The U.S. Children's Bureau's 1935 study showed that most children who sold papers earned between 82 cents and $1.82 for a fifteen-hour work week. Only 7 percent earned at least $4 per week, and these workers were generally older boys like the striking newsies in the Bronx. The youngest newsies tended to work the longest hours for the least money.[30] When the Fair Labor Standards Act became law in 1938, it exempted "independent merchants." But the shift in newspaper marketing had already spelled the end for urban newsies. By the close of the Great Depression it was no longer common to see boys selling newspapers on the nation's downtown streets.

Industrial Workers

Factories were another source of jobs for many children and adolescents in the 1930s, but the decade signaled important changes for these young workers too. The Labor Department's figures for the early 1930s showed that legal reforms had helped keep most workers under fifteen out of the nation's factories and had almost eliminated children under sixteen from mining. Comparing strikes by young mill workers, one in 1903 and another in 1933, reveals some of the important changes in public attitudes and policies that affected the lives of young factory workers by the 1930s.

In the spring of 1933 workers at the Penn-Allen Shirt Company in Allentown, Pennsylvania; the D. & D. Shirt Company in Northampton, Massachusetts; and dozens of small contract shops in eastern Pennsylvania walked off their jobs. They demanded higher pay and shorter working hours, noting that the area's high unemployment rate left them particularly vulnerable to exploitation by employers. The press dubbed the mill workers' walkout a "Baby Strike" because most of the strikers were adolescent girls—almost 40 percent were fourteen, fifteen, or sixteen years old.[31]

This was not the first strike by young Pennsylvania textile workers to gain the public's attention. Almost exactly 30 years earlier, on May 29, 1903, an even bigger strike began that also involved adolescents and even younger children connected to eastern Pennsylvania's textile mills. By the end of June 1903, 100,000 workers—children, adolescents, and adults—had walked off their jobs, involving 7 of every 10 of the region's mill workers. The workers demanded a pay raise, shorter working hours, and the elimination of exploitative child labor. The fiery union activist Mary Harris "Mother" Jones joined the protests, but after more than a month the workers had made little headway. Local newspapers generally ignored the strikers' complaints, and government officials were unsympathetic to the workers' cause.

Jones came up with an idea that she hoped would attract public attention and sympathy. On July 7, some two hundred to four hundred striking textile workers gathered at Torresdale Park on the outskirts of Philadelphia. The group included men, women, and children. About half the crowd consisted of youngsters ten through fifteen years of age; eyewitnesses described the other half as "adults," though many of them were probably sixteen- and seventeen-year-olds. The protesters planned to march through the streets of Philadelphia, then make their way a hundred miles north to New York City. Jones called it "The March of the Mill Children."[32] She and her supporters hoped that seeing child strikers crossing through the towns, villages, and cities of the eastern United States would move ordinary Americans to condemn the mill owners and push government officials to do something to help the striking workers.[33] About 10 percent of textile workers in the district were eight to fifteen years old, and some two-thirds of these young workers were girls. A few newspapers ran stories about the march, noting that many observers were surprised to see children among the demonstrators. But their sympathy did not translate to support for the strikers. A Cincinnati newspaper called Jones and her marchers "a gang of lunatics." Public officials were slightly more sympathetic, but they continued to do nothing to end the strike.[34]

By the time the child marchers reached New York City, the group had dwindled to about sixty. The *New York Times*, which like all newspapers at the time relied on young workers as its primary sales staff, took particular pleasure in describing the march's disappointments. On the evening of July 23 thousands of New Yorkers watched Jones and the demonstrators walk up Second Avenue by torch light as six hundred policemen stood by "to maintain order." Jones took an even smaller group to Theodore Roosevelt's home on Oyster Bay in an attempt to get the president's support, but he refused to see them. Mill owners successfully broke the strike within the next few weeks, ending the 1903 "March of the Mill Children" in failure.[35]

Or was it? In 1905 a new state law in Pennsylvania prohibited the employment of youngsters under fourteen years of age in factories. It also outlawed most night work for fourteen- and fifteen-year-olds and spelled out penalties for anyone falsifying a youngster's age in order to secure employment for the child. Even the young strikers had carried signs suggesting that children under fourteen should be in school rather than at work. In 1913 Pennsylvania's Women's Labor Law limited work schedules for all females, including adolescents, to no more than fifty-four hours per week. Two years later Governor Martin Brumbaugh strengthened the state's child labor law by signing a bill requiring work permits for young workers and prohibiting fourteen-year-olds from getting a job until they had completed the sixth grade. Adolescents who qualified for work permits under the new law could work only limited schedules of nine hours a day and no more than fifty-one hours per week. The same legislation made it illegal for anyone under eighteen to work at night and for fourteen- through seventeen-year-olds to hold jobs in certain "hazardous" industries. In 1925 the Pennsylvania legislature created a Bureau of Women and Children to help enforce the state's new child labor regulations. Growing technological changes in the region's industries combined with state laws to consistently reduce children's participation in Pennsylvania's workforce in the 1920s.[36]

Nevertheless the new "Baby Strike" that took place in Pennsylvania's Lehigh Valley in 1933 demonstrated that the onset of the depression threatened the progress of the 1920s. This strike eventually resulted in the extension of prohibitions against child labor to 14- and 15-year-olds, a measure that some of the young strikers may not have wanted.[37] According to the U.S. Department of Labor, the 1933 protest involved more than 40 separate facilities employing 3,200 workers, approximately 25 percent of them 14 and 15 years of age. One shop in Allentown had only three employees over 14. During the months following the 1929 stock market crash, factory owners from Philadelphia and other East Coast cities went in search of cheap labor and low rents. Several mill owners established sweatshops based on piecework wage schemes in the Lehigh Valley. Local families hurt by rising adult unemployment sent their daughters and a few sons to work in the relocated mills. Cigar factory owners also copied the model. Secretary of Labor William K. Doak warned that such factories were taking jobs from adults in America's cities and giving them to children in the rural countryside.[38]

The reactions of the mayors in the two communities involved in the new "Baby Strike" illustrate the importance of the early 1930s as a period of transition in the attitude of government officials toward unions and, specifically, young workers. Allentown's Mayor Fred Hart was sympathetic to the young strikers and quickly established a local committee composed of the community's "leading citizens" to investigate conditions in the factories. Northampton's Mayor Charles Fox, on the other hand, blamed the walkout on "agitators" and promised the factory owners "police protection." Fox, referring to food aid for poor families, told newspaper reporters, "If I had my way, I'd give no food orders to unemployed persons who urged factory workers to strike." His wife, who oversaw unemployment relief in Northampton, agreed, concluding, "I don't believe the strikers should be entitled to any unemployment relief because they don't have souls." Despite such blatant opposition to the young protesters from two of Northampton's officials, a member of the local council responded that if the factory owners paid "decent wages . . . police protection would not be necessary."[39]

At the state level, officials enthusiastically embraced Mayor Hart's attitude and rejected Fox's. Pennsylvania's Republican governor Gifford Pinchot responded by establishing his own "Sweatshop Commission" to investigate the workers' charges of low pay, abuse, and long hours. A parade of young workers testified about their experiences in the factories, and journalists relayed their stories to the public. One boy told investigators that he spent most days from 7 a.m. until 5 p.m. in the factory, then returned to work three nights each week from 7 p.m. until 3 a.m. Other young workers revealed that employers often told them to hide in cellars or on fire escapes when state inspectors arrived at the factories. Stephen Raushenbush

from the state factory inspection bureau explained that it was difficult under current state law to rectify the situation since most
young workers were paid by the piece. The state knew, he said, that
"hours of labor in many of the Pennsylvania sweatshops range from
fifty to ninety a week and the wages start at 50 cents and go to $10.
. . . This deplorable condition is responsible for $1.98 silk dresses,
3-for-10-cent cigars, 39-cent silk hosiery, $10 suits and top coats,
and 25-cent shirts and neckties."[40]

The *Winston-Salem* (North Carolina) *Sentinel* explained how
the piecework system exploited young workers. A featured article
told the story of "Mildred Sweeney . . . a thin, snub-nosed little
Irish girl, who ought to be thinking of nothing more serious than
basket ball [sic]." Instead, "at 15, [she] has been the sole support of a
family of ten for the last year. From 7 o'clock in the morning until 5
in the evening, Mildred trimmed shirts in a factory in Allentown.
The highest wages she made in one week for all her long hours of
work was $1.10. . . . One week she made just five cents." The article
went on to describe how Sweeney often came home too tired to eat,
with only 50 or 75 cents to show for a full week's work. Owners got
away with such low wages because employees like Mildred Sweeney
were paid one-half cent to 2 or 3 cents for a dozen trimmed shirts,
not by the hour. Mildred complained that the piecework system
was bad for workers, but there is no evidence that she believed it
was wrong for her to hold a job. Instead her words suggest that she
wanted to continue to work, but at a fair wage. "The week that I
just got a nickel, I had to go everyday, just like always, and wait to
see if there was anything to do. Sometimes we'd wait all day and go
home at night without earning anything. But if you don't come
everyday, they fire you."[41]

Newspaper and magazine editors condemned the factory owners
and offered sympathy to the strikers. But the solution to the problem of worker exploitation put forward by the press may not have
been what young strikers like Mildred Sweeney had intended. For

example, the *Toledo Leader*, in an article headlined "Sweatshop Conditions Force Children's Strike," explained: "Child labor exploited to unbelievable limits by unscrupulous bosses during the depression, has revolted. And America—the richest nation in the world—is witnessing its first strike of 'baby workers.'" According to the *Leader*, "hundreds of underfed, overworked, and grossly underpaid children, employees of the shirt and pajama factory sweatshops which infest that district are on strike against wages as low as 15 cents a week and working condition [sic] which would make the overseer of a Soudan slave camp blush with shame." The reporter appeared to support the right of the young workers to strike by noting that "the children are engaged in active and effective picketing, and are receiving the support of decent-minded citizens." He argued that the strikers' demands were "modest, very modest. . . . All they are asking for is the 'prompt payment of wages,' a 10 percent increase in piecework schedules, restoration of a recent pay cut [rates had been cut from 6 cents a dozen to 3 cents], and recognition of 'a union.'" But finally, the article concluded that although the strikers' cause was just, high adult unemployment rates and terrible factory conditions provided good reasons to restrict *all* wage labor for adolescents.[42]

In a similar tone, *The Nation* magazine praised Pennsylvania state officials for attempting to eliminate child labor as part of an overall strategy to improve working conditions for adult workers. "SHOCKING conditions in the sweatshops of Pennsylvania, where 200,000 men, women, and children work long hours for starvation wages, became front-page news through the efforts of the 'baby strikers' of the Lehigh Valley," wrote journalist Paul Comly French. The hearings, French argued, showed a situation with "tales of hideous working conditions, long hours, and miserable wages, comparable only to those which obtained in the earliest years of the Industrial Revolution . . . as well as a story of lost youth and saddened childhood." Only the elimination of child labor would rectify the situation.[43]

Garment factories hired adolescent girls and boys to do low-paid piece-work in what critics called "*shocking* conditions." Newspapers described the labor struggle by young garment workers in Pennsylvania's mills in 1933 as a "Baby Strike," reflecting the public's rising concern that children under sixteen should not be permitted in the workplace. *(University of Maryland, Baltimore County)*

The public hearings in Northampton and Allentown included moments of great drama. As reported by the newspapers, they undoubtedly swayed readers against the sweatshop owners and in favor of calls for stronger child labor laws. During the hearings that took place on April 28 in Northampton, Nathan Dashefsky, one of the two brothers who owned the D. & D. Shirt Company, "boasted that he was armed." Officials required him "to unswing his pistol and keep it unloaded during the rest of the hearing." Dashefsky did as he was told but defiantly informed the investigators that he did not believe "employees had the right to bargain . . . collectively on any matter." He claimed that all the young workers who had testified were simply "liars." Hale A. Guss, a Northampton borough manager, added excitement to the scene by charging that the Dashefskys' language in front of their young female employees was what "only the scum of the earth would use." Charlotte E. Carr, deputy secretary of the State Department of Labor and Industry, agreed with Guss's fiery accusation and noted that several of the striking girls said they were too embarrassed to tell the full truth about working conditions in the factory in front of the men present at the hearings. In response, officials decided to hold a separate hearing conducted solely by women investigators, including the governor's wife, Cornelia Bryce Pinchot. At the closed-door hearings, girls testified that they were regularly sexually harassed by their employers and forced to accept unwanted "attention." A girl who earned 55 cents a week testified that her male supervisor offered to double her earnings if she would agree to have sexual relations with him three times a week. Other young girls reported that mill owners took them to New York hotels on weekends to entertain potential buyers.[44]

After the hearings, Cornelia Pinchot and Charlotte Carr summarized the young strikers' testimonies and offered an overview of the strike for board members of the Pennsylvania Department of Labor and Industry. Clearly the young workers had described terrible conditions in Pennsylvania's sweatshops, but the board also needed to consider the legal issues of the strike. Pinchot and Carr argued that the strikers were conducting a legal job action. Their picketing had "followed within complete conformity of the law and . . . both adults and minors cooperated in this effort." This was an important point since it supported strikers' accusations that factory owners had violated state law by firing employees who had walked off their jobs.

Another point especially important for young workers involved school attendance. School authorities had argued that the state's compulsory school attendance law required that fired workers under sixteen must return to school, even if they held work permits. If the board judged the workers' strike illegal, such young strikers could be charged with truancy. Feeling pressured, the group voted to delay a decision.[45]

Meanwhile Cornelia Pinchot marched with a group of young strikers in Harrisburg on May 11. She also gave speeches at various venues, replete with sad stories about the working conditions for girls in the factories.[46] Throughout the 1930s Pinchot acted as a champion for organized labor's efforts to end sweatshops and the employment of fourteen- and fifteen-year-olds. And unlike during Mother Jones's heyday, such ideas were accepted as mainstream. By the time the Pennsylvania Board of Labor and Industry met again, it was clear that public opinion opposed the factory owners but wanted stronger child labor regulations. State education officials attended the meeting and argued that the state's chief interest should be to keep children in school, not to protect their rights as workers. Members of the board agreed but concluded that they were bound by current law to protect the legal rights of workers, even those only fourteen and fifteen years of age. Perhaps because it was looking for a loophole that would allow it to avoid full support for the child strikers, the board delayed its final decision. Instead, on July 12, 1933, it passed a general resolution prohibiting the hiring of strikebreakers and ordered that minors engaged in a legal job action against their employers should not lose their work permits during a strike or lockout.[47]

In the end, the Dashefsky brothers broke the strike at their factory in Northampton. But even before the governor's hearings, workers at the Penn-Allen Shirt Company in Allentown signed a contract that included a 10 percent pay increase and recognition of the Clothing Workers Union. The situation in other factories mirrored the divided circumstances in Northampton and Allentown.[48] Even in the depths of the Great Depression, at least some of the young Pennsylvania strikers achieved their goals of higher wages and union recognition, though pressure from unemployed adults and organized labor continued to push government officials to prohibit the employment of fourteen- and fifteen-year-olds in industry.

It is reasonable to assume that at least some of the young Allentown-Northampton strikers were unhappy when the Pennsylvania legislature passed a new law in 1935 raising the minimum age to sixteen for factory employment. The law also limited sixteen- and seventeen-year-olds to an eight-hour day, forty-hour week, and restricted the kind of work sixteen-to-twenty-one-year-olds could do on the job. Pennsylvania lawmakers also passed a new and stronger compulsory school attendance law for children under sixteen. These changes and the atmosphere surrounding the 1933 strike showed how public attitudes had changed about the employment of children and adolescents since 1903. The shift reached Washington in 1938 with the passage of the Fair Labor Standards Act.

Children's Wage Work at the End of the Depression

It should not be surprising that in the 1930s adolescents like Slim Collier wanted paid work. Until then, many boys his age had sought jobs in the transition from childhood dependency to the world of adult independence. And popular lore had long celebrated the childhood work experiences of American heroes such as Benjamin Franklin, Andrew Jackson, and Thomas Edison. Between the late nineteenth century and the end of the 1930s, however, reformers concentrated their attention on the dangers of paid employment for children and adolescents in the nation's mines, fields, factories, and streets. During the Progressive Era muckraking journalists like Jonathan Spargo and Jacob Riis, along with child welfare organizations such as the National Child Labor Committee and the U.S. Children's Bureau, increasingly questioned the wisdom of having a large proportion of American children forgoing school in exchange for long hours at often dangerous and low-wage jobs. Such reformers maintained that the only acceptable "work" for individuals under sixteen years of age was "schoolwork" or "age appropriate family-based chores." They also sought to encourage sixteen- and seventeen-year-olds to stay in school by calling for restrictions on legal work even for older adolescents.[49]

From 1870 through 1910 the number of ten-through-fifteen-year-olds employed for wages in the United States rose from 740,000 (13.2 percent of the age cohort) to 1,990,225 (18.4 percent). The actual number is likely to have been much higher since the Census did not count workers younger than ten, those who did piecework at home or were illegally employed, or many youngsters who were involved in the street trades. By the 1920s a number of factors had combined to reduce the proportion of children and adolescents working for wages. These included changing public attitudes toward the social value of children, wage labor for young workers, and education. By the third decade of the twentieth century, states were placing a stronger emphasis on the enforcement of compulsory school attendance laws and child labor regulations. And new technologies were reducing the profitability of employing young children in certain industries. In 1930, despite an overall growth in the population of ten-through-fifteen-year-olds, the number of children from this group who worked for wages declined to 667,118, or 4.8 percent of the age cohort.[50]

It may appear that by the mid-1930s all adolescent workers had been removed from the paid labor force, but that was not the case then nor for the balance of the twentieth century. Children and adolescents continued to work in the hidden economy as shoeshiners, as scavengers, in the street trades, and doing odd jobs for neighbors and business owners. Many, especially those in Mexican-American, Filipino, Chinese, and African-American families, worked in agriculture, an industry exempted from federal labor regulations. There is no data measuring the overall contribution of children and adolescents to the economy during the 1930s, but it is clear that passage of the Fair Labor Standards Act marked a significant change in attitude for lawmakers and the general public about the appropriateness of paid employment for adolescents. Loopholes in the new law left some young workers outside federal protection, but passage of the FLSA, coupled with shifting public attitudes, state compulsory school attendance laws, and high unemployment rates, removed the vast majority of adolescents from full-time employment in the 1930s. In 1940 the Census Bureau counted more fourteen-through-seventeen-year-olds in school than in wage work. Among this group, 4.3 million attended school and only 209,347 worked full- or part-time (70 percent fewer than in 1930). Even among sixteen- and seventeen-year-olds, 3.4 million were in school and only 662,967 worked at full- or part-time jobs.[51] The data does not reflect the hidden economy of adolescent employment; and a cynical view suggests that the improved figures had more to do with high unemployment rates among adults than with concerns for the welfare of children and adolescents. Still, by the end of the 1930s school had become the only socially acceptable full-time work of modern American childhood.

CHAPTER THREE

Transient Youth:
On the Road to Nowhere?

✒ THE CHANGING cultural definitions of work and American childhood did not alter the lives of all young Americans overnight, especially during the Great Depression. The decade's high unemployment rate and hard times for many American families left many adolescents and youth in desperate circumstances. By the early 1930s, for many Americans, an increasingly visible army of transient teens and youth in their early twenties underscored the worst consequences of the depression for children, families, and the country's future.

In the spring of 1929, fifteen-year-old Clarence Lee was living with his parents and younger siblings on a dairy farm in rural Louisiana. A few years earlier the Lees had lived a more comfortable life in Baton Rouge, where Clarence's mother took in laundry and his father worked as a laborer. The family reluctantly turned to sharecropping when Clarence's father lost his job in the mid-twenties. Many African-American families clinging to the bottom rungs of the economic ladder found that the depression came their way before the 1929 crash. Clarence remembered that moving to the dairy farm ended any childhood freedoms he had enjoyed in Baton Rouge. On the farm he awoke each morning at 3 a.m. to help his father milk the landowner's dairy cows, then spent the rest of his day doing fieldwork. Lee's parents found it difficult to feed and clothe their children on the meager earnings the family received from sharecropping. When Clarence turned sixteen, his father explained that it was time to "go fend for yourself." He remembered being very hurt by his father's words. Clarence wanted to stay at home and continue to help his family, but as he explained in an interview conducted more than sixty years later, "There was nothing I could do. I had to go."[1]

Turned out of his family's home, Lee was one of an estimated 250,000 adolescents and youth in their early twenties who hit the road in the 1930s. Young transients hopped freight trains, hitchhiked along highways, begged, stole, and even prostituted themselves in order to survive. Some did not travel very far, but others roamed across the entire country. These young wanderers seemed to epitomize the hopelessness and insecurity that gripped much of the nation during the depression. Lee remembered spending several months on the road, where he suffered from hunger, exposure to the elements, and the special dangers associated with being a young black male traveling in the Jim Crow South. In 1931, however, Lee was luckier than most young transients because his work experience helped him land a job on a dairy farm in another part of Louisiana. Since there were no minimum wage laws and he was desperate for work, Lee agreed to work for only 10 cents an hour. Even at that low wage, Clarence Lee eventually saved enough from his earnings to pay off his parents' $111.40 sharecropping debt, freeing them from the servitude that embraced both black and white sharecropping families. Without debt, they were free to move if they could find work elsewhere. It was too late, however, for eighteen-year-old Clarence to go home. He continued to work, and in 1933 his persistence paid off with a well-paying job at a New Orleans 7-Up bottling plant.

For many Americans, the estimated 250,000 adolescents and youth who hopped freight trains and hitchhiked along the nation's highways symbolized the "youth problem," which seemed to be one of the worst consequences of the economic depression. *(Library of Congress)*

Despite Lee's ability to take care of himself, improve his personal situation, and eventually help his family, he remembered his time as a struggling young transient as "a destructive experience. . . . When I was riding the freight trains, I didn't feel like an American citizen. I felt like an outcast. I wasn't treated like a human being. I was nothing but dirt." It seemed that the "Depression would never end."[2] The earliest New Deal programs underscored the fact that America's adolescents and youth had been hit hard by the nation's economic crisis. This recognition suggested that during such hard times the federal government had a responsibility to help young Americans, especially males, in their transition to adult independence. At the same time, however, the limitations of New Deal efforts reveal important ambivalences about the changing definition of childhood among policymakers and the general public.

America's Youth Problem

For most of American history the vast majority of young people had begun to find more autonomy during their mid-teen years. That trend began to change in the mid-nineteenth century as a growing number of urban middle-class parents provided the means for their sons and daughters to graduate from high school. By the early twentieth century a wave of new compulsory school attendance laws encouraged more and more adolescents to remain in school longer than ever before, but such change was slow and unevenly distributed. For example, in 1914 more than 85 percent of Iowans from ten through seventeen years of age were in school, but in some Southern states the rate was less than 30 percent.[3] As late as 1929 less than 20 percent of all Americans had completed four years of high school. Many teens continued to follow the traditional path into the job market rather than stay in school beyond the elementary grades. The Labor Department estimated that more than four million teenaged job seekers could not find paid work during the worst years of the depression. Throughout the 1930s the unemployment rate among sixteen-to-twenty-year-olds climbed to twice that of adults.[4] Duval Edwards's experience was typical among young job-seekers. Edwards ran away from home in 1932 partly because he felt that he was a burden on his family. In Bossier City, Louisiana, he saw a help-wanted sign in a restaurant window that read, "Dish-washer wanted—only college graduate need apply." Edwards could not believe that someone needed a college education to wash dishes, so he asked for the job anyway. "We mean it, sonny," the owner replied. "We are helping those who have finished college and can't find any other work."[5]

Homeless transients, hoboes, and tramps were not new to the country, but the rising number of young wanderers who hit the road during the early 1930s paralleled the worsening economy. Most young wanderers were males in their teens and early twenties; females constituted only about 10 percent of the group. It had always been more socially acceptable for adolescent males to leave home in search of work. It was also more common for girls, even from poor families, to stay home in order to care for younger siblings, ill parents, or elderly relatives.

While most young Americans did not leave home during the 1930s, the decade's visible pool of roving boys and girls led many adults to focus on what became known as "America's Youth Problem." Youth activists and concerned adults argued that the presence of so many young transients was an ominous sign of something terribly wrong in America. Such critics feared that the Great Depression might produce a class of disaffected and radical youth that presented a danger to America's future. As one author noted, "It's an old story—the conflict of the older and younger generations. . . . Old Story or new story: the question is what are we going to do about it?"[6] Reformers began to call for government intervention to help ease the problem.

Hitting the Road

Why did so many teens and youths take to the road in the 1930s? As already noted, some were told to leave, and others felt they were a burden on struggling parents. Young transients often said they were unable to find jobs in their home communities and hoped to get work elsewhere. Many came from families living on the edge of survival even before the onset of the depression, and leaving home seemed a good alternative to continuing to suffer there. Some young wanderers reported running away from abusive parents or guardians. Others simply wanted to avoid unwelcome responsibilities or trouble with the law. And finally, in a decade darkened by economic depression and an uncertain future, many young transients saw the open road as a path to adventure and excitement.[7]

The lure of adventure was a strong pull. In the spring of 1930, thirteen-year-old Harold Hoopes searched for some way to alleviate what he described as the boredom of living in Paradise, Kansas. His family had moved into town after the bank foreclosed on their farm. Harold was happy to be relieved of farm chores but found town life boring, with "nothing for kids to do." He jumped at the chance for adventure when a seventeen-year-old neighbor announced that he planned to hop boxcars to California. The older boy had heard there were jobs there; he thought Harold and another boy might like to come along. Harold quickly gathered some things for the trip: "a comb, scissors, a razor (which I didn't need at 13), ropes, belts, etc.," and twenty-five cents.

Harold and his two companions began their journey by walking from Paradise to the nearby town of Russell, where they hopped their first freight train. Inexperienced at this business, the boys did not get far. In Colby, Kansas, a railroad bull (a popular term used to describe private security guards hired by the railroad companies) turned them over to the local police. The trio spent the night in jail and the next morning were ordered to pull weeds in a large field for several hours in the hot sun. When lunchtime approached, a police officer told the boys they could quit working. He bought them hamburgers and then walked them to the edge of town. There he sternly ordered them to go home and not come back. The officer "thought he was heading us home," Harold explained, but Paradise was actually in "the opposite direction so we kept on walking." They hiked all afternoon and finally reached the next town by evening. There they cooled their tired and burning feet in a large stockyard watering tank. Hungry, the boys went in search of food and found a sympathetic baker who gave them a "whole sack of bread and rolls." They stuffed themselves, rested, and caught the next freight train north. Harold and his companions had quickly learned the tricks of the road. They never made it to California, but they spent the next several weeks "hoboing" in Colorado.

Unlike Clarence Lee, Harold Hoopes had no regrets about his time on the road. Hoopes remembered being awestruck by Colorado's mountains and intrigued by the many different people he met. He recalled times when some people looked at him with distain, but overall the experience was a grand adventure. As the warm days faded into autumn, he grew homesick and headed back to Paradise. When his mother saw her dirty and disheveled son walk into the yard, she exclaimed, "'Oh! My God!' and fainted dead away." Harold's mother was rightfully surprised to see him. She and her husband had heard that their son, like far too many young transients, was dead—run over by a train.[8]

Ina Máki was also looking for adventure when she became a young transient. She left Virginia, Minnesota, where she remembered there was "little else to do." After graduating from high school in the spring of 1939, she told her Finnish-born father that she planned to spend the summer hopping freight trains. His only response was to warn her that the trip would "be dangerous." Ina was one of the few girls who took to the road, and her father's casual attitude about the adventure may seem unusual. But many parents felt empathy for their older children who were forced into idleness and boredom by the nation's high unemployment rate. In this case, Ina's father had been a young transient himself, immigrating from Finland to the United States. Ina did as she planned and returned home in time to go to college in the fall of 1939. Like Harold Hoopes, Ina Máki recalled her time on the road as an exciting experience she was glad to remember.[9]

Despite such positive examples, tragedy and loss were not uncommon among young transients. Girls and boys on the road were always in danger of being raped by older and stronger men. They were also vulnerable to crime and violence from strangers, and local authorities often threw young wanderers in jail without provocation, as part of crime prevention efforts. The trains too were a danger. Orphaned at age eleven, in 1932 seventeen-year-old Gene Wadsworth was living with an uncle and five cousins in Burley, Idaho. He didn't feel welcome in his uncle's house and was so depressed by his situation that he contemplated suicide. Instead he decided to run away by hopping a passing freight. Things went well at first. Gene met a boy named Jim and the two became fast friends. Gene Wadsworth's heart was broken, however, when Jim was killed in a train accident. The boys were hopping a freight train when, as Gene recalled, "I heard Jim let out a muffled moan, as he fell" from the train. "I whirled round and made a grab for him. He had on a knit cap. I got the cap and a handful of blond hair. Jim was gone. Disappeared under the wheels." Gene Wadsworth was sick with grief and felt that the experience changed him forever. "From then on, I was a loner."[10]

Young transients quickly learned about the dangers associated with riding the rails, but many were injured or killed in the process. Trains traveled at high speed, and everything on the railroad was big, heavy, and potentially dangerous. Railroad bulls posed a major threat to a young wanderer's safety and comfort. Duval Edwards decided he preferred hitchhiking after seeing a bull rob a young wanderer at gunpoint. Bulls also shot at individuals jumping on and off trains. Beatings were another popular means of control.

Most communities turned a blind eye to the harsh treatment of young wanderers by railroad bulls and local police. Many people feared that unattached young people on the road were simply criminals. As a 1934 article argued, young people on the road and those without work or in school "had a great deal of time in which to get into trouble." Another observer noted an "increase in crimes committed by boys between sixteen and nineteen." Without work, many young transients resorted to stealing and begging in order to get by.

Local authorities looked suspiciously on them all. In 1934 "Ellen" hitchhiked from Florida to Chicago over a four-month period. During her travels she was arrested thirty-one times for vagrancy. When she got to Chicago, the police arrested her again, putting her in jail with "prostitutes that wanted to kinda straighten up. . . . Of course I was no prostitute," Ellen explained, "but I had no visible means of support, and [the police] didn't know what else to do with me." Girls were most likely to be picked up for vagrancy and prostitution. Authorities usually charged boys with vagrancy or theft.[11]

Americans' fears about hoboes and tramps increased as their numbers rose along with the nation's unemployment rate. And from 1933 to 1935 newspaper headlines throughout the United States highlighted what seemed to be a spreading wave of violent crime, including armed robberies and murders committed by the likes of the Brady Gang, John Dillinger, Charles Arthur "Pretty Boy" Floyd, and the Romeo and Juliet of the criminal set, Bonnie Parker and Clyde Barrow. Gun-related violence was growing worse. The *New York Times* reported in May 1934 that four of the city's on-duty police officers had been killed since January 1. Only three New York City policemen had been murdered during all of 1933. Innocent bystanders were sometimes caught in the crossfire between criminals and the police. A sixteen-year-old girl and two boys, one seventeen and the other only ten months old, had been wounded in a gun battle that left one police officer dead. All three young bystanders survived, but the bullet that struck the girl left her paralyzed.[12]

Media coverage of crime brought Americans to demand that police and the courts get tougher with criminals. The number of individuals incarcerated in state and federal prisons increased 39 percent from 1930 through 1940, while the nation's total population grew only a little over 6 percent.[13] Death-penalty convictions for murder and other serious crimes resulted in the execution of 1,791 individuals, 54 percent of whom were black. The depression in fact saw the highest number of executions in the United States since the Justice Department began collecting such data in 1930. It is difficult to know exactly how many of those executed for murder or other crimes were juveniles at the time of their execution or conviction, but trends in the historical application of the death penalty from the 1930s through the 1960s suggests that approximately 2 percent were under eighteen.[14] Many people pointed to the nation's growing army of young transients as evidence that the United States was experiencing a moral crisis, with a crime rate that seemed out of control.[15]

During the first years of the depression Washington policymakers, politicians, and the popular press were slow to recognize adolescents and youth among the nation's growing transient population. Those who attended President Hoover's 1930 White House Conference on Child Health and Protection did not even mention young transients. Nor did the *New York Times* and popular magazines talk about the trend. But by the summer and early fall of 1932 this changed. Images of transient "children" in the press became common representations of a national "Youth Problem." An article in the September *Ladies' Home Journal* claimed that "200,000 Vagabond Children" were wandering aimlessly throughout the United States. The October 23 *New York Times Magazine* included a collage of seven photographs indexed under the words, "Wandering Boys Become a Social Problem in America." The page's main headline read, "A Tragic Aftermath of the Days of Prosperity: The Army of Homeless Boys Now Roaming the Country." A caption next to a photograph of several boys explained that the picture showed "Young Americans, some of whom have forsaken the hardships of home for the hardships of travel: Itinerant Youths." Another informed the newspaper's readers that "the problem of the increasing army of destitute boys, first called to the government's attention by the railroads, is being studied by the President's Organization for Unemployment." The *Times* described the boys pictured on its pages as part of the "ragged army cut loose from home surroundings and unable to adjust themselves to the hard times of the present." The newspaper used the phrase "A Free Ride on a Journey to Nowhere" to describe a photograph showing boys hopping into an empty boxcar.[16]

Much press and government attention to the problems of transient youth expressed empathy for the young travelers. But youthful hoboes were viewed as at least potential juvenile delinquents if they were not already full-fledged criminals. Young African Americans faced special prejudices reinforced by racial stereotypes that portrayed all black males as the sexual predators of white females. Clarence Lee remembers barely escaping with his life while riding a train outside Denham Springs, Louisiana. He was fortunate to meet a sympathetic white conductor and engineer who told him that "a white woman had been raped near Denham Springs." Lee recalled many years later, "I fit the description, my color, my height, the way I was dressed." But the conductor and engineer "figured I was innocent" because they knew "I was in the boxcar . . . when the woman was raped." The two men put Clarence off the train in a swamp outside Denham Springs before he could be arrested or lynched.[17]

The Scottsboro Boys

Clarence Lee's fears of being a special target because he was a young black male on the road were well founded. The infamous Scottsboro Boys case is probably the most often-cited example of blatant racial injustice in the 1930s. It also confirmed the fears and hysteria directed at young wanderers who hitchhiked along the nation's highways and rode its freight trains during the Great Depression. And it illustrates the special dangers young black males faced on the road.

The long ordeal of the Scottsboro case began on March 25, 1931. A young white transient walking across the top of a railroad tank car traveling through rural Alabama stepped on the hand of Haywood Patterson, an eighteen-year-old black also hitching a ride on the train. Haywood had been riding the rails from the time he turned fourteen and had learned to stand up for himself, even to whites. He cursed the youth who stepped on his hand and a fight broke out between eight white and ten black transients as the train slowed to enter a railyard. The blacks eventually forced all but one of the whites, Orville Gilley, from the train. Patterson saved Gilley's life by pulling him into a moving boxcar as the train quickly accelerated out of the railyard.

The white boys who had been forced from the train told the stationmaster in the railyard that they had been attacked by a gang of blacks. The stationmaster telegraphed ahead to the town of Paint Rock, Alabama, where a sheriff's posse stopped the train. Two white females, twenty-one-year-old Victoria Price and eighteen-year-old Ruby Bates, were also riding in the train's freight cars that day. When confronted by the sheriff, Price and Bates said that a group of twelve black males with knives and pistols had raped them and attacked their friend Orville Gilley. The sheriff's posse searched the train and found nine black adolescents scattered throughout its freight cars. All were arrested, taken to jail in Scottsboro, Alabama, and charged with raping Price and Bates.

The press dubbed the nine African Americans arrested in the case the "Scottsboro Boys." Probably they were called "boys" because they were black, but all were still in their teens: Charles Weems and Andy Wright, nineteen; Haywood Patterson and Clarence Norris, eighteen; Olen Montgomery and Willie Robertson, seventeen; Ozzie Powell, sixteen; Eugene Williams, thirteen; and Roy Wright, twelve or thirteen at the time of his arrest. Their ages underscore the reality that many transients during the depression were adolescents.

Emotions surrounding the case ran high, and the nine defendants were nearly lynched the day after their arrest. A grand jury indicted the nine boys for rape on March 30; their separate trials began on April 6. The prosecution's evidence was flimsy from the start: a physician who examined Price and Bates concluded that it was highly unlikely either had been raped. The doctor also noted that one of the defendants, Willie Robertson, was severely handicapped by a serious case of syphilis and walked with a cane. Robertson's condition made it painful for him to have intercourse and almost impossible for him to move quickly from the scene of the alleged rape to the boxcar where he was arrested.

Despite weak evidence and the physician's testimony, the stage was set for convictions. The prosecution named Haywood Patterson as the group's ringleader and, according to the *New York Times*, the presiding judge instructed the juries in the cases that any defendant who they believed was in the boxcar at the time of the rapes "was guilty whether [he] had laid hands upon the women or not." The all-white, all-male juries believed the testimony given by Price, Bates, and Gilley. In a series of hasty verdicts, the juries convicted all nine defendants and sentenced eight to death. The youngest, Roy Wright, brother of Andy Wright, escaped a death sentence only on a technicality.[18]

The Scottsboro case became an international cause célèbre for civil rights when Northern newspapers reported on the trials. Lawyers from the International Labor Defense (a Communist-led legal group) and the National Association for the Advancement of Colored People (NAACP) competed for the right to appeal the convictions. Several of the Scottsboro defendants' mothers toured the United States and Europe seeking support for their sons' appeals and emphasizing that they were just boys. Black and white celebrities also became involved in the media circus. In January 1932 one of the girls, Ruby Bates, recanted her original story, maintaining that the black teens were actually innocent. Despite her change of heart, a rising groundswell of support for the boys, and a series of legal appeals, all the boys remained in jail.[19]

In July 1937 Alabama authorities finally acknowledged the weak evidence against four of the defendants by dropping charges against Willie Robertson, Roy Wright, Eugene Williams, and Olen Montgomery. The *New York Times* reported that the "boys" were welcomed to New York's Pennsylvania Station by a crowd of an "estimated 2,000 . . . welcoming Negroes. . . . Several women wept; others sought to touch the boys' arms. Everybody yelled." One person asked Roy Wright if he was frightened by the enthusiastic crowd. "Ah ain't nevah been afraid," the newspaper quoted Wright, "Ah wasn't afraid in 1931."[20]

The five Scottsboro Boys who remained in jail were not as fortunate. Reopened jury trials resulted in new convictions and death sentences for Norris and Patterson. Norris's sentence was reduced to life in prison by a gubernatorial declaration in 1938. Patterson went to trial two more times and escaped from jail twice, the second time living underground in Michigan. He told his story to the journalist I. F. Stone who published it in 1950 in *The Scottsboro Boy*. Federal agents soon recaptured Patterson, but Michigan's governor refused to grant Alabama's call for extradition after a nationwide letter-writing campaign pleaded for Patterson's release. He soon found himself in trouble again. In December 1950 a Michigan jury convicted him of manslaughter, and Patterson died in prison of cancer in August 1952.

At his second trial, young Andy Wright received a sentence of ninety-nine years in prison. Charlie Weems got seventy-five, and Ozzie Powell agreed to plead guilty in exchange for a twenty-year sentence. All three were eventually paroled. Clarence Norris had the dubious honor of being the last defendant in the Scottsboro case released from jail when Governor George Wallace pardoned him in 1976.[21]

In the 1930s many Americans were appalled by the clear civil rights violations in the Scottsboro case, but their reaction could not prevent the years of misery suffered by the eight defendants who spent much of their young lives in prison. Racism played a huge role in the case, but fears about transient youth shared by many

Americans during the depression also fueled the injustice. The Scottsboro case highlighted the concerns many people had about the generation of Americans coming of age during such hard times. Homeless young people who aimlessly wandered the nation presented new dangers that might spread to an entire generation. As President Franklin Roosevelt argued in 1932, "Any neglected group . . . can infect our national life and produce widespread misery."[22]

Recognizing America's Young "Gypsies"

In 1932 the U.S. Children's Bureau released its first report on the problem of transient youth spurred by the onset of the nation's economic depression. The bureau concluded that the new wave of young wanderers did not fit the stereotype of hoboes and tramps common in American society since the late nineteenth century. They were not simply irresponsible runaways, illiterates, alcoholics, drug addicts, or social dropouts; most were in fact looking for work, and many had spent at least some time in high school; a few had even gone to college. Officials from small towns in California and the temperate southwestern states were used to seeing adult hoboes, but they told the Children's Bureau that since 1929 local soup kitchens and homeless shelters were being flooded with transient boys and girls looking for food and shelter. One superintendent of a soup kitchen in Yuma, Arizona, reported that from November 1, 1931, through March 15, 1932, his organization had fed 7,500 transient "children."[23]

The nineteenth-century phrase "Go West, young man" was part of America's historical memory. Many Americans were tempted to see the latest generation of transients as simply following in the footsteps of earlier generations who had left home in search of opportunity. But sociologists and child-welfare advocates insisted that the old model did not apply in modern America. In his 1935 pamphlet *Youth in the Great Depression*, the renowned sociologist Kingsley Davis reminded Americans that "the last frontier disappeared some forty years ago. When young men now want to move on, they find there is no place to go." Davis maintained that "the machinery by which young people are drawn into the work of the nation had broken down; and youth, bearing the burden of this breakdown, were seeking blindly for some way out." Under such circumstances, he warned, rising crime rates were unavoidable and revolution was a real possibility.[24]

The secretary of the Cleveland Travelers Aid Society, Frances W. Hawes, expressed similar sentiments. She feared that the United States was in danger of creating an entire "generation of men with incomplete educations, who have never known the independence of regular jobs, and who feel that the government owes them a living."[25] *Scribner's Magazine* compared the nation's young transient population to the "disaffected and violent youth of the 1917 Russian Revolution." An article in the September 1933 *Survey Graphic* called unattached transients "An Army of Boys on the Loose." Child-welfare experts argued that rising juvenile delinquency rates were evidence of growing disaffection among American youth. A study of twenty thousand transients conducted in Buffalo, New York, from December 1933 through August 1935 found that one-third were teens and that these "boys and girls are close to becoming gypsies, if not bandits and criminals. . . . What will they be like when they have had a score or more in which to develop their unusual habits and allegiances?"[26]

In January 1933 Congress also brought new attention to the issue of young transients during committee hearings on unemployment relief. At one of the sessions, Senator Bronson Murray Cutting, a Republican from New Mexico, asked the Child Welfare League of America's executive director how many homeless children were riding the nation's railroads and hitchhiking along its highways. C. C. Carstens responded that no one knew for sure, but estimates ranged from 200,000 to 1,000,000. In another session, an official from the Southern Pacific Railroad reported that since 1927 the company had experienced a dramatic increase in the number of trespassers ejected from its property (78,099 in 1927, and 683,457 in 1932). He guessed that up to 75 percent of the violators were transient boys and youths under twenty-five. An Interstate Commerce Commission report on injuries to railroad trespassers noted that of 5,962 trespassers injured or killed during the first ten months of 1932, 1,508 had not reached their twenty-first birthday.[27]

During the same Senate hearings, the chief of the U.S. Children's Bureau, Grace Abbott, warned that wandering boys and girls "get used to the dangers and hardships; to the lack of opportunity for cleanliness; they overcome their abhorrence of begging." Being on the road shaped impressionable young people in undesirable ways. "Their interest is in 'getting by,' and they come to make a game of beating the authorities. The danger is not only what is happening to them now, but they can easily become confirmed in the habit of vagrancy and become what is called the American hobo."[28]

Conclusions like this confirmed fears of a fundamental problem that threatened American security. A 1933 study conducted among social workers, probation officers, teachers, and other professionals who regularly worked with children and youth in New York revealed that of all age groups, boys and girls over sixteen were most vulnerable to the depression's hardships. The report concluded that older teens and young people in their early twenties were being left behind, even with the minimal relief efforts in place.[29] A letter to Secretary of Labor Frances Perkins showed how this could easily happen. The letter writer explained that because his father was unemployed, the county provided a relief allowance for all the children in the family under sixteen years of age. Recently, however, when he had reached his sixteenth birthday, the county had eliminated the portion of the allowance that covered him. He tried to earn money to make up the difference, but, as he lamented, "I couldn't get a job for even one day." Feeling like a burden on his family, he hit the road in search of work and had been wandering from town to town, unable to find a job.[30]

In February 1933 President Hoover received a similar letter, this time from a parent who pleaded with the president to help America's young people. The letter's author, J. Newton Cloe, was a minister and father from Newport, Kentucky. Cloe explained that he was "an admirer and staunch supporter" of the president and "deeply disappointed" that Hoover would soon be leaving the White House. He urged Hoover, as a "humanitarian," to support legislation during his final days as president that would help the "thousands of American youths that are stranded and scattered, helplessly, hopelessly and heartlessly, throughout this country." Cloe argued that these young people were "not of an inferior class, but from our best homes." He offered the example of his own son, nineteen-year-old Delmar, who was "an Eagle Scout with most every available merit badge, a member of the Red Cross Life Saving Corps." A high school graduate, Delmar had attended the University of Cincinnati's cooperative education program. In the past year he had fruitlessly "traveled over ten thousand miles—'hitch-hiked'—in search of an honorable and lucrative position." Cloe pleaded with the president to do something "NOW" for boys like his son. "This is but the humble request of an anxious citizen, the heartfelt anticipation of a minister, who has given over thirty years of service to the uplift and spiritual welfare of youth and the fearful anxiety of a parent for the future of our country . . . as vested in the youth of today." Hoover responded that he was "intensely sympathetic in the matter" and believed that Congress would soon do something to help.[31]

Wild Boys of the Road

The release of the Warner Bros. film *Wild Boys of the Road* in the fall of 1933 helped focus public attention on the issue of young transients and America's youth problem. The film's themes were certainly predictable, but they reflected attitudes that help explain why Americans generally endorsed New Deal programs for America's youth by the time Franklin Roosevelt entered the White House in the spring of 1933. The movie's director, William A. Wellman, hoped the film would also act as a cautionary tale for boys and girls who might be thinking about taking to the road.

Wild Boys of the Road stars sixteen-year-old Frankie Darro as Eddie Smith, an earnest and optimistic teenager from an unnamed town in the Midwest. Eddie is an only child who shares an idyllic and loving relationship with his parents. His father has a supervisory job at a local cement plant that supports the family's middle-class life. Eddie knows he is much luckier than his best friend Tommy, played by a young-looking, twenty-year-old Edwin Philips. Tommy lives with his caring but apparently widowed mother who ekes out a meager living by taking in boarders. Eddie is seemingly oblivious to the depression's threats to his own family and instead tries to help his friend Tommy get a job at the cement plant.

Eddie's optimism is dashed when he learns that his father has been laid off. Wanting to help, he sells his beloved "jalopy" car for twenty-two dollars and gives the money to his father. Eddie's father is deeply touched by his son's generosity but can do little more than thank him.

Eddie now convinces his friend Tommy that they should hit the road in search of jobs. The boys hop a freight train and soon see that they are not the only young Americans on the road looking for work. They have a fight with a "boy" who is actually a freckle-faced girl named "Sally," played by nineteen-year-old Dorothy Coonan. Eddie, Tommy, and Sally join forces and agree to travel to Chicago in search of Sally's aunt. A happy reunion scene in Chicago is interrupted when police raid the brothel where Sally's aunt works. Having been told earlier by police not to remain in Chicago without jobs or a place to stay, the three friends feel they have no choice but to hop another freight and move on.

The film's next scenes illustrate the dangers and difficulties that faced young transients. Things get a little better for the protagonists when they find friendship and support among other adolescents on the road. Local authorities, however, offer no help and instead violently evict the young squatters from a Columbus, Ohio, railroad yard. As boys and girls scatter amidst the chaos, Eddie and Sally watch in horror when Tommy's leg is cut off by a passing train when he falls on the tracks. Tommy is hospitalized and survives, but in order to help his friend, Eddie becomes a criminal when he steals an artificial leg from a local store. The sad situation, he explains, justifies his crime.

In the movie's final scenes, Eddie, Tommy, and Sally make their way to New York City. Eddie finally finds a job, but he needs money to buy a uniform. While panhandling to earn the needed three dollars, Eddie and his friends become victims of adult criminals who easily manipulate them into unwittingly committing a crime. The three are arrested and charged with "vagrancy, petty theft, resisting police, breaking and entering, and hold up." They appear before a juvenile court judge but are unwilling to give their full names. Asked by the judge what he has to say for himself, Eddie passionately responds:

> Sure I got something to say. I knew that all that stuff about you helping us was baloney! I'll tell you why we can't go home. Our folks is poor, they can't get jobs and there isn't enough to eat. What good will it do for you to send us home to starve. You say that you've got to send us to jail to keep us off the streets. Well, that's a lie. You're sending us to jail 'cause you don't want to see us; you want to forget us. Well, you can't do it 'cause I'm not the only one. There's thousands like me and there's more like me hitting the road every day!

Tommy chimes in:

> You read in the papers about people giving help. The soldiers get
> it! The banks get it! The breweries get it! They're always yelling
> about giving it to the farmers! What about us! We're kids. . . .

Tommy's speech refers to early New Deal legislation—the Beer and
Wine Revenue Act, the granting of World War I veterans' bonuses,
and the Emergency Banking Act. Eddie argues that he and his
friends also deserve help because they are not juvenile delinquents
or tramps, just good kids who are innocent victims of bad times.

> I'm not a bad boy, neither is Tommy. Us three kids been traveling
> around the country looking for work. You don't think we like the
> road, do ya? I only did it because I wanted to work. Go ahead.
> Lock me up. Jail can't be any worse than being on the road.

Eddie's tough exterior unravels to reveal a vulnerable boy. He
breaks into uncontrollable sobs, which moves the judge to dismiss
the charges and promise that Eddie will start his new job. The judge
then tells Sally that he will help her get work as a domestic. This is
an important change since it suggests that life will now be closer to
normal: Sally will no longer have to pretend she is a boy. The judge
laments that it will be harder to do something for Tommy but
promises a solution. Not only will the friends be receiving immediate help, but the judge assures them and the movie audience that
"Things are going to be better now." Roosevelt's election meant that
"unemployed parents would be going back to work soon."[32]

A *New York Times* reviewer criticized *Wild Boys of the Road* as
"disappointing" because it "over sentimentalized" the tragic condition of the nation's young transients. Further, the reviewer complained, the film's "happy ending . . . robbed it of its value as a social
challenge." Despite these shortcomings, the critic noted that the audience was touched by the film's message, with "audible sob-stifling
and feminine murmurs of shock and grief." Twelve-year-old Robert

Symmonds was touched in a different way. He saw *Wild Boys of the Road* in a Seattle theater but came away with a view exactly opposite what the film's director had intended. "Seeing *Wild Boys of the Road*," Symmonds recalled, put "ideas into your head. . . . Kids loved it." When school was out in June 1934, Symmonds and a friend took their first of many illicit train rides. The boys jumped into a Great Northern Railway boxcar in Seattle that took them five hundred miles to Portland, Oregon. They tried to ride back to Seattle the following evening on another train but instead ended up in Vancouver. There they hopped a tank car, holding on for dear life in a hair-raising ride to Centralia, where they were finally able to move to a boxcar when the train made a brief stop. Despite their frightening experience, Symmonds remembered arriving in Seattle feeling "like conquering heroes."[33] There is no way to know how many other young viewers shared Symmonds's reaction to *Wild Boys of the Road*. But the movie was among the growing calls for government intervention to help solve the nation's youth problem.

Boy and Girl Tramps of America

In 1934 Thomas Patrick Minehan added to the national discussion by publishing *Boy and Girl Tramps of America*. The book provided one of the few opportunities to hear the voices of young Americans who had become transients. From 1931 to 1933 Minehan had been a graduate student in sociology at the University of Minnesota. He completed the work that became the basis of his 1934 book as part of his master's thesis.[34] Minehan conducted 1,465 interviews (1,377 boys and 88 girls) and documented 509 case studies (493 boys and 16 girls) with young transients. He described his research as "500 life histories of boys and girls I had met on the bum, 1,000 samples of conversations, and over 2,500 opinions, ideas, and attitudes expressed by all classes of transients under all conditions." Minehan used only nicknames to identify the young people he encountered, but *Boy and Girl Tramps of America* provides important insights into the everyday lives of transient youth.[35]

Minehan hoped his book would stimulate the development of long-term policies to "reclaim the youth which we are losing" to the hardships of the depression. In the Introduction, he explains how he got interested in studying homeless transients. One evening in November 1932 he put on some "old clothes and stood in a bread line in the cold and the rain." The experience "was memorable," he wrote. "I can still see the ragged cold line of men shivering in the rain and slime of an alley. . . . Here I decided was a possibility of getting ideas, attitudes, and viewpoints of the mass of men hit most cruelly by the depression." He began to hang out with homeless transients and soon discovered that many were not men but boys. Broadening his study to hobo jungles (makeshift squatter camps near railroad yards), Minehan also met a few girls, "children really— dressed in overalls or army breeches and boys' coats or sweaters— looking, except for their dirt and rags, like a Girl Scout club on an outing."[36] He asked young wanderers why they had left home, how they traveled, how they obtained food and clothing, and where they slept. He also tried to learn about their educational experience, sex lives, religious beliefs, and political philosophies. His findings supported the claims of child-welfare experts that most young transients were looking for work and were being left behind by an America suffering through its worst economic crisis in history.

The young people in Minehan's sample were primarily adolescents and youth whom many Americans would recognize as the average girl or boy next door. Of the 548 individuals he identified by age, 291 were 13 through 16; 282 were 17 through 21; and only 4 were under 13. All 29 girls in the study were under 19. Ninety-five percent of the transients in Minehan's sample were born in the United States and most claimed to be Protestant, Catholic, or Jewish. Sixty-two identified themselves as "nonbelievers." Reflective of their generation, only a minority had earned a high school diploma (27), but over half had graduated from at least the eighth grade, and 25 had taken at least a few classes in college. Most had been on the road more than six months but less than two years. They came from both rural and urban America and hailed from 30 different states.[37]

"Hard times" was the most frequent reason young transients gave for why they had left home. Of those interviewed, 321 reported that either one or both of their parents had died, and another 89 said their parents were divorced. Among the teens whose parents were still alive, a majority of fathers had been unemployed for more than 12 months.

Some young transients said they simply wanted to travel. Others hated school. "Nothing I ever did ever satisfied anybody in school," one girl told Minehan. "I hated them all," she added. A boy nicknamed Omaha Red explained that he ran away because, "All my life I hated school." A few left home to escape a violent parent or stepparent. Asked "if he ever got a licking at home," a boy named Nick told Minehan, "That's all I ever got. The old man would lick me if I did something. The old lady if I didn't."[38]

"Some trouble with a girl" was also a reason offered by a few young male transients. A former college student recounted that he had decided to leave town after the father of a girl he knew came "over to our house and began to raise hell. . . . He thought I ought to marry her I suppose. But I couldn't see it that way, when she was a push-over for every guy in the fraternity row. So I beats it. Being on the bum is better than being married anyway—especially to something like that."

Many of the girls Minehan met on the road were traveling with boyfriends. "We were going to get married anyway," one girl explained. Another recalled that her father, "the old man," caught her "necking too heavy on the back porch one night." He barred the girl's boyfriend, Joe, from coming near his daughter again unless the two got married. "Joe says he didn't want to get married just yet 'cause he liked to be free kinda. But he was pretty hot for me too and one day he asks me to scram and we scrammed."[39]

As *Boy and Girl Tramps* confirmed, the longer young transients stayed on the road, the more likely they were to develop attitudes and behaviors contrary to mainstream American values. In a society that had long disdained charity for the able-bodied, young transients willingly accepted handouts and ate most of their meals at missions run by the Salvation Army and other private philanthropies. Other times they begged or stole what they could, justifying their crimes as acceptable during times that seemed to unfairly target the young. Backyard clotheslines were a favorite "fishing" location for something to wear. Many boys and girls developed creative and dishonest scams for getting what they needed. A boy nicknamed Happy Joe said that when begging for food it was a good strategy to "tell them you got a sick mother and a lot of younger kids at home hungry. . . . That way you get more and will have a nice lunch for later." Young transients stole from farmers' chicken coops, gardens, and orchards, and few seemed to feel guilty about their unsociable behavior. Stealing was better than starving or going without needed comforts. A few talked openly about injuring others or even killing someone in order to get what they believed was rightfully theirs.[40]

Sexuality among young transients also defied social norms, Minehan showed. "Prostitution is regarded as a normal occupation by both boys and girls," he wrote. In one incident, a sixteen-year-old girl was willingly having sex with most of the males on a freight train. Worried that she might get hurt, Minehan complained about the situation to a railroad brakeman. The brakeman went to the boxcar where the girl was having sex with several men and demanded to know if she was all right. She "came to the door a little bit drunk and very undressed." Cursing the brakeman the girl yelled, "You big fat fool. You Y.M.C.A. dummy. Why do you have to spoil it all? Why can't you let a girl alone when she isn't hurting you? Everything was fine, all right, and now you've spoiled it all." Minehan maintained that transients had few inhibitions when it came to sexuality or other temptations that they might otherwise have been curbed in mainstream society. Masturbation and homosexuality were not uncommon. Some young transients also became the victims of pedophiles. Minehan wrote that many of the kids he met learned to avoid "certain older men [who] become friendly with a lonely boy and attempt[ed] to seduce him."[41]

Life on the road contributed to the cynical attitude many young transients held about politics, politicians, and business. Minehan said he often heard such comments as, "Show me a politician and I'll show you a crook," and "Listen, they got more honest men behind bars than they have on the bench." When Chicago Mayor Anton Cermak was shot in Miami on February 15, 1933, during a public appearance with President-elect Franklin Roosevelt, there was little sympathy from the young people Minehan encountered. After Cermak died from his wounds, a transient boy known as Boo Peep gleefully exclaimed, "Geez, they got somebody at last . . . and maybe Hoover too." Boo Peep mistakenly thought the mayor's assassination marked the beginning of what he and his friends believed was a welcome and inevitable revolution.[42]

Minehan hoped to scare the public into doing something to help American youth. "Although still very young," Minehan concluded, many of the transients he met had "already acquired the outlook of the chronic tramp." Other observers expressed similar opinions. A journalist traveling through the United States during the mid-1930s believed that transients were only the most visible part of a "lost generation" of Americans who were like "runners delayed at the gun. They have lost so much time at the start that only the exceptional can challenge at the finish." Others, like Minehan, were not as pessimistic and instead suggested solutions for America's Youth Problem. In his book's conclusion, Minehan argued that the generation could be saved if Americans were willing "to examine not only our present policies of handling youth but our entire economic and social system, the philosophy and practices which have driven youth into vagabondage."[43] "Anything to get off the road," a homeless boy known as Texas told Minehan. "I've seen enough of the country. One city is just like another. And if a guy keeps traveling around too much, he becomes a bum. And I don't want to be a bum."[44] Minehan hoped that Americans would offer boys like Texas a better future.

Roosevelt and America's Youth Problem

In May 1934 a police detective arrested sixteen-year-old John Domanski in a New York City train station on a pickpocket charge. John was not a transient—he lived with his parents—but many Americans would have identified him as part of the country's youth problem. According to the detective, the boy was acting as a lookout for a younger boy who was attempting to steal the wallet of a man sleeping on a public bench in the terminal. Asked why his parents were not at court with him, John replied, "I don't want them to know. I'll defend myself." The court magistrate persuaded John to go home and ask for help because, he explained, "it was silly for a fellow in trouble to keep it from his parents." Arthur Baletti, owner of a Washington Market trucking firm, overheard the discussion and offered to help secure John's $500 bail. Baletti told a *New York Times* reporter that he did so because "I hate to see a kid start off on the wrong foot."[45]

By the time Franklin Roosevelt entered the White House, a growing number of Americans felt like Arthur Baletti. On March 21, 1933, Roosevelt asked Congress to approve a new work-relief program for unmarried males aged eighteen through twenty-five. Unemployed veterans of any age were also eligible for the program. The

Roosevelt's Civilian Conservation Corps was one of the first and most popular New Deal work-relief programs. Many Americans liked the CCC's emphasis on discipline, hard work, and work-relief as part of the remedy for the plight of America's older male teens and youth. *(Library of Congress)*

president's plan envisioned "a civilian construction corps to be used in simple work, not interfering with normal employment, and confining itself to forestry, the prevention of soil erosion, flood control, and similar projects."[46] The CCC (the letters ultimately stood for Civilian Conservation Corps) was Franklin Roosevelt's pet project. In 1935 Congress expanded the eligible age range for CCC enrollees to include seventeen-year-olds, but the effort never included those under age seventeen. It is also difficult to say that many transients entered the CCC since enrollees had to be living with their families who were already on relief rolls. Nonetheless some boys and young men must have decided to join the CCC rather than become a transient. The CCC excluded females of any age.[47] The president's first New Deal program for youth fit the gender stereotypes that shaped all federal programs during the Great Depression.

In 1935 Roosevelt added another New Deal relief program aimed at older teens and youth. His Executive Order 7086, signed on June 26, 1935, established the National Youth Administration (NYA) as part of the Works Progress Administration. Although also a relief program designed to meet the needs of young people, the NYA was not a residential program like the CCC. Instead it emphasized keeping young Americans connected to their families and extending their education.[48] The NYA's establishment and implementation clearly showed that while the Roosevelt administration was concerned for the plight of young Americans who were coming of age during the depression, its formula for success was to keep teens in school, not in the workplace.

An American youth movement that began on college campuses throughout the United States in the 1930s put growing pressure on the Roosevelt administration to do even more to help the nation's teens and youth. Left-leaning groups such as the American Student Union (ASU, 1935–1941) and the American Youth Congress (AYC, 1934–1941) attracted students from diverse social and ethnic backgrounds. The AYC became the nation's largest student activist organization, holding its first national meeting in Washington, D.C., in 1934 and reaching a peak membership of 4.5 million in 1939. The group also advocated world peace, anti-fascism, and gender and racial equality. Because the voting age in the United States was twenty-one, the AYC had to devise means other than voting power to promote its goals. AYC members participated in international meetings on youth issues and sponsored peaceful protests on various campuses and in Washington, D.C. Most important, AYC leaders formed alliances with prominent adults such as Eleanor Roosevelt, who raised money and served as an advocate for the organization within the administration. By 1935 this friendly relationship had deteriorated when the group criticized the NYA as an important but grossly inadequate measure that helped only a small fraction of the estimated eight million needy teens and youth. Even among those who were part of the program, the AYC noted, stipends were too low to allow students from the poorest families to remain in school. The AYC was also unhappy about the persistence of racism within the NYA, despite Mary McCleod Bethune's appointment as head of the agency's Colored Division. On July 4, 1936, the AYC presented a "Declaration of the Rights of Youth," which outlined a broad agenda of political views about young Americans and their families.

> On the Fourth of July one hundred and sixty years ago our forefathers declared their independence from despotic rule in order to realize their inalienable rights to life, liberty, and the pursuit of happiness. Today our lives are threatened by war; our liberties threatened by reactionary legislation; and our right to happiness remains illusory in a world of insecurity. Therefore, on this Fourth day of July, 1936, we, the young People of America, in Congress assembled, announce our own declaration—A Declaration of the Rights of American Youth.[49]

The AYC's declaration went on to oppose government policies that destroyed agricultural products (in an attempt to remove surpluses and stabilize prices) "when so many Americans went hungry." It denounced campus officials who tried to curtail student and faculty protest activities. It endorsed unions and the right of workers to engage in protest. Finally the AYC declared American youth's "right to happiness!" This included "the right of freedom from toil for children for whom labor can only mean physical and mental harm." Among older youth the AYC declared "a right to work" and "the right of proper preparation for work . . . without discrimination, poor as well as rich, Negroes as well as white, through free scholarships and government aid to needy students." Specifically, the nation's "educational system should provide for vocational training at adequate wages, under trade union supervision." The AYC said it recognized that "young people do not constitute a separate social group," but members argued that the problems and aspirations of America's younger generation were "intimately bound up with those of all the people." The statement ended with a declaration of loyalty to the United States and an optimistic view of the future. "We look at this country of ours. We love it dearly; we are its flesh and marrow. Therefore, we the young people of America, reaffirm our right to life, liberty and the pursuit of happiness. With confidence we look forward to a better life, a larger liberty and freedom." AYC members did not expect to be handed a better life, but they felt it was their right to earn one. "To those ends we dedicate our lives, our intelligence and our unified strength."[50]

By the late 1930s the number of young transients dropped as a rising proportion of young Americans remained in high school and went on to college. And more young people were staying home as government relief programs provided at least the bare essentials for many families. A slightly improved job market also enabled some parents to find work, making it possible for their children to stay in school. The success of the CCC and the NYA also made a difference. From 1933 through 1942, 3 million young men served in the CCC. The NYA enrolled more than 4 million young Americans, about 10 percent of the nation's student body. The drop in the overall unemployment rate also helped some young jobseekers find employment, especially those who earned at least a high school diploma.[51] As students of American history know, however, it was the United States' move toward entrance into the Second World

War that helped end the Great Depression. A memo prepared by U.S. Children's Bureau staff in 1940 estimated that 3.9 million Americans aged fifteen through twenty-five were still looking for a job. Of those, approximately 60 percent were male and 40 percent female. While still a large number, the data also reveals a significant change from the pre-depression era: only 2 percent of the estimated group was under sixteen, and sixteen- and seventeen-year-olds constituted less than 17 percent of the total pool of young jobseekers.[52] By 1940 many young people who might have dropped out of school and hit the road had decided that attending high school was a better, and feasible, choice. The dwindling number of young transients reflected the growing possibility of a brighter future for America.

CHAPTER FOUR

The Importance of
Being Educated

JOE PENNIGER wanted the best for his three daughters and three sons. "I want them all to graduate from high school and get some kind of business education," Penniger told a Federal Writers' Project interviewer in 1939. "I'll send them to college if they want to go. I didn't go to school any after I finished the seventh grade. I quit for the lack of sense, I guess, because my father tried to get me to stay in school." Penniger's experience and attitude toward education were typical of many adults during the closing months of the Great Depression. Like Penniger, most had not attended school beyond the elementary grades themselves, but many had changed their minds about the value of their children earning at least a high school diploma. "I see a lot of things differently since I've grown up," Penniger explained. "Kids who go to school have more advantages. . . . My oldest girl has a job in the Court house that she would not have been able to get or keep if she had quit school like I did."[1]

In the 1930s parents like Joe Penniger, politicians, popular culture, and policymakers learned to pay greater attention to the links between poverty and the lack of school-based education. By the end of the decade this shift fueled by the depression's economic crisis led to expanded access to school-based education for both children and adolescents. National debates over school curriculums and modernization linked the nation's future progress with the establishment of better schools.

Since the late nineteenth century, child-welfare advocates and educators had recommended extending school-based education for all American children. By 1930 their efforts had been only partly successful. That year the Census counted 95 percent of children age six through thirteen in school full-time. Every state had enacted compulsory school attendance laws for youngsters in this age group, and a majority extended the requirement to sixteen-year-olds. But only 51 percent of fourteen-through-seventeen-year-olds remained in school beyond the elementary grades. That was an improvement over the 1920 figure for teens that counted only 35 percent still in school, but the 1930 figure did not meet the goals of education advocates.

Many observers also lamented that American schools varied enormously in quality and accessibility. The poorest schools could be found in Southern states, where limited tax revenue, low incomes, and racial segregation hampered the efforts of progressive educators. Jim Crow segregation also hindered improvements, and reformers were quick to note that the South had the nation's highest illiteracy rates. A majority of the country's rural areas continued to offer only the most rudimentary school-based education for children. The one-room schoolhouse remained the only educational facility in many communities located outside towns and cities. Further complicating the picture, by the early 1930s American schools faced the worst budget crisis in their history. While the depression created a new concern for education, America needed to embrace new strategies if schools were to become the public cornerstone of the modern childhood ideal.

Despite desperate times, after Franklin Roosevelt's election the federal government joined the states to channel more money into public schools than ever before. By 1940 more young Americans were staying in school longer than at any time to that point in history. The growth in school attendance among fourteen-through-seventeen-year-olds is striking evidence of this shift. The rate jumped 25 percent among adolescents in just the early years of the depression (to 64 percent in 1933). It increased 43 percent over the decade, with the 1940 Census counting 73 percent of fourteen-through-seventeen-year-olds still in school. From 1930 to 1940 the number of high school graduates in the total population almost doubled, from 667,000 to 1,221,000.[2] For the first time in American history, staying in school long enough to earn a high school diploma became the norm rather than the exception.

The influx of money and increasing public support for education also produced a rise in the overall quality of America's schools and a shift to schools organized by ages and grade levels. In addition, the New Deal selectively implemented unprecedented programs at the federal level that paid teachers' salaries, offered educational instruction to needy children and adolescents, and funded the construction of new school buildings and libraries. Communities consolidated resources to build bigger, fancier, and better-equipped schools. The number of school buildings actually shrank as states closed one-room schoolhouses to open new age- and grade-level schools, many of which were paid for with the help of federal funding. New federal educational programs also provided money for preschools for children from poor families and dispensed stipends to needy older teens and college-age youth. By 1940 these changes in school-based education had expanded opportunities for a generation of young people. Increasingly they expected to attend elementary, middle, and high school as part of the universal experience shared by all children and teens in the United States.[3]

Trends in America's Schools

Some common themes shaped American education for children and adolescents in the 1930s. Hiroko Kamikawa, born on July 11, 1920, in Fresno, California, remembered that throughout her childhood her Japanese-American parents emphasized school-based education as an important tool for adult success. In 1926, when Hiroko was six years old, she entered first grade at Lincoln Elementary, the public school located in her neighborhood. Fresno was a town of about 150,000, and like most communities of its size, it had several elementary, middle, and high schools. Throughout the United States, students at local elementary schools generally reflected the demographic makeup of the surrounding community—unless legally enforced racial segregation overruled neighborhood boundaries. Black students attended inferior racially segregated schools in Jim Crow states, and San Francisco operated separate schools for Chinese-American children.

Fresno did not practice legally enforced racial segregation; Lincoln Elementary reflected the social makeup of its surrounding neighborhood. In Hiroko's case that meant she attended school with children of Japanese or Chinese heritage and a few from European immigrant families. Like most children who attended school in their own neighborhoods, Hiroko knew her classmates well and felt quite comfortable in school. She was a good student and popular among her peers.

Samuel Prince's memories of his years in elementary school are similar to those of Hiroko Kamikawa, though the two lived at opposite ends of the United States under very different personal circumstances. Samuel spent several years in New York's Hebrew National Orphan Home (HNOH) and went to P.S. 403. The subjects at P.S. 403 were virtually the same as those taught at Lincoln in Fresno. Like Hiroko, Samuel felt safe at school and liked being there. Going to school for him meant "doing something important, where good effort was rewarded."[4]

Children at schools like Lincoln and P.S. 403 often recognized ethnic and racial differences, but these distinctions acted more as curiosities than divisions among the younger students. Hiroko remembered one incident that illustrated this point. One day her teacher reprimanded her and two German boys for chewing gum. As punishment, Hiroko and her classmates had to stand in front of the other children and sing songs while prominently displaying on their noses the wads of gum taken from their mouths. Since Hiroko's parents spoke no English at home, she knew more Japanese than English and chose to sing a Japanese folk song entitled "Hato Popo." For similar reasons the twins picked a German tune. Contrary to the teacher's intent, Hiroko recalled that all three had a good time, and the other students in the class enjoyed hearing the traditional folk songs.[5]

In the 1930s school authorities often disciplined children through tactics of humiliation, like those used by Hiroko Kamikawa's teacher. They also sent notes home to parents and ordered students to complete repetitious writing assignments. Teachers and principals sometimes meted out physical punishment—a hard rap on a child's knuckles with a ruler, or paddling a student on the behind. Attending school in rural Nebraska, Walter Schmitt remembered watching a fellow student have his mouth "scrubbed out with soap" as punishment for uttering "language that he shouldn't have used." Misbehaving students sometimes received detentions, suspensions, and expulsions. Such punishments were serious, but by the 1930s school officials generally placed less importance on strict discipline than earlier generations of educators had done.[6]

The move to age- and grade-level education was an even more important change in American schools. Urban areas had chosen to build age- and grade-level schools since the late nineteenth century. But most rural areas could not afford such programs, or their school-age populations were too small to justify the model. In the 1930s districts throughout the United States shifted to the urban age- and grade-level model. Curriculums for elementary and middle schools, however, changed little. Most students began school at age six, when they entered first grade. Some urban districts included kindergartens, but they were still rare in American elementary education. History, geography, grammar, mathematics, and penmanship dominated state-sanctioned school curriculums in the lower grades (sometimes referred to as grammar school for grades one through eight). Yet teaching styles, materials for students, and the quality of school facilities were very different from one school district to the next. Still, most schools offered the same basic subjects.

In the 1930s, as part of an effort to attract adolescents who found little practical value in the classical liberal education offered in American high schools, urban districts added vocational and business courses to the curriculum. The vocational education movement had begun during the second decade of the twentieth century. In 1911 Charles Prosser became the first secretary of the new National Society for the Promotion of Industrial Education. Prosser envisioned the establishment of vocational "continuation schools" throughout the United States. He believed that such facilities should be separate from traditional high schools and offer classes two or three nights a week to fourteen-through-eighteen-year-olds who had already left school for full-time employment. Prosser believed vocational training would provide "deserted" adolescents with work-related skills that could benefit the larger society as well as individual teens.

Most education policymakers agreed that vocational classes were a good idea, but they feared that Prosser's model would encourage even more adolescents to drop out of school. So instead of separate night courses for working teens, reformers devised plans to integrate vocational education curriculums into the existing public high school model. By the 1930s this second approach had won out over Prosser's idea. Circumstances during the depression further increased the popularity of publicly funded vocational curriculums within the traditional high school. Vocational programs were sometimes located in separate buildings, or they co-existed as separate tracks within the same facility.[7]

Before the 1920s and 1930s, most adolescents who sought vocational training left school for courses offered through private organizations such as the YMCA or YWCA, or for on-the-job training. Advocates of the new two-track high school model argued that all adolescents should stay in school through high school graduation, no matter what their career goals. In practice the system was not as equitable as it sounded since students were often tracked into either the vocational or the college preparatory track based on their race, ethnicity, gender, or socioeconomic status rather than their academic ability. Catholic high schools generally did not offer vocational education at all, primarily due to scarce resources. As demand for vocational education increased during the 1930s, private organizations such as the YMCA and YWCA reinvigorated their educational activities, concentrating on business skills such as bookkeeping, shorthand, and typing.[8]

By the 1930s many teens were willing to leave their neighborhoods in order to attend a high school that better met their needs. Hiroko Kamikawa's dream of going to college led her to seek out a high school that offered a traditional classical curriculum. So she transferred from Edison, the secondary school closest to her home, to Fresno High School, the county's college preparatory institution located across town.[9]

Opened in 1899, Fresno High School was the oldest and most prestigious secondary school in the area. High schools that offered the classical liberal curriculum remained the best that American secondary education had to offer. In the prosperous 1920s many communities had spent lavishly in constructing new state-of-the-art high schools. New buildings, especially those built for schools that offered the traditional classical curriculum, often included swimming pools, gymnasiums, football fields, track-and-field facilities, auditoriums and stages, and specialized classrooms. Fresno County officials had followed the trend by proudly opening a new building for Fresno High School in 1922. This is where Kamikawa spent her high school years and where she earned a diploma in 1938, graduating among the top ten in her class.[10]

While finding the right high school might mean avoiding a school closer to home, adolescents living in many rural communities did not always have the luxury of choice. Many students in the segregated South, even those in urban communities, also had few options. Still, the growing willingness among many students to travel longer distances for a more specialized education underscores the increasing importance that teens and their families placed on high school during the depression.

Another important element of the shift in secondary education was a growing attention to extracurricular activities as an essential part of adolescence. High schools urged students to participate in adult-controlled team sports, clubs, and various social activities. Since the turn of the century, child-welfare advocates had promoted the regulation of adolescents' social lives as well as their academic education. High schools became the focus of such reforms during the early decades of the twentieth century, but at the time many teens did not attend high school. Extracurricular activities were well entrenched by the 1930s as part of what educators called "the equalization of opportunity" promoted in the nation's secondary schools. They also touched the lives of more Americans as an increasing percentage of teens remained in school through high school graduation. School principals responded to a survey asking about their support for extracurricular activities by noting their primary motivations: socialization, training for social cooperation, experience of group life, improvements in discipline, and training for leadership in a democracy.[11]

In the April 1930 issue of the *Pictorial Review*, Eleanor Roosevelt pointed to high school and its extracurricular activities as part of good citizenship. In answer to the question, "What is the purpose of education?" Mrs. Roosevelt agreed with the traditional argument that education's dual goals were "vocational skills" and "good citizenship." She took her discussion further by endorsing extracurricular activities as part of the fundamental educational process for all young people. "The other school contacts—social activities and athletics—develop team play, cooperation, and thought and consideration for others. These are all essentials in good citizenship," she declared. Every adolescent, no matter what his or her individual plan for the future, needed to go to high school and participate in extracurricular activities. "The practical side of good citizenship," Mrs. Roosevelt argued, "is developed most successfully in school because [there], in miniature, one is living in a society, and the conditions and problems of the larger society are more easily reproduced and met and solved."

Going further, she explained that "Learning to be a good citizen is learning to live to the maximum of one's abilities and opportunities." This meant that in America's schools "every subject should be taught every child with this in view." Adults must "take a constant interest in all educational institutions and remember that on the public school largely depends the success or the failure of our great experiment in government 'by the people, for the people.'"[12] In other words, schools ought to nurture each individual student's full potential. A diversified curriculum and schooling beyond the elementary grades was no longer a luxury but a necessity for the future of American democracy.

The curriculum details alluded to by the first lady became the center of a significant philosophical debate over education in the 1930s. The decade's economic crisis had fostered new criticism of many traditional American values that linked free enterprise and big business with democracy. Critics such as Father Charles Coughlin and Huey Long blamed unregulated capitalism and its uneven distribution of wealth for causing and continuing the depression.

Groups like the American Legion and the National Association of Manufacturers (NAM) worked through America's schools to fight such criticism. Consumerism, business, and patriotism, they contended, were essential parts of "the American Way of Life."

NAM distributed pamphlets, booklets, films, and other educational materials in America's schools. The NAM campaign also used billboards and magazine advertisements to sell the idea that "free enterprise . . . free speech, a free press and free religion [were] integral parts of democracy." The American Legion called for the dismissal of "disloyal teachers" who taught "subversive" ideas in their classrooms. Many politicians seemed to agree. In 1935 twenty states required teachers to take loyalty oaths, and Congress passed an appropriations bill that included a rider forbidding school districts from paying teachers "spreading communist doctrine." The act was repealed in 1937 after protests from free-speech groups and objections by officials within the Roosevelt administration, but the issue did not go away. School board members in Bradner, Ohio, burned textbooks they considered unpatriotic. Towns in New York and New Jersey banished social studies texts considered "un-American." The influence of the American Legion and NAM was felt in schools across the United States. By the late 1930s school curriculums, especially at the high school level, increasingly linked free speech, consumerism, and patriotism.[13]

Schools also served as the primary means to advance ideas about children's and teens' health care. More than ever before, students received sight and hearing tests at school. Districts employed nurses who checked young bodies for lice, worms, or other parasites and weighed and measured elementary school students to see if they were getting adequate nutrition. Some public health officials implemented immunization programs in elementary schools for diseases such as diphtheria. High schools expanded public health efforts to include basic information about sexuality and adolescent health care. Living "the American Way" also meant brushing your teeth regularly—preferably with commercial toothpaste—and using other health-care products. For many youngsters, schools were the only place they received preventive health care. The attention to children's health was also part of an overall trend linking school-based education, recreation, consumption, and good citizenship with overall health.[14]

Lessons Learned Outside of School

Age- and grade-level schools became a larger part of the lives of children and adolescents during the 1920s and 1930s, but there were also important educational lessons to be learned outside the classroom. This was especially true for children who were members of ethnic, religious, and racial minorities. Like most Japanese-American young people growing up in California, Hiroko Kamikawa attended *Gakuen* (Japanese language school) held at the local Buddhist temple where she went to religious services on Sundays. Most of the Japanese-American and Chinese-American children in Hiroko's neighborhood attended *Gakuen*. Interestingly, two black and two white children also took advantage of *Gakuen*'s offerings. Parents looked to the private school as a supplement to their children's "American" education. Hiroko, though, found the language classes quite difficult. Her assessment seemed on target since the U.S. Army discovered during World War II that few American-born Nisei had the skills necessary to work as interpreters, though many had attended Japanese language classes at a neighborhood *Gakuen* as children and teens.[15]

It is likely that most young Japanese Americans shared Hiroko's frustration with the language classes but understood her enthusiasm for the extracurricular activities that took place at the Buddhist temple. Most Japanese-American parents prohibited or strictly controlled the social activities of their children. Hiroko remembered joining a club for adolescent girls called the Lumbini. Such groups offered companionship and opportunities for chaperoned interaction with the opposite sex. She also played basketball and remembers games against teams sponsored by other Buddhist churches in the Central Valley. The historian Valerie Matsumoto has counted more than four hundred Nisei youth organizations in the 1930s in southern California alone.[16]

The United States has a long history of special clubs and schools organized along religious, ethnic, and racial lines. In the nineteenth century the Roman Catholic church fought to retain the right to establish parochial schools. It strengthened such efforts during the 1920s as part of the resistance against growing anti-Catholic prejudice. Groups like the Young Men's Hebrew Association (YMHA) also expanded. YMCAs and YWCAs looked for new avenues of influence. For example, the Baltimore YMCA taught sex education to young men and their parents "as a natural part of the programs."[17] In an era when strong racial and ethnic prejudices persisted throughout the nation, parochial schools and private ethnic, religious, and cultural organizations provided important opportunities for children and teens to learn social and leadership skills in a comfortable setting among others like themselves. For Hiroko, "belonging to the Buddhist church was like being embraced by a protective shield, spiritually and emotionally."[18]

The Depression's Threat to America's Schools

As noted earlier, basic educational trends were not uniform throughout the United States at the onset of the depression. Changes occurred because of the national crisis that affected America's schools during the first years of the 1930s. The 1930 White House Conference on Child Health and Protection created a "Children's Charter," which included a declaration that every child in

America had the right to attend "a school which is safe from hazards, sanitary, properly equipped, lighted, and ventilated." Younger children had the right to "nursery schools and kindergartens," and every child had the right to "an education which, through the discovery and development of his individual abilities, prepares him for life; and through training and vocational guidance prepares him for a living which will yield him the maximum satisfaction." The conference's Committee on the School Child devised guidelines that encouraged states to fund the construction of schools and foster academic curriculums around "the interests, needs, and abilities" of students. Local government officials and school administrators were urged to provide health programs and "desirable leisure time activities." Above all, the committee maintained, "equalization of opportunity [should be] sought in all schools, by all possible means, for all school children . . . this applied to all schools whether urban or rural, to Negro Schools, Indian Schools, and all other types of schools in the United States and . . . territories."[19]

But neither the 1930 White House Conference nor the Hoover administration lobbied Congress for the funds to help states and their schools implement these programs. In the 1920s states had expanded access to public education, but the 1930s presented serious funding problems for schools.[20] The lower birthrate of the early 1920s helped ease the pressure on schools in the first two years of the depression, but by the spring of 1932 there were clear signs of serious trouble.

That May the U.S. Senate held special hearings on what Chicago school officials called "a unique situation." The city's school board was out of money and owed its public school teachers two months' pay. Irvin A. Wilson, president of the Chicago Principals Club, appealed to the senators' sense of patriotism and pointed to the White House Conference's endorsement of school-based education as a right of childhood. Chicago teachers and administrators, he explained, "believe that education and citizenship must go hand in hand. . . . Certainly the ideals of America support public education. We are willing to make any sacrifice, and we have made all sacrifices in order that the schools of [Chicago] remain open." Wilson did not believe the nation could "afford to permit 500,000 boys and girls to remain out upon the streets of the second largest city. . . ." The senators expressed sympathy but offered no financial aid and seemed not to realize that Chicago's problem was only the canary in the mine shaft signaling the onset of a national school crisis.

Funded primarily by property taxes, school districts across the country soon found themselves in the same situation as officials in Chicago. They lost their major source of revenue as a rising number of home and business owners defaulted on local tax payments. In the months following the congressional hearings, the situation in Chicago and elsewhere only worsened. On April 16, 1933, more than twenty thousand students, teachers, and parents formed a mile-long march through Chicago's streets protesting that teachers had not been paid in eight months. A policeman told an impatient motorist delayed by the marchers, "These teachers have waited nearly a year for their pay; you can afford to wait an hour for their parade."[21]

Faced with shrinking budgets and higher demand, especially at the high school level, school officials and states across the country solicited the federal government for help. The Hoover administration continued to do nothing, but early in the new presidency, the Roosevelt administration approved construction projects and funneled grants and loans to school districts through the Federal Emergency Relief Administration (FERA). Primarily these programs provided work-relief for unemployed adults, but children and teens also benefited from the attention and money that came to the schools. Work-relief projects, funded by the Works Progress Administration (WPA) and the Public Works Administration (PWA), built hundreds of new elementary and secondary schools and libraries throughout the United States. The Roosevelt administration also introduced the first federally funded nursery schools for poor children (WPA Emergency Day Nurseries) and established educational programs for needy older teens and youth in the Civilian Conservation Corps and the National Youth Administration.[22] None of these programs by themselves saved America's schools, but they were part of an overall shift in public policy and attitude toward education.

The Depression as a Stimulus for Education

Higher school attendance rates were the most visible sign of a change in attitude among Americans toward school-based education. Hard times made it difficult for some children and teens to go to school, but overall more American children and adolescents were in classrooms for more years than ever before. Besides the new attitude, other factors contributed to the improvement. New technologies eliminated many of the economic advantages previously enjoyed by employers who hired workers under fourteen years of age. High adult unemployment rates also led most states to enforce existing bans on children's employment and to strengthen mandatory school attendance laws. States and local communities scrambled for federal work-relief dollars, many of which were used to build schools in places with no or inadequate facilities.

Still, parental attitudes were key. By the late 1930s a growing number of working-class adults shared the sentiments of parents like Margaret Newton, the mother of three young children—eight-year-old Joanne, five-year-old Betty, and two-year-old Jack. Although the Newtons did not have much money, Margaret and her husband were trying their "best to have a good home for our children and [we] want them all to have a good education and go to school and maybe, to college." Margaret's husband had a high school diploma, but she had quit school after completing only the eighth grade. "My folks were ailing and I was badly needed at home to help with the work, but I want my children to have a better chance." A twenty-eight-year-old mother in Miami expressed similar sentiments. "We do want the children to have at least a high school education. It will mean so much to them as they grow older."[23]

In the past such parents may have considered it more advantageous to keep adolescents who had finished elementary school at home, or send them to work where they could earn money and gain vocational training. The depression furthered changes in attitude like those expressed by Margaret Newton by highlighting the uncertainty of capitalism's competitive job market. To an increasing number of Americans, earning a high school diploma looked like the minimum a young person needed to secure a better future. Leaving school early seemed like a poor choice.[24]

Despite progress, access to a high school education remained difficult for some of the nation's teens. Tilda Guy's story was typical of many Americans growing up in poor and isolated communities. Born in 1925 in Guy Hollow, Tennessee, located in rural Campbell County near the historic Cumberland Gap, Tilda's family moved when she was a baby to a mining camp in Harlan, Kentucky. They relocated back to Tennessee, to Johnny Ridge, when she was ready to start first grade. Tilda walked three miles each way to and from Primroy Elementary, a one-room schoolhouse headed by a single teacher who oversaw forty-five to fifty children from age six through fourteen. Despite such primitive conditions, Tilda loved her time at Primroy and felt it "was one of the happiest times I ever had in my life, because we had a really good time going to school." Her family moved again when she was nine years old, this time back to Guy Hollow. Tilda started fourth grade at King School, "so called," she explained in her autobiography, "because so many people in the area were 'King' by name." King School was another one-room schoolhouse and Tilda loved it there too.

She was a good student with big dreams that included going on
to high school and becoming a missionary and teacher. But her efforts were thwarted when geography proved to be a more difficult
challenge than academics. As she explained, her family "lived so far
back in the mountains, I couldn't go to high school. There was no
transportation, and the nearest high school was twenty-five miles
away. I [would have] had to walk three miles to get to a county
road, which was no more than a wagon road, and then there wasn't
any school bus service, even on the county road." Disappointed,
Tilda took advantage of the only available alternative and repeated
the eighth grade. By the spring of 1939, however, she had no choice
but to leave school. She spent the next several years at home, helping her parents, and married in 1944 at age nineteen.[25]

Like Tilda Guy, Jim Hardison believed that graduating from
high school was a good idea. He seemed luckier than Tilda Guy because he lived in a North Carolina town with a modern high
school. He hoped that a high school diploma would help him get a
better job than the one his father had in the local cotton mill. His
father's earnings of eighteen dollars a week were barely enough to
put food on the table. There was no money left over in the family's
meager budget to pay for school clothes and supplies. Willing to
help himself, sixteen-year-old Jim got a job with the CCC during
the summer of 1937. He told his mother not to worry about him
coming back for school in the fall because "there wasn't anything
that could keep him from finishing high school." He asked his
mother to save the twenty-five dollars that CCC officials sent
home each month from his pay so that he "could have things like
other boys" when he returned for his last year of high school. At
least that was Jim's plan. But a strike at his father's cotton mill
dashed his dreams. When school began in the fall, Jim was still
working at the CCC camp. As his mother explained, "The $25 a
month he sent home was all me, Otis, and the other three boys had
to live on." Loyal to his family, Jim Hardison probably felt he had

little choice but to give up school and continue to work. His distraught mother sadly described the situation.

> You couldn't imagine unless you'd been through with somethin' like it yourself how we suffered. We didn't have half enough to eat and no clothes at all. Day after day I had to sit and think of my boy in the CCC camp while his heart was set on finishing high school. And, Claude, the second one, wouldn't go to school because he didn't have decent clothes to wear. I thought I'd go crazy seeing him look so sullen and bitter, and thinking maybe he blamed me because I had persuaded his Papa to stick by the Union.[26]

One of Jim Hardison's neighbors, sixteen-year-old Lusette Smith, finished high school despite her family's hard times, but it was not an experience she liked to remember. "Most people look back on their Senior year as a pleasant time in their lives, but I won't." With no money for bus fare, each day Lusette walked three miles to school and three miles back home. "The walking wouldn't have been so bad," she recalled, "if I hadn't been afraid each day that my ragged shoes would fall apart before I could possibly get to school. Then, too, walking in the early morning can make you awfully weary when you haven't had any breakfast and not much supper the night before." Embarrassed by her situation, Lusette kept a low profile at school. "Without decent clothes and without enough food I went every day and heard my classmates discuss their plans for the future. I didn't talk any because I was afraid even to think what my future might be."[27]

Russell Baker's family also faced money problems after his father died in 1931. His mother gave up one of her children to childless relatives and struggled as a single parent to raise Russell and his sister Doris. Baker's mother had always encouraged her academically talented son to do well in school, telling him it would help pave the way so that he could "make something of himself."[28] Baker knew he had the ability to succeed in high school, but could his family afford to send him? Despite his disadvantaged situation, he had three things in his favor. First, his mother's recognition of the importance of earning a high school diploma. She did not ask her son to quit school early so that he could help support the family. Second, Baker wanted to stay in school, and he sold newspapers to cover his expenses for supplies, clothes, and lunches. Third, he lived in Baltimore, home of City College, one of the most prestigious public high schools in the United States.

Opened in 1839, only Boston Latin and Philadelphia Central had operated longer than Baltimore's City College. In 1928 the city's school board relocated the school to "one of Baltimore's snootiest neighborhoods," spending $2.6 million on a dramatic new Gothic stone building that accommodated twice as many students. City College offered working- and middle-class "bookworms" like Baker access to the same quality education available at expensive private high schools. Perhaps most important, attending City College helped Baker realize what Eleanor Roosevelt had called "the maximum of his abilities and opportunities." Students who hoped to go to City College had to have a good academic record and score well on a special exam.

Surrounded by other talented boys, Baker thrived. City College gave him many of the tools necessary to "make something of himself," but nearing his graduation he worried that his classical education had not prepared him for the life open to a working-class boy. Instead he was ready for college—but that path seemed out of reach. "It was assumed I would get a job" after high school graduation, Baker wrote in his Pulitzer Prize–winning autobiography, *Growing Up*. "Boys of our economic class didn't ordinarily go on to college."[29] He was ready to give up on the idea of college until a friend said that schools might offer him a scholarship. Baker found the idea hard to believe, but he was not about to let any opportunity slip by without at least trying. He applied and re-

In the 1920s many cities had built large, cathedral-style high schools and imposing elementary schools like School 64 in Baltimore. But in the early thirties, school districts faced enormous budget deficits and could not provide for many rural adolescents who still had no access to secondary education. *(University of Maryland, Baltimore County)*

ceived a full scholarship to Johns Hopkins University. His outstanding performance at a prestigious public high school had earned him a place among the nation's educated elite, a circumstance that was not as unusual for children of his generation as it had been for their parents.

Although City College was a public high school, it was not open to everyone. It admitted only boys, and it was all white. Baltimore also operated public college-preparatory schools for academically talented girls, but females were not admitted to City College or its rival, Baltimore Polytechnic Institute, until the 1970s. Baltimore operated public junior and senior high schools for black students, but neither institution received the funding or held the academic status of the city's all-white high schools.

Despite progress, gender, race, geography, and class hindered the democratization of public education in the 1930s.[30]

Civil Rights and America's Schools

The rising value of school-based education led some Americans to challenge the status quo on access to public education. By 1930 eighteen states had legalized some form of racial or ethnic segregation in public schools. During the next ten years several court cases challenged the "separate but equal" doctrine that rested at the heart of segregation in many public schools.[31]

One successful challenge involved Chicano and Chicana students living in Lemon Grove, California, a small multi-ethnic community about ten miles outside San Diego. The case is not technically a racial desegregation case, but it contains important links to civil rights and education.

Residents from the eastern United States and northern Mexico began settling in the Lemon Grove community at the turn of the century. A few Japanese and Chinese families from other parts of California also relocated there. A 1926 newspaper article touted Lemon Grove as "one of the prettiest spots in the San Diego suburban district," adding that "it would be hard to find a better class of people anyplace." Lemon and orange groves covered the picturesque hills surrounding the community's residential and business district. The town had an active women's club, an energetic chamber of commerce, a golf course, paved roads, and a public school for the first through eighth grades housed in "a fine new building . . . with every facility of the well-equipped schools."[32]

More than fifty Mexican families lived in Lemon Grove. Like their Anglo neighbors they paid taxes, owned property, raised children, and built a strong network of mutual support. Lemon Grove's Anglo landowners, businessmen, and housewives depended on the community's minority population to work on the region's farms, in the local packing plant, and as domestics in private homes. Despite this economic interdependency there was little social interaction among Anglo and Mexican adults. Most Chicano families lived in the community's northern section while the majority of Anglo families resided closer to the Lemon Grove Grammar School on the east side of town. As is usually the case, however, the social division among adults did not transfer as readily to their children. Every child in the first through eighth grades attended the Lemon Grove Grammar School. David Ruiz, a Chicano student at the school in the 1930s, recalled that the children got along well. In 1930 and 1931, however, a few influential Anglo parents caused a rift in the community that became known as the "Lemon Grove Incident."[33]

During the late summer of 1930 the Anglo-controlled Lemon Grove Parent-Teacher Association and members of the chamber of commerce proposed the establishment of a separate school for Chicano and Chicana children. The idea was not unusual: a number of communities in California and other parts of the West already segregated black, Asian, and American Indian children in public schools. The first segregated schools for American Indian children had been established in the nineteenth century. The California Supreme Court's 1885 decision in *Tape v. Hurley* made it illegal to exclude children of Chinese descent from the state's public schools, but the ruling paralleled the U.S. Supreme Court's 1896 *Plessy v. Ferguson* decision which was broadly interpreted by many Western states as permitting racially segregated "but equal" schools for Asians, blacks, and American Indians.[34] Pro-segregationists found it more difficult to blatantly establish separate schools for Mexican-American children since individuals of Mexican heritage were generally considered "white" under federal law. Nonetheless, by the early 1930s many Western communities got around this legal detail by establishing separate "neighborhood" schools for children of Mexican heritage. Supporters argued that such schools fostered neighborhood cohesion, but in reality a child's parentage generally trumped a child's residence. In Texas the number of Mexican neighborhood schools doubled between 1922 and 1932. By the early 1930s in California, children of Mexican-American heritage constituted 90 to 100 percent of the student bodies in sixty-four separate schools located in eight of the state's counties.[35]

Anti-Mexican prejudice rose during the 1930s as many Americans searched for scapegoats to blame for rising unemployment and declining wages. A series of articles published in popular newspapers and magazines in 1930–1931 demanded the creation of new government policies that would specifically limit Mexican immigration to the United States. Los Angeles newspapers featured articles on "the alien problem," a code phrase referring to all people of Mexican descent living in the United States. No distinction was made between individuals who had immigrated from Mexico and those born in the United States. In 1931 the Hoover administration fueled anti-Mexican prejudice by implementing the National Repatriation Program. Over the next eight years almost half a million people of Mexican descent were deported to Mexico under this federal repatriation program. The action directly violated the constitutional rights of the many naturalized or native-born American citizens who were also swept up in the deportation program. In this atmosphere the Lemon Grove School Board decided to remove all children of Mexican parentage from the community's grammar school.[36]

On January 5, 1931, after the Christmas break, 169 students returned to classes at the Lemon Grove Grammar School. The school's principal, Jerome T. Green, met the students at the school's entrance and called the 75 Mexican-American students in the group aside, refusing to allow them to enter the building. He explained that Mexican-American students would now attend a separate two-room school on Olive Street. The students felt dejected and humiliated by the announcement, but they and their parents had already heard that the school board might try to send them to a segregated school. Instead of obeying Principal Green, as previously discussed with their parents, the children went home and refused to return to school until permitted to attend the Lemon Grove Grammar School.

Mary Smith Alvarez, one of the children who disobeyed the school board's order, understood that the segregation plan was a formula for an inferior education. David Ruiz, another Chicano student, recalled that the segregated students and their parents were very unhappy with the new Olive Street School because it "wasn't a school. It was an old building. Everyone called it 'La Caballeriza' (the barnyard)."

The Chicano parents promptly organized the Comite de Vecinos de Lemon Grove (Lemon Grove Neighbors Committee). The Mexican consulate in San Diego helped by arranging for attorneys Fred C. Noon and A. C. Brinkley to file a suit against the school board on behalf of the students, arguing that the new policy violated their civil rights. Twelve-year-old Roberto Alvarez was chosen to represent the community's Chicano and Chicana children. "The exclusion was clearly an attempt at racial segregation" that illegally separated "the children of Mexican parentage," the suit maintained. The attorneys argued that since Chicano children were white, the school board had "no legal right or power to exclude [Alvarez] from receiving instruction upon an equal basis." The petition also documented that Alvarez and 95 percent of the excluded students were American citizens "entitled to all the rights and privileges common to all citizens of the United States."[37]

The school board answered the charge by claiming that the decision to remove the children was necessary due to overcrowding at the Lemon Grove Grammar School. The board argued that the Olive Street School was equal in quality, with a fully equipped playground and two qualified teachers. The board also emphasized that because the school would concentrate on Americanization, it was better equipped to help Spanish-speaking students improve their language skills. As a final argument, board members noted that the Olive Street School was closer to where most of the community's Chicano and Chicana students lived and therefore made the trip to school safer since the youngsters would no longer have to cross a main street to get to school.

The Americanization argument became a special target of criticism because it failed to recognize that the policy required all Mexican-American students to attend the Olive Street School, even children like Alvarez who had excellent English-language skills. Alvarez testified during the trial that he understood and spoke English very well, and that at least one of the Chicano students sent to the Olive Street School spoke *only* English. Another irony was the fact that white students who failed their academic studies at the Lemon Grove School were kept in a lower grade but were not segregated from their peers into a separate school. In contrast, the board's new policy segregated all Chicano and Chicana students simply due to their ethnicity, no matter their academic performance.[38]

On March 30, 1932, San Diego's Judge Claude Chambers decided the case in favor of the students. Chambers explained,

> I understand that you can separate a few children, to improve their education they need special instruction; but to separate all the Mexicans in one group can only be done by infringing the laws of the State of California. . . . I believe that this separation denies the Mexican children the presence of the American children, which is so necessary to learn the English language.

Further, Chambers maintained that the school board had no legal basis to segregate the Mexican-American children because they were not part of a racial group designated for legal segregation ("Orientals, Indians, or Negroes").

The minutes of the next Lemon Grove School Board meeting simply noted that it had lost the court case and that the old system would be resumed. The Mexican-American students and their parents had successfully defeated the effort to restrict the children's civil rights by using an argument later incorporated in the 1954 *Brown v. Board of Education* decision. The court's decision in the Lemon Grove case was not typical of the 1930s, but the incident reveals the growing importance many students and parents placed on access to quality school-based education.[39]

Donald Murray's case was another step in the effort to democratize access to public education. In 1935 Murray returned to his home state of Maryland after graduating from Amherst College in Massachusetts. He applied to the University of Maryland's Law School, his home state's only publicly funded law school. Although he was well qualified, the university denied Murray admission because he was black. Murray enlisted two NAACP lawyers, Charles Houston and Thurgood Marshall, to file a suit on his behalf against the university. It appeared that Maryland had violated the separate-but-equal doctrine because it offered no public law school for African Americans. On June 25, 1935, the Baltimore District Court ruled in Murray's favor and ordered his admittance to the University of Maryland's Law School. The university appealed, but the Maryland Court of Appeals reaffirmed the lower court's decision. The appeals court noted that Murray was denied admission to "the only school provided."[40] The decision did not condemn segregated public education, but it served as an important step in the NAACP's drive to achieve equal access to publicly funded education.

Fourteen-year-old Margaret Williams became the center of another significant civil rights case that also originated in Maryland in the 1930s and had the help of the same NAACP lawyers linked to Donald Murray's case. The Williams case is further evidence of the increasing demand for access to quality education by children and their parents, regardless of their race or ethnicity. Born September 28, 1921, in Cowdensville, Maryland, a small black community in southwest Baltimore County, Margaret Williams attended Colored

School #21, a racially segregated one-room schoolhouse in Cow-densville. At the end of the 1934–1935 school year her teacher rec-ommended Williams for promotion to the eighth grade, along with the only other seventh graders in the school, Lucille Scott and Ed-ward Fletcher. Baltimore County's superintendent rejected the rec-ommendation, arguing that only the boy, Edward Fletcher, should move on to the eighth grade. In his mind there was "no reason to pass the girls, because by the time [they] were fifteen or sixteen years old, [they] would be having babies." Margaret thought the su-perintendent's words were "unfair to say to a person," and her "par-ents were tremendously upset."

Gender discrimination was real, but all three students faced the problem that Baltimore County operated no public schools for black children, boys or girls, who wished to study beyond the sev-enth grade. The county had a sad history of public education for African-American children; it had not even operated elementary schools for black children until 1895. For many years a majority of black families in the area understood that the city of Baltimore pro-vided better opportunities for education and employment. The 1930 Census counted 124,565 residents in Baltimore County, of which 90 percent were white and only 9.4 percent black. In con-trast, the city of Baltimore had almost eight times as many residents (804,874) with approximately 82 percent of the city's population counted as white and 17.4 percent black.

In 1926, under increasing pressure to accommodate the needs of older black students, county officials had offered a tuition plan enabling "qualified" black students to attend Baltimore's all-black junior and senior high schools. To be eligible, interested black stu-dents had to successfully complete the seventh grade, be recom-mended by their teacher for promotion, and earn a passing score on a special examination. Baltimore County required no such test for white students, and the board had built several all-white high schools. The subtle inequity of the plan meant that the county had no obligation to provide schooling beyond the seventh grade for black children who failed the special examination, but all white students would be accommodated within the county. County officials knew that the tuition plan was cheaper and easier to administer than building a county high school for black students in order to maintain racial segregation. Officials believed that few black children were capable of doing high school work, and that therefore there was no need to build upper-level schools for African Americans. From 1926 through 1931 the board's convoluted logic seemed justified by the fact that fewer than one hundred black students took the special examination each year, and of those only one in three earned a passing score.[41]

Just before the start of the new school year in 1935, Thurgood Marshall met with Margaret Williams's and Lucille Scott's parents to discuss their situation. Like many Americans in the 1930s, the girls and their parents understood the value of a high school education and enlisted the help of lawyers to ensure what they believed to be a right. The girls had taken the county's special examination for black children who had completed the seventh grade, but like most students who chose to take the test, both failed to earn a passing score. Marshall suggested that the girls challenge the obviously unfair tuition-based program by trying to attend the county's public high school located nearest to their homes, the all-white Catonsville High School. On September 12, 1935, the two girls, accompanied by Joshua Williams (Margaret's father) and the girls' minister, the Reverend James E. Lee, went to Catonsville High School. Williams's father handed the school's principal, David Zimmerman, the girls' report cards showing that they had been recommended by their teacher for promotion to the eighth grade—the same requirement demanded of all white students admitted to Catonsville High School. Zimmerman treated everyone with courtesy, but he refused to admit the girls to the school. He agreed that the girls' academic record qualified them to attend a

Baltimore County high school, but he explained that county policy prohibited blacks from attending the school.[42]

Marshall next stated his intention to file a lawsuit on the girls' behalf against the Baltimore County School Board. Meanwhile Margaret Williams began the eighth grade at Baltimore's all-black Booker T. Washington School. She was soon forced to quit, however, when city officials asked her to pay the fifty-dollar tuition fee required of noncity residents. She returned to Colored School #21 and repeated the seventh grade, hoping that taking the classes again would better prepare her for a second try at the county's special examination.

On March 14, 1936, Marshall filed his suit, *Williams v. Zimmerman*, demanding that the court require the Baltimore County School Board to admit Margaret Williams to the high school nearest her home. Marshall fed information about the case to a sympathetic Baltimore newspaper reporter, explaining that his suit's goal was to force Baltimore County to build a "Negro" high school, not integrate its all-white schools.[43] Marshall had decided that desegregation was still too controversial, so he was relying instead on the established separate-but-equal doctrine. It is also possible that Margaret or her parents were not anxious to be integration pioneers. She took the special examination a second time and failed. The suit was the only answer if she wanted to attend a public school in Maryland.

Unlike the judge who heard Roberto Alvarez's lawsuit, Baltimore Circuit Court Judge Frank I. Duncan seemed disinterested in sorting out the details of the case that came before him in September 1936. Marshall had submitted a mountain of research outlining the inequities in the tuition program and the fundamental unfairness of the county's special examination. "The eyes of all the White people in the courthouse were always on Lucille and I," Margaret Williams remembered. Despite her bravery and Marshall's meticulous research, on October 23, 1936, Judge Duncan ruled in favor of the Baltimore County School Board, stating that since Williams had failed the special examination she required no redress from the court. The Maryland Court of Appeals reaffirmed the lower court's decision, adding that while requiring black students to take a special test might be unfair, "admitting . . . a child" to Catonsville High School "who is not fitted for it" was not the solution. The appeals court noted that "carefully prepared" examinations were given to children of both races for various purposes and that differences in the examinations were "only a minor importance" that did not justify the lawsuit.[44]

Lucille Scott retook the county's required examination and passed. Finally eligible for the county's tuition program, she attended Baltimore City's Booker T. Washington Junior High School and graduated from Frederick Douglass High School in 1941. Margaret Williams did not go to public school but did earn a high school diploma from St. Frances Academy, a comprehensive elementary-through-secondary school run by the Oblate Sisters of Providence (a Roman Catholic Order of African-American nuns founded in Baltimore in 1829). The case of *Williams v. Zimmerman* did not end Baltimore County's racist tuition program nor integrate its schools. Nonetheless Margaret Williams's challenge to the status quo did make a difference. At the end of the spring term, the city of Baltimore decided to no longer to accept noncity residents in its increasingly crowded schools. Fearing another expensive lawsuit, the Baltimore County School Board opened three "separate but equal" secondary-school facilities for black students at the start of the 1938–1939 academic year.[45] Margaret Williams had not achieved her own goal, but her challenge had opened the door to a high school education for other black students in Baltimore County.

The history of American Indians and their schools involved another kind of problem that often limited access to a high-quality public school. Since the nineteenth century, many Indians had attended boarding schools. These facilities did not feature college preparatory curriculums but often offered the best vocational education available to Indian children and teens. They were, however, notorious for their blatant Americanization programs designed to erase Indian traditions and culture. Some children living on reservations attended day schools, but most of these facilities offered a poor education. Congress's passage in 1934 of the Indian Reorganization Act and the Johnson-O'Malley Act made substantial changes in federal policy for American Indians living on reservation lands. The new laws included important alterations in the operation of day and boarding schools. John Collier, Commissioner of Indian Affairs from 1933 to 1945, oversaw these reforms, but the new policies never fully reached the lofty goals of fair treatment and equality that Collier advocated.[46]

Lorenzo Mattwaoshshe's years in school provide some insights into the difficulties of American Indian children in gaining access to quality school-based education both before and after the New Deal. Lorenzo was born on February 21, 1916, at the Patowatomi Prairie band reservation in Jackson County, Kansas. When he turned five, his parents sent him to the Haskell Institute, a boarding school for Indian children in nearby Lawrence. This was a situation very different from that of most American children who went to school in the 1930s. Lorenzo remembered being homesick even though his siblings also attended the school. He rarely saw his brothers and sisters since students were segregated by age and gender. The adjustment to school was especially difficult for Lorenzo because of his age and the fact that he spoke no English upon his arrival. His childhood friend, James Wabaunsee, also attended the Haskell Institute and recalled that teachers "washed your mouth out with soap" if you spoke anything other than English.

Lorenzo's parents likely sent their children to Haskell because it offered a better education than the Whichaway day school, the only facility available to Indian children on the reservation. Lorenzo had to go to Whichaway for a time when his parents ran out of tuition money for Haskell, but eventually they saved enough to get him into another boarding school, this time in Genoa, Nebraska. There Lorenzo's poor preparation at the day school proved to be telling, and by age fifteen he had completed only the fifth grade. "We had a class picture," an adult Lorenzo told the historian Marilyn Holt. "I was right in the middle of the back. All the rest of the young ones in front of me. See, I was fifteen years old! Fifth grade! They used to tease me about that. Who's that in the middle? Is that the teacher?" The picture was taken in 1931, the same year Lorenzo quit school. He was born too early to benefit from even the small improvements in Indian education under the New Deal. New educational provisions granted Indians living on reservations certain rights of home rule and provided funding for counties to help expand educational opportunities for Indian children. In 1969 a congressional report concluded that even though the 1934 legislative intentions were admirable, the changes did not end discrimination or inferior school-based education for Indian children.

The New Deal did offer Lorenzo another educational opportunity in 1933 when he found a job with the Works Progress Administration. At the Genoa school he had learned some construction skills, and the WPA paid him to teach at the local reservation school.[47] As the stories of Alvarez, Williams, Scott, and Mattwaoshshe show, schools still had a long way to go before they were accessible and of good quality, especially for young Americans hindered by rural isolation or policies that reinforced traditional discriminatory practices.

Student Publications and Peer Culture

What did student publications say about going to school in the 1930s? Of course, school officials had ultimate control over what appeared in yearbooks and newspapers. Such publications nonetheless offer some insights into student culture and administrative policies in the schools. Yearbooks and school newspapers from the 1930s exude optimism and the idea that through playing by the rules, working hard, and staying determined, young people could secure a brighter future for themselves and their country. Schools were portrayed as oases, insulated from the problems of the larger society. Despite this image, school publications also reveal competition among students and the difficulties some young people felt about fitting in with their peers. Generations of high school students would identify with this contradiction.

Some publications recognized that the depression presented special challenges for young people, but optimism remained the major theme. The 1933 yearbook editors at Catonsville High School, the same all-white Maryland high school where Margaret Williams failed to gain admittance in 1938, explained that the editors had chosen Mickey Mouse as their publication's mascot because, "In these days of depression, people have turned to Mickey Mouse as a means of dispelling gloom, as an escape from cares, and as a reminiscence of their childhood." The introduction continued, "For like reasons, the editors of the JUNE BUG offer this book that in the future the reader may find it a pleasant diversion and an amusing recollection of high school days at Catonsville." In another section the editors praised members of the school's Student Council for their "attention to Student Aid work which is making school privileges possible for a number of needy students."[48]

Bob Oetting, a student journalist for the newspaper at Riverside High School in Milwaukee, noted in November 1931: "At the present time, Milwaukee, as well as the other cities of the nation, is in the midst of a great economic depression. This will mean many unemployed men, poverty, and suffering in our city this winter." In light of the situation, he explained, the school's Household Arts Club had expanded its fund-raising. In the past the club had used proceeds from candy sales and a Christmas bazaar to help "provide lunches for needy students at the school." Now the club added a clothing drive due to a growing need among students and in the broader community. Club members collected and "reconditioned" donated clothing for "the use of the poor." Oetting praised the students for exhibiting "the true Riverside spirit [since] to carry on this work, the girls in the club have voluntarily and unselfishly abandoned their personal projects." The same issue reported that Riverside High School's enrollment had increased by 276 students in 1931 over the previous year, but student newspaper subscriptions were down due to the "business depression." At Milwaukee's Washington High School, one of its newspaper reporters asked students about lowering the cost of admission to school basketball games. Five of six students were for it, expressing sentiments similar to sophomore Hazel Thurner: "Many pupils like to see basketball games, but they can't afford the admission price."[49]

Hard times also affected the number and quality of school-sanctioned social activities described in some publications. The 1932 Catonsville yearbook asked, "Whom are you going to take?" to the junior-senior prom. "What are you going to wear?" "What orchestra is going to furnish the music?" The questions were typical of any high school decade, but the editors cautioned that this year, "entertainment is eliminated," primarily because of "Old Man De Pression and the class is just plain broke, a much worn phrase."[50] The quality of the publication itself could also suggest the state of a school's financial resources as well as the students' ability to purchase what was produced. St. Frances Academy, the Roman Catholic parochial school for black students in Baltimore, did not have the money to produce a commercially printed yearbook, and it is likely that most of the school's students could not afford to buy one. Nevertheless the students' desire to conform to the mainstream model of wealthier high schools was strong. St. Frances students self-published a mimeographed version of a "yearbook" built on the familiar format followed by wealthier schools.

Reading between the lines of yearbook pages and newspaper articles, one can see that not everything was as congenial as it might first appear, especially in the peer culture that developed in high schools. While most elementary schools were able to avoid sharp divisions among students, competition among adolescents was often based on class, ethnicity, religion, race, or a combination of all four. It seemed that as students matured, they looked for ways to distinguish themselves from their peers, even in racially and ethnically homogeneous schools.[51] Most yearbooks, for example, included individual portraits of the school's senior class. Many student editors attached nicknames and brief editorial descriptions to the photographs. Their choices suggest that they tried to find something positive to say about each student, but some also include biting comments that may not have been welcomed by the teens singled out by their yearbook peers. Celebratory sections with headings such as Hall of Fame, Most Likely to Succeed, Cleverest, Most Athletic, and Best Looking are stark contrasts to less distinguished "honors" such as Plumpest, Thinnest, Most Fickle, Most Argumentative, or Most Bashful.

The structure of high schools promoted a strong hierarchy based on grade level, also reflected in 1930s high school yearbooks. In 1939 the ninth-grade editors writing in Maryland's Towson High School yearbook admitted that they and their peers felt discriminated against by older students and by the school's administration. "Most school activities are closed to us," the editors noted. Still, wanting to show their support for the school and their optimism for the future, the freshman editors explained that they and their classmates did "not resent the exclusions from extra activities [because] we know that we must prove our worth, that our freshman year is a probation period."[52]

Playing by the rules was an important idea promoted by school officials and students. A survey conducted in Oakland, California, high schools in the 1930s showed that many students from poor families believed that self-confidence, hard work, and persistence would help them get ahead even during hard times. A student identified as "Paul" wrote, "You have to have ambition—you just can't have ability and personality; you have to work." "Bill" argued that "any boy who had the will or ability to get ahead in the world will certainly succeed." Interestingly, girls from poor families who participated in the study seemed less optimistic. Perhaps they understood that the larger society limited career options for females and that a girl's looks may have been valued more than her academic achievements. The study's examiners concluded that "negative changes in a child's appearance symbolized a loss in status, which had special significance for the social experience of girls and typically developed out of constraints on the purchase of clothes and shoes." In some cases "limitations also extended to hygienic practices; to the frequency of clothes washing, the availability of soap and heated water for baths, etc.," all of which hurt girls more than boys. Socially contrived distinctions among students were real, but the Oakland study concluded that, overall, "the elimination of such inequality was a primary concern of staff members and student leaders in the junior and senior high schools."[53]

Despite the best efforts of many well-intentioned individuals, many people who went to school in the 1930s remember being discriminated against by peers, faculty, and administrators. Being a member of a racial or ethnic minority made many students easy targets. Prejudices based on class differences were more subtle but nonetheless visible. Eleanor Roosevelt received hundreds of begging letters from teens worried that their worn clothing would keep them from being accepted by peers. One letter to the first lady from a fourteen-year-old girl living in Dows, Iowa, in 1934 expressed the insecurities about appearance shared by many teens. "Will you please send me some cloths or some money for some if you can. My girl friend wrote to. We both don't have any cloths. The kids at school all make fun of you if you can't dress just so." Another girl from Alliance, Ohio, asked Mrs. Roosevelt what she did with the clothes she no longer wore, adding, "Would you send your old ones so mother could make me a couple of dresses for School or anything." The girl explained, "I am writing this letter in school and have one eye on the teacher so I am not Writing as nice as I can . . . (Please do not publish this)."[54] Peer pressure to conform was also reflected in controversies over high school sororities and fraternities. By the 1930s most public junior and senior high schools did not sanction such organizations. In the 1940s some state legislatures outlawed them in public high schools.[55]

Instead of sororities and fraternities, many teens looked to a wide range of extracurricular activities as a way to gain a sense of belonging. Most adolescents at some time felt left out, but John D. McKee of Emporia, Kansas, faced the special challenge of being "different." He suffered from a spastic muscle condition called cerebral palsy. Through hard work and determination, coupled with the unflinching support of his parents, he learned to walk and attended public schools in an era when many children with physical or mental handicaps were consigned to special educational facilities. John's parents supported their son's desire to live life as close to that of other children as possible. When he reached high school, John played drums in the school band and was a star researcher and speaker on the debate team. Unable to qualify for sports teams, he was proud of the honor letter he earned for his participation on the debate team. "Winning that letter made up in large measure for not being able to play football or basketball, to run or jump as a member of the track team, or to do more than paddle around in the shallow end of the swimming pool," he wrote. It allowed him to feel that despite his physical limitations he was in some way "doing what my friends were doing."[56]

School publications suggest that being on any team was an important part of growing up. School clubs included organizations as diverse as the Appropriate Dress Club, Cartoon Club, Debate Team,

Small rural schools in the Midwest devised "six-man football" in response to the sport's growing popularity among teens. Note the cars parked at the edge of the field: rural teens were more likely to have access to an automobile than their city cousins. *(Library of Congress)*

Dramatics Club, Mythology Club, Natural History Club, Quilt Club, Scouting Club, Story Book Club, and Travel Club. Athletic teams were among the most popular extracurricular activities and were becoming increasingly important for boys as an expression of male maturity. Boys' sports teams generally received more notoriety than girls' athletic activities, and many small communities used high school sporting events as a major form of public entertainment. Nonetheless the extravagantly supported male high school teams bolstered by cheerleading squads, common to the post–World War II years, were unfamiliar to most Americans in the 1930s. Instead, local tastes and available funding influenced the kinds of sports teams that schools offered students. By the 1930s football was a popular sport for high school boys in most parts of the United States, but it was also expensive to field a full team and demanded a large pool of players. During the depression, rural districts in Nebraska developed six-man football as an alternative game for small schools with few students and little money or time for travel. East Coast schools were less likely to include a football team. Lacrosse for boys was a more popular sport for high schools east of the Appalachians and north of Virginia, but in other parts of the country few high schools outside American Indian reservations played the game. Basketball and baseball attracted both boys and girls in every part of the United States, but male and female teams played under different rules and used different equipment.[57] While school yearbooks and other student publications celebrated the accomplishments of student athletes, student editors encouraged teens to belong to any kind of school-sanctioned club.

Through extracurricular clubs and teams as well as events such as dances, high schools across the United States attempted to conform to the ideal of adolescence that placed adult-monitored activities at the center of teen social life. Yearbooks and student newspapers touted their efforts. Student editors went out of their way to promote the idea that high schools offered opportunity and equality consistent with America's democratic ideals. They sometimes pointed to the special problems facing the generation coming of age during the Great Depression, but the key message suggested that staying in school and playing by the rules ensured the best path to adult independence for every young American. [58]

Quitting School

Despite the positive image portrayed in school publications, some children and adolescents simply disliked going to school. As noted earlier, in 1930 about half of all American adolescents quit school before earning a high school diploma. Ralph G. Marshall's recollections of going to school in the 1930s were not the kind of memories recorded in school yearbooks or newspapers.

I hadn't taken to schoolin' much, the days I wasn't playing hookie, my mind was out in the fields and draws huntin' game as its hard to think on an empty stomach. I did manage, however, to get passing grades right up until the eighth grade, which I failed by one point and when the school started in September, I just didn't show up figuring it was more important to find a way to keep eatin'.[59]

Simon Martinez also admitted to "skipping" school and, like Ralph Marshall, failed to graduate. Instead of going to classes, Simon and his friends would "go down on the river, go fishing. Go steal watermelons . . . [or] go to the movies in the afternoon, then come home." Despite his inconsistent attendance, Simon always did fairly well in school, but even as a young student he was not fully engaged. In the second grade he was expelled for drinking alcohol. He had stolen a bottle of homemade cherry wine from a woman in his neighborhood, taken the bottle to school, and hidden it in the boys' bathroom. "Every once in a while I'd raise my hand and tell the teacher I had to go to the bathroom. I'd go to the bathroom and drink some of that cherry wine," he later admitted. The teacher recognized the situation when Simon staggered into the classroom after his third or fourth visit to the bathroom. The principal eventually allowed him to return to school, but Simon never felt it was that important. Entering high school in 1939, he explained that the hard times also contributed to his lack of enthusiasm, especially for extracurricular activities. "It was the end of the depression. Most kids had to work and so consequently we didn't have free hours that most kids have today." Simon Martinez did not graduate and joined the navy in 1941 at age seventeen.[60]

It is impossible to know how many of the students who quit school did so because they hated it. Some were expelled by school officials for persistent truancy, violence, or other anti-social behavior. Girls who became pregnant could not remain in school once they "started to show," a popular euphemism of the time that described the later stages of pregnancy. Researchers examining high school attendance in Muncie, Indiana, in the 1930s concluded that many students left school when their parents relocated trying to find work. Some of these students probably enrolled in school in their new communities, but others never returned to the classroom.[61] Many teens worked or helped out at home while going to school, and some found the burden too heavy and simply stopped going to class. Others ran out of money to pay school expenses or to buy the clothes they believed they needed to be accepted among their peers. Not having enough money for bus or streetcar fare, lunches, or supplies kept some teens out of school. A sixteen-year-old girl living in East Point, Kentucky, was typical of many adolescents affected by the nation's rising unemployment rate. In 1930 she had to quit school "on account of the depression." Four years later she was still not in school. "Financial difficulties have kept me from going to school anywhere, even a public school."[62]

Despite the hard times, some teens from poorer families found ways to work, attend school, and become active participants in extracurricular activities. Robert Omata of Hanford, California, had worked behind the meat counter in his family's small grocery store from the time he was twelve. Despite having to work, Robert found time to play football and qualify for the National Honor Society at Hanford Union High School, where he graduated in 1938. He liked high school and never considered quitting. Another boy who worked in a grocery store, fifteen-year-old Jasper Harrell, lived with his mother in Marion County, South Carolina. When Jasper was still young his father deserted the family, leaving the family in dire circumstances. No one in Jasper's family had ever graduated from high school, and his two older brothers quit school in the sixth grade. In 1939 Jasper had already surpassed their achievement and was doing well in the eighth grade. He seemed determined to continue his education through high school. Each morning he went to school and then rushed home to eat in time to report to his job at Robert's Grocery. He worked in the store each day from 3 p.m. to 6 p.m., then went to a neighbor, "Mrs. Green," for help with his studies. Leaving her house about 8:30, he returned to the grocery store to help clean up and close the business for the day, finally arriving home at about 11 p.m. He earned two to three dollars a week working at the store and used the money to pay for school supplies and other expenses. Jasper's mother was proud of her youngest son's determination and did what she could to keep him in school.[63] Going to high school became an integral part of life for a growing proportion of young people in the 1930s generation, and many were willing to make great sacrifices in order to gain what they believed was the path to a better life.

School by Age and Grade

A tragedy in New London, Texas, in 1937 ironically highlighted the shift to larger age- and grade-level schools that had spread across in America by the late 1930s. New London was a blue-collar community filled with families that depended on fathers' wages earned in the region's oil fields. In the 1920s the area contained several small, old-fashioned schools. In the mid-1930s the surrounding community combined state, county, and federal New Deal money to build a modern million-dollar school complex that drew children from the first grade through high school for both vocational and college preparatory curriculums. The campus was a source of community pride, a clear statement that parents who earned their living in the oil fields understood the importance of building and maintaining modern educational facilities for their children.

On March 18, 1937, a massive explosion hit the school when natural gas used to heat the building and provide hot water ignited, "first [making] the walls bulge out . . . then the roof lifted up and crashed in with a deafening roar," the *New York Times* reported. The building was fireproof, so flames died quickly, but the strength of the blast and the massive volume of falling debris killed almost everyone inside the building instantly. Seven hundred children from nine through eighteen years of age and forty teachers were in the structure when the explosion occurred. More than five hundred students and teachers were killed, with fewer than two hundred escaping with injuries. Most of the children and teachers were gathered in the auditorium "when the blast wrecked the school as though a bomb from an air-raider had found its mark." Horrified mothers who were gathered for a PTA meeting in a cafeteria three hundred feet from the auditorium helplessly watched the building collapse on their children.

> Screaming hysterically, the mothers raced across the campus. With bare hands they clawed at the debris, trying desperately to reach children whose cries could be heard from beneath the crumbled structure. As darkness fell on the ruins of the school, the community center for this region of scattered oil camps and small hamlets, the campus presented a macabre scene. Sightseers crowded elbow to elbow with grief-stricken parents, watching the rescue crews at work with acetylene torches beneath floodlights from the football field and a string of electric bulbs hastily put in place above the wreckage. Alongside the tragic pile, an ever lengthening line of white told the magnitude of the disaster. The bodies of the little victims. . . .

Doris Derring, a fifteen-year-old student in the eighth grade, found shelter under a desk. She told a reporter about seeing her teacher buried alive. Doris saw "100 of her classmates blow from their desks into the schoolyard."

The new school that had given the children and families in New London so much pride instead became the center of the community's heartbreak. Despite the large investment in the building of the school complex, an investigation after the blast raised serious questions about dangerous shortcuts that planners had taken to save money on long-term utility costs. The story of the disaster also led some observers to question the wisdom of putting so many children together in large schools. A *New York Times* article dismissed such fears, arguing that the new "consolidated schools are of sand and stone, have stairways of slate and cement, and are classed as fireproof. Broad corridors, fire towers, fire escapes, sprinkling systems are provided. They furnish a striking contrast to the wooden firetraps still used as schools. No structure, however built, when converted into a holder for inflammable gas, as was the Texas institution, can be made to resist explosion." Many parents and educators agreed that "the consolidated school is the antithesis of the little red school house." For rural communities, "it provides facilities held equal to those of city schools, [through] enabling sparsely populated districts to combine in one well equipped school."[64]

The disaster in New London did not slow the spread of more modern consolidated schools throughout the United States. By the late 1930s poorer communities had used the new influx of federal funds to expand access to school-based education. Urban districts benefited as well from new attention from the federal government and the general public. Modern high schools and rising graduation rates served as sources of civic pride. In June 1939 the *Gary Post Tribune* reported that the city's downtown streets were filled with thousands of "proud fathers and mothers, sisters and brothers, uncles and aunts and other relatives and friends of 1,156 young men and women who, wearing mortarboard caps and gowns, marched down Broadway to Memorial auditorium for the fifth annual convocation of the graduating classes of the Gary public high schools and junior college." Gary, Indiana, had been moving toward this day for several decades, but most of its progress occurred in the 1930s. The graduating class of 1939 recorded the highest number of graduates to date in this industrial community of 100,000. In the 1920s Gary had hired new teachers, enrolled more students, and

The WPA school hot lunch program fed millions of needy children, many of whom were not getting adequate meals at home. *(Library of Congress)*

built new facilities. Good schools symbolized the height of social and economic progress, and Gary was well known for its cutting-edge public schools.[65]

But the depression found school officials struggling to keep Gary's schools open. As in other communities throughout the United States, they were surprised by the economic crisis. As tax revenues collapsed, Gary cut operating budgets. Teachers endured pay cuts and layoffs. Programs were eliminated. New construction stopped, and funds for building maintenance shrank. The quality of teaching declined as more students were crammed into existing classrooms.

After 1934 new federal and state programs funneled money to Gary's schools. By the end of the decade, the changes mirrored those in many parts of the United States. The state contribution to Gary's public schools rose from 10 percent to 30 percent of the local school system's annual budget. Federal money from the FERA paid some teachers' salaries and funded new construction to house the community's growing school population, especially in the upper grades. Inequities based on race, ethnicity, and gender continued, but overall schools remained intact and gained prestige during the decade's hard times.[66] By the end of the 1930s more girls and boys in Gary and elsewhere experienced school-based and age-graded education as an integral part of their childhood through their teens. In 1916 a fifth of the schools in the United States employed only one teacher. By 1940 that figure had fallen to just over 11 percent. In the next three decades school systems eliminated the romanticized one-room schoolhouse in favor of the consolidated schools popularized by reformers and educators during the 1930s.[67] Money from the federal government helped. The record-breaking graduating class of 1939 in Gary symbolized the growing support for public education, from the elementary grades through high school, that took hold in the United States during the depression years.

Players and Consumers
in Popular Culture

🖋 LIKE SCHOOL-BASED EDUCATION, play and entertainment were essential parts of the modern childhood ideal popularized during the Great Depression. Children and adolescents became the focus of new marketing strategies developed by the purveyors of commercial popular culture. On one level, popular culture and consumerism are reminders that there were other things going on in the lives of young Americans besides the deprivations brought on by the depression. At another level, a close examination of play and entertainment for children, teens, and youth shows that advertisers and entertainment executives made deliberate decisions in response to the depression that contributed to the development of a universalized popular culture for young Americans. The choices made by young American consumers indicate that they played at least a part in this shift and were not simply the pawns of business interests. Still, some adults worried about the trend, and by the mid-1930s their efforts contributed to a more sanitized version of popular culture for all Americans.

John Smith Barney has fond memories of growing up in tiny Wheelersburg Village, Ohio. John and his playmates did not have much money, but they still found ways to have fun. Listening to the radio was one of John's favorite pastimes. He was six years old in 1930 when the first children's adventure program, the *Little Orphan Annie Show*, began broadcasting from Chicago's WGN. The NBC network picked up the show in 1931, sending it to affiliates across America. Run as a weekly serial adventure program from 1931 to 1950, the *Little Orphan Annie Show* had its roots in the famous newspaper comic strip of the same name. Unlike the newspaper version that attracted fans of all ages, the radio show targeted youngsters in elementary and middle school. Its success prompted other radio producers to copy the format. Soon fifteen-minute adventure programs like the *Little Orphan Annie Show* aired each weekday afternoon before dinner, during what broadcasters called the "children's hour." In many ways the decision by radio executives to add children's programming to their daily schedules built on the model established by publishers of popular literature, who began adding books and magazines for young readers during the late nineteenth century.

Radio turned out to be an even more effective medium for stories aimed at young Americans than print media. It also offered new opportunities for links between children's entertainment and consumerism. John Barney's recollection of a cold winter morning during the mid-1930s reveals the clever way advertisers used radio to further commodify children's entertainment. "I was ready by eight o'clock," he recalled. "I had eaten two big bowls of WHEATIES and drunk some Ovaltine, but had to finish up one jar before Mom would buy me a new jar; no new jar meant no protective inner-seal to send in to Little Orphan Annie." Proofs of purchase, like the Ovaltine protective seal or boxtops from cereals like Wheaties, could be mailed in to the programs for "free" gadgets touted by radio serial heroes. John liked chocolate-flavored Ovaltine, but other children, such as Minneapolis's Ralph Luedtke, hated the stuff. Still, Luedtke could not resist participating in the special offers for young radio fans. He asked his mother to buy Ovaltine so that he could get the premiums mentioned on his favorite program.[1]

What historians have described as the youth culture of the late nineteenth and early twentieth centuries developed within the growing commercialization of adult popular entertainment. Consumerism continued to prosper during the 1920s but suffered badly in the first years of the depression. By the fall of 1932 advertising revenues had fallen by half, toy sales had plummeted, and one-third of America's movie theaters had closed their doors. Advertisers looked for new ways to sell products in a shrinking market. As one solution they began paying more attention to children and adolescents, who thus became more important as independent consumers. For the first time in American history, teens became identified as a discrete market apart from young children and adults.[2]

Some adults worried about this growing emphasis on children as consumers. They argued that the purveyors of radio, movies, and other commercial products put profit before the best interests of America's children.[3] Such complaints about popular culture were not new, but examining the rising wave of criticism that arose during the 1930s underscores the pervasiveness of popular culture directed at children and teens in the depression years. Critics seemed to understand that commercial culture had become an unavoidable part of modern childhood. Instead of calls to shut down movie theaters, radio stations, and other commercial entertainment, reformers concentrated on shaping the content of popular culture. They called for a celebration of what many identified as all-American values of loyalty, patriotism, obedience to authority, community service, perseverance, clean living, democracy, freedom, and good sportsmanship. Advocates demanded that Hollywood and radio broadcasters portray the idyllic middle-class American childhood that for decades had been touted by child-welfare reformers. Critics also demanded the elimination of what they identified as excessive images of violence, criminal behavior, rebellion, and sexuality in films, radio, and other aspects of popular culture.

While hard times clearly made life difficult for many young people and their families, most young people found ways to share in at least part of the fun.[4] And, like earlier generations, children and adolescents invented their own amusements that often altered or ignored the intentions of adults to control young people's entertainment.

A Threat to American Youth?

From 1929 to 1932 researchers in the Payne Center at Ohio State University conducted a series of studies examining the effects of commercial culture, especially movies and radio, on the psychology and behavior of America's children, teens, and youth. In 1933 Henry James Forman summarized the findings in a book entitled *Our Movie-Made Children*. Reprinted seven times over the next two years, the book argued that movies and radio were gigantic, highly effective educational systems. Easy access to commercial culture enhanced its importance as a source of lessons about values and normative behavior for children, adolescents, and youth. For example, interviews conducted with eighteen hundred college-age males and females revealed that many described movies as an important source of information about kissing and sexual petting. Examination of diaries and journals kept by more than four hundred high schoolers confirmed that sexuality in films influenced even younger viewers' ideas about sexuality. A tenth-grade girl's comment, "I have learned quite a bit about love-making from the movies," was typical of many feelings expressed in the teens' writings.

Another Payne study tested a group of second- and third-graders on their ability to absorb and retain information they saw in movies. Researchers tested the children immediately following their

Children often adopted behaviors from commercial popular culture, particularly films and radio, in their play. In 1939 a New Deal photographer captured these boys engaged in a "gun fight" in Boscobel, Wisconsin. *(Library of Congress)*

viewing of a film, then retested them six weeks later. On the second test the children recalled 90 percent of the same information they had remembered immediately after viewing the film. Listening to radio broadcasts produced similar results. Children and teens were clearly learning from movies and radio, but what were the psychological consequences of the information they were absorbing? Some signs seemed to warn of possible ill effects from the content of commercial media. One study reported that children and adolescents who went to the movies four to five times a week had higher rates of "truancy and delinquency" than those from similar social and economic circumstances who saw films less frequently.[5]

Such findings reinforced adult assumptions about the harmful effects especially of Hollywood movies in the early 1930s. An Irish-American shoe factory worker in Lynn, Massachusetts, told a Federal Writers' Project investigator, "I don't believe in too much movies for young ones. Movies are made for grown up folks, that is most a them are, and young ones gets the wrong ideas [from] the things they see. All them gangsters and shootin' and stuff. People ought ta know what kinda show a young one's goin' ta see, 'for they give 'em the money ta go."[6] A man living in New York asked the U.S. Children's Bureau for advice about an eleven-year-old female relative who was "very much interested in movies and particularly in movie actors and actresses." He noted that the girl "avidly reads all sorts of movie magazines [and] can discourse for hours on various movie stars and pictures, their personal life, etc." Up until "about six to eight months" ago, the letter writer claimed, the girl had been "tractable, amiable, thoughtful and very sweet in manner and disposition." Suddenly she became "abrupt to her elders, exceedingly thoughtless, careless, and disobedient." Furthermore the girl, "though only eleven years old, [had] become much interested in 'boy friends' and thinks that she is quite in love with a very nice youngster of her own age." Perhaps most revealing of all, the man noted, the girl had "ambitions to be an actress."[7]

Faced with dwindling profits and shrinking audiences after the 1929 stock market crash, radio and movie producers pushed the limits of Americans' tolerance for sexually suggestive, violent, and otherwise racy entertainment. Several popular magazines and newspapers at the time drew attention to the growing controversy over movie and radio content. Beginning in 1933, *Parents Magazine* featured articles condemning violence in radio's serial adventure programs for children. A cartoon in the magazine depicted a frightened young girl listening to a radio blaring, "Scram! Don't Shoot! Kidnapped! They're Going To Kill Me! Help! Murder! Bang! Bang! Kill Him! Police!"

Critics maintained that the capitalist business model was the heart of the problem. Some advocates suggested that Great Britain's government-owned public radio was a better model than the commercial radio format developing in the United States. Commercial radio broadcasters certainly felt threatened by such ideas.[8] They opposed government ownership and in 1934 took their argument to the public through a campaign entitled "Radio as a Means of Public Enlightenment." The Federal Communications Commission (FCC) responded by holding hearings to investigate the debate over public versus commercial radio. During one session, the president of the Columbia Broadcasting System (CBS), William Paley, testified that keeping America's commercial radio model was more democratic and would provide a better service to the public than government ownership. If the public wanted more educational programming, Paley said, broadcasters would be happy to provide it. He noted that in just the first nine months of 1934 his network had devoted 2,207 hours to what he broadly defined as educational programming. "We conceive of education by radio not in the narrow classical sense, but in the broadest humanitarian meaning," the CBS president explained. "Nor, in our democratic society, is culture merely a matter of learning the difference between Bach and Beethoven . . . but it is equally a knowledge of how to rear a family in health and happiness—or to spend leisure wisely and well."[9]

As radio's popularity expanded, the debate over the content of children's shows continued. In May 1935 Franklin Roosevelt asked the FCC to pressure broadcasters to clean up their programming or face greater government control. Hoping to avoid federal dictates, CBS and NBC announced self-censorship codes—a direct response to critics' concerns about the moral values being delivered to young listeners. CBS's code stipulated:

1) The exalting, as modern heroes, of gangsters, criminals, and racketeers will not be allowed.

2) Disrespect for either parental or other proper authority must not be glorified or encouraged.

3) Cruelty, greed, and selfishness must not be presented as worthy motivations.

4) Programs that arouse harmful nervous reactions in the child must not be presented.

5) Conceit, smugness, or an unwarranted sense of superiority over others less fortunate may not be presented.

6) Recklessness and abandon must not be falsely identified with a healthy spirit of adventure.

7) Unfair exploitation of others for personal gain must not be made praiseworthy.

8) Dishonesty and deceit are not to be made appealing or attractive to the child.[10]

Movie studios also responded to growing calls for government censorship. In 1933 the Roman Catholic church established the Legion of Decency, aiming to pressure movie executives and the government to "disinfect . . . the pest hole" threatening American children and youth. Several states and local communities had already implemented censorship boards. By 1933 the New York Board of Censorship was threatening to prohibit the showing of objectionable Hollywood films in New York City. Movie industry executives turned to a self-censorship code as part of their effort to avoid such reactions.

Perhaps to the surprise of many filmmakers and broadcasting executives, the decision to clean up America's movie screens and airwaves proved to be a boon for business. Concentrating on "All-American values" and eliminating much of the violence and sexuality in films resulted in a more sanitized and homogeneous commercial culture for Americans of all ages.[11] From the mid-1930s forward, an entire generation of young Americans absorbed this image as the normative model of idyllic life in the United States.

Turn the Radio On!

Sales of most manufactured products declined drastically after the stock market crash, but that was not the case for the radio industry. In 1930 only half of all U.S. households had a radio. Ten years later the figure had risen to 83 percent. Ownership among urban families was nearly universal. Rural households were less likely to have a radio, but 70 percent of those in the rural countryside had joined the national trend. The average cost of a radio receiver ranged from thirty dollars for a simple table unit to hundreds of dollars for fancy console models. So buying a radio could be costly, but in the 1930s it became a choice that a clear majority of American families found the means to afford. Many Americans considered owning a radio a necessity of life as the medium matured over the decade.[12]

Having the money to buy a radio, however, did not solve the difficulty many families faced in trying to enjoy their favorite programs. While over 90 percent of urban households had access to commercially produced electric power as early as 1930, less than 10 percent of rural families did. New Deal programs like the Rural Electrification Administration and the Tennessee Valley Authority brought electricity to many rural areas in the late 1930s and 1940s. A small portable generator or strong batteries also solved the problem of powering a radio for families who continued to wait for electric lines to reach their homes.

New programming encouraged radio's popularity. In the 1920s reception was often poor, broadcast hours limited, and most programming consisted solely of music. In the early 1930s four national networks increased their broadcast range and added new types of programs to their schedules. In addition, 743 local radio stations offered an array of broadcasts. By 1937 radio programming could be heard by almost all Americans twenty-four hours a day, seven days a week. The medium became the nation's major source of popular entertainment.[13] Broadcasters devoted an increasing amount of airtime to comedy and variety shows, soap operas, dramas, sports, and programming created specifically for young listeners. They also learned that designating some of each day to children and adolescents provided new avenues of advertising revenue that had been overlooked earlier.

"Oh Boy! Daddy bought us a new little radio!" shouted the cartoon image of a little boy to his smiling brother in a 1932 Davega Radio City Stores advertisement printed in the *New York Times*. A 1934 advertisement for Westinghouse's "World Cruiser" console model was another typical use of children's images to promote radio sales. The Westinghouse ad pictured a well-dressed middle-class family of four (mom, dad, and a boy and girl) excitedly examining world maps while listening to the radio. The accompanying caption read, "We're planning a world cruise with our Westinghouse World Cruiser!" The message was clear: owning a radio provided entertainment as well as educational opportunities for children and adults.[14]

While educators, politicians, and some parents debated radio's content, for most young listeners the medium was simply fun. After morning breakfast shows and early-afternoon soap operas aimed at housewives, radio stations filled their late-afternoon broadcasts with the serial adventure programs designed to attract elementary- and middle-school-aged children like John Barney and his friends. Some of the programs' characters, like Little Orphan Annie, were already familiar to young listeners from the comics, but radio's version placed the eternally optimistic ten-year-old in exotic locales where she engaged in life-threatening adventures that were more exciting than what appeared in the daily newspaper comic strip. Daddy Warbucks, Annie's wealthy benefactor, provided the money and influence she needed to access this imaginary world of thrilling and endless possibilities. The Great Depression was not a problem for Annie.

Similar programs were based on adventure and the promotion of loyalty, friendship, obedience to authority, service, perseverance, clean living, democracy, freedom, and good sportsmanship. Evil-doers existed in the world of radio adventurers, but the good guys always won out in the end. *Jack Armstrong, The All American Boy* (1933–1950), became one of the most successful of the new entries. The show's name suggests the link between the values promoted on the program and those touted as all-American by media critics. The program's main characters, the high school–aged heroes Jack Armstrong and his friends Billy and Betty Fairfield, thwarted evil villains and traveled to even more exotic locations than those described on the *Little Orphan Annie Show.* Program titles like "The Country of the Head Hunters," "The Zambo Anga Adventure," and "The Luminous Dragon Eye Ring" drew young listeners with the promise of spine-tingling tales in settings far from their everyday lives. Billy and Betty's wealthy Uncle Jim served the same role as Little Orphan Annie's Daddy Warbucks. The Great Depression was not a problem for Jack, Annie, or any of the other adventure series radio heroes. Wealthy benefactors helped, but story lines suggested that the secret to success rested in the all-American values of the programs' main characters.

With the exception of the *Little Orphan Annie Show,* adventure programs featured white males like Jack Armstrong as the main hero, but scriptwriters also included female buddy characters like Betty Fairfield. Broadcasters surmised that it was probably best not to challenge the dominant image of white males as society's leaders. They also believed that including female characters would help keep their programs open to both boys and girls. Because radio adventure shows contained so many similar themes, scriptwriters used the programs' locales to set them apart. *The Lone Ranger* (1933–1956) and *Tom Mix* (1933–1943) took place in the American West. *Buck Rogers* (1932–1947) offered space travel in the twenty-fifth century, and *The Green Hornet* (1936–1952) worked city streets as a newspaper journalist by day and a crime-fighting, costumed crusader by night.[15]

While self-censorship resulted in more sanitized themes and story lines in children's radio programming by the mid-1930s, commercialization did not suffer. Sponsors continued to use the children's hour to promote their products to young fans. Boxtops or other proofs of purchase could be exchanged for premiums such as toy silver bullets from the Lone Ranger, interplanetary maps from Buck Rogers, decoder badges from the Green Hornet, and decoder rings from Little Orphan Annie. Owning a souvenir like these identified a young person as someone who knew what was keen. The Skelly Oil Company's early sponsorship of the *Captain Midnight* program (1938–1949) is an interesting example of the strategies used by advertisers to attract children's loyalty and new revenues for business. The show's young listeners could not drive, so Captain Midnight encouraged his young fans "to tell their dads" to take them to the local Skelly gas station so they could pick up the "official Flight Patrol membership card and brass badge." The pledge printed on the membership card included the all-American values promoted to a generation of radio listeners: "As a Junior Pilot of the Captain Midnight Flight Patrol, I pledge myself to be Honest in all things, Fair to all others, Brave in the face of danger, Courteous to my superiors and elders and Alert at all time to the fine principles of our Flight Patrol."[16]

Children's weekend programming drew even younger listeners than the weekday shows but also included fantasy. Beginning in 1932 Ireene Wicker was the star of the *Singing Story Lady*, a program created for pre-kindergarten-aged children. *Let's Pretend* (1934–1954) attracted a slightly older audience but still younger than most of the youngsters who listened to the weekday adventures. *Let's Pretend* featured a group of young actors known as "The Pretenders" who acted out familiar fairy tales and stories sent in by listeners.[17]

Some shows broadcast outside the children's hour attracted young listeners at the other end of the age scale. For example, *The Shadow*, which first aired in 1930, was canceled in 1932 because it failed to find an audience. A twenty-two-year-old Orson Welles brought the program back to life in 1937 by appealing primarily to adolescents. Welles was the same radio broadcaster who caused a sensation with his infamous October 30, 1938, science-fiction drama "War of the Worlds." Some Americans panicked when they heard what they believed to be a real-time news report detailing an attack by Martians on the East Coast of the United States. It appears that most of the people who were frightened out of their wits were adults; younger listeners understood that the show was fiction because they recognized Welles's voice from his role on *The Shadow*.[18]

Many evening radio programs also attracted children and teens. Families listened to the radio together the same way a later generation would embrace television. Younger and older Americans waited each week for the unavoidable calamity that happened when someone opened the door to the overflowing closet on *Fibber McGee and Molly* (1935–1959). Situation comedies featuring vaudeville stars such as George Burns, Gracie Allen, and Jack Benny captured the interest of whole families. Programs like *Nashville's Grand Ole Opry* (1925 to the present), *Your Hit Parade* (1935–1959), and weekly classical music broadcasts appealed to a wide range of tastes and age groups. Sports broadcasts also drew a diverse audience. Millions of Americans listened to baseball's World Series games over the radio, and Friday night boxing matches were popular entertainment. A vast majority of Americans of all ages tuned in their radios on June 22, 1938, to hear the heavily promoted rematch between heavyweight boxers Joe Louis and Max Schmeling. The German Schmeling had defeated Louis, an African American, four years earlier in a match that Nazi propagandists used as proof of Aryan racial superiority. In the rematch Louis knocked out the German in the first round. The victory seemed to symbolize a fatal weakness in Nazi racial logic; Louis, only the second African American to hold the championship boxing title, became an American hero.[19] Unlike Jack Johnson, the first black heavyweight champion, Louis represented the all-American virtues.

Despite the wide array of choices on radio, programming did not mirror the complexities of America's cultural landscape. The few minority voices that could be heard in dramatic or comedy programs reflected racial and ethnic stereotypes common to the 1930s. For example, the Lone Ranger's loyal American Indian companion, Tonto, was clever but spoke only broken English and was best known for uttering the fictitious phrase "kemo sabe" (supposedly, "friend"). The Green Hornet's sidekick, Kato, also spoke broken English and was first described as a Filipino of Japanese ancestry. He became more Filipino than Japanese after the December 7, 1941, attack on Pearl Harbor but never improved his ability to speak English. Two white actors, Freeman Gosden and Charles Correll, played the most popular African-American characters on radio, *Amos 'n' Andy* (1926–1960). Americans of all backgrounds listened to this very long-running program, but much of the show's comedy relied on popular racial stereotypes that portrayed blacks as uneducated, lazy, and slow. Gosden and Correll sometimes appeared in photographs and at promotional events in blackface makeup, and the show's scripts included "Negro-dialect." The NAACP protested the program's racial stereotypes, but *Amos 'n' Andy* remained a popular part of the nation's radio airwaves for many years. Its images undoubtedly influenced children's beliefs about race, but it is unlikely that most children knew of controversies over the program.[20]

For an entire generation, radio became a necessity that connected them to a commercial market increasingly divided into age-based categories. The medium also provided cheap entertainment for a generation of Americans whose ability to consume was limited by the depression. Listening to the radio could be a solitary experience, but many children also shared it with friends and family. Even children and teens who listened alone knew they were sharing their favorite programs with others. Radio lessened feelings of isolation and deprivation that so many young people endured. A thirteen-year-old girl from Oklahoma, writing in 1935, explained its appeal: "We live five miles from town, and we are poor. We have no money for boughten amusements. There is not a radio around in the country and I get terribly lonesome in summer." Getting a radio "would mean enjoyment for all my friends as well as me."[21]

The Movies, Child Actors, and Young Audiences

Young Americans also made movies an essential part of growing up in the 1930s. Hollywood helped attract children and teens to theaters by putting more young faces on America's screens than ever before. Movies gave the generation coming of age during the depression a collection of shared images they carried with them the rest of their lives. Movies also portrayed a world of possibilities that many would not have seen without the increasingly popular medium. Jean Lobe grew up in Milwaukee during the depression and was a huge film fan. She remembered that going to the movies "was a great thrill" that always left her coming "out of the theater completely dazed to be back in my own life."[22]

Despite their popularity, films had been controversial with some Americans from the time Thomas Edison's studio released the first images at the turn of the century.[23] By the 1920s the Christian evangelist Billy Sunday and the automobile executive Henry Ford had become highly visible and vocal critics of American movies. Their criticism also reflected a growing nativism and anti-Semitism that spread during the period and remained part of American society in the 1930s. In 1921 Ford told the *Dearborn Independent*, "As soon as Jews gained control of the 'movies,' we had a movie problem, the consequences of which are not yet visible. It is the genius of that race to create problems of a moral character in whatever business they achieve a majority." In an effort to quiet such critics, in 1922 the eight major film companies responded by creating the Motion Picture Producers and Directors Association of America (MPPDA). They named a well-known Protestant politician, Will Hays, as the organization's head. Hays turned his office into a public relations agency for the movies. He lobbied the Boy Scouts, Camp Fire Girls, Girl Scouts, General Federation of Women's Clubs, International Federation of Catholic Alumnae, National Education Association, YMCA, and other groups in a dialogue that he hoped would end calls for government censorship of Hollywood films. As a result of these conversations, in 1930 Hays devised a set of guidelines that spelled out themes and behaviors recommended by the MPPDA to filmmakers. Faced with shrinking audiences, from 1930 to 1933 most directors and studios ignored the new code and instead added to the amount of sex and violence in films. But audiences failed to materialize, and calls for government censorship mounted.

In 1934 Hays tried a different strategy. The MPPDA began to enforce the "Hays Production Code" by refusing to put the organization's stamp of approval on films that did not follow its guidelines. This was a significant threat since the film companies owned or had very close business relationships with most of the major movie theaters in the United States. *Tarzan and His Mate* became the first movie censored under the newly enforced code. Like the radio industry's guidelines, the film studios' Hays Production Code sanitized the industry's products.[24]

Walt Disney's *Snow White and the Seven Dwarfs* (1937) is representative of the Hays Code's prescription for films aimed at children and families. The film adapted a classic fairy tale of good winning over evil, an idea consistent with the all-American values promoted by critics. Furthermore the story involves a beautiful and helpless young woman who is saved from a life of drudgery and exploitation by the romantic but brief kiss of a handsome prince. The tale of Snow White reinforced traditional gender stereotypes, was romantic but not sexy, and avoided overt depictions of violence while providing a dramatic storyline. The Great Depression may have put many young Americans in unhappy circumstances, but in films like *Snow White and the Seven Dwarfs* hope for a better future springs eternal.[25]

Besides romance and fairy-tale endings, filmmakers also used new technologies and marketing strategies to draw audiences to theaters. By the 1930s children, teens, and adults escaped the summer heat in air-conditioned movie theaters; in winter they could sit in warm comfort. "The talkies," movies with sound, had entered theaters in the late twenties, but in the 1930s studios improved audio quality and added color. *The Wizard of Oz* and *Gone with the Wind* (both released in 1939) were extravagantly expensive color movies that paid off big at the box office and became favorites of children and teens. New animation techniques boosted the popularity of cartoons and encouraged Disney's release of its first full-length animation movies. Warner Bros. created the first Daffy Duck cartoon in 1937 and followed in 1940 with Bugs Bunny, a character that often escaped the peering eyes of censors.[26]

Lower ticket prices also helped draw children and teens to movie theaters. By 1932 theater owners had dropped the average ticket price twenty cents, making it possible to sit in a dark theater all afternoon or evening for as little as a dime. Saturdays became kids' day at movie houses across the United States, and going to "the picture show" was a weekend ritual for many young Americans. As Bill Schulz told his peers in his Milwaukee high school newspaper, going to the movies was cheaper "in the long run" than almost any place else a boy could take a girl on a date. Sometimes movies were even available for free: business owners sponsored outdoor movies in the hope they would attract retail customers from the rural countryside into town on weekdays. The rural Nebraskan Walter Schmitt remembers going to the nearby town of Gresham on summer evenings to watch free movies. "If any small town didn't have it," Schmitt recalled, "why [everybody would] point at 'em, They don't even have a free movie."[27]

Shirley Temple became an icon of modern American childhood in the 1930s as the decade's most popular movie star. *(University of Maryland, Baltimore County)*

In 1935 the publishers of the *Chicago Tribune* decided to use the popularity of movies to help sell newspapers. The *Tribune* offered a twenty-two-inch Shirley Temple doll to anyone able to sell five annual subscriptions. One frustrated little girl quickly learned that this was not easy. She wrote to Eleanor Roosevelt asking for help. "You have millions of friends," the girl noted. "Couldn't you please ask them to take for one year at 65 cents a month the Daily Chicago Tribune. I don't know how I'd ever thank you if you got them. I know one thing. I'd pray with all my heart in Holy Mass and when receiving the Holy Communion pray to God to bless you and all.

Please do help me," the girl pleaded. "If you do get them send them as soon as you can."[28] She really wanted that Shirley Temple doll.

Shirley Temple is perhaps the best-known child film star of all time. In the 1930s her image became an icon of American childhood; no film or stage star's likeness was more marketable. A singing, dancing, and acting phenomenon, the precocious little girl began making film shorts in 1932 when she was only three years old. Her 1934 film releases, *Stand Up and Cheer*, *Little Miss Marker*, and *Now and Forever*, secured her reign as the most popular box office star of the decade. Her dimple-cheeked, curly-topped film persona seemed to offer just the right combination of sentimentalized childhood that appealed to children and adults hungering for happy endings and a brighter future. Often playing an orphan, or at least a child who had lost her mother, Temple exhibited fortitude and exceptional wisdom that often surpassed that of the adult characters in her films. Young moviegoers identified with her spirit, and adults found it comforting to see that children held the promise of a brighter future. At the height of her popularity, Temple received sixty thousand fan letters a month. In 1933 alone, toy manufacturers sold 1.5 million Shirley Temple dolls. The Academy of Motion Picture Arts and Sciences recognized the young actor's contribution to the film industry's remarkable turnaround by awarding her a special miniature Oscar.[29]

At the start of the decade studio executives already knew that child actors could successfully draw audiences into movie theaters, but they took things one step further as part of an overall strategy to combat the depression. Six-year-old Jackie Coogan became a film star when he joined Charlie Chaplin in the 1921 silent film classic *The Kid*. Coogan made fifteen feature films from 1921 to 1927. His parents sold his image to a clothing manufacturer that promoted Coogan's working-class film persona as the ideal fashion statement defining middle-class childhood dependency—overalls, a sweater, and an oversized duckbilled cap. In 1930 Coogan starred as Tom

Sawyer in the film version of Mark Twain's classic depiction of idyllic small-town American childhood. He scored his last box office success at age sixteen in the 1931 film *The Champ.* Coogan's pioneering career paved the way for an explosion of films featuring children and adolescents.[30] Besides Shirley Temple, well-known child and adolescent stars in the 1930s included Judy Garland, Roddy McDowall, Mickey Rooney, Ann Rutherford, Lana Turner, and Jane Withers. Children and adolescents also performed in group ensemble productions such as the *Little Rascals* and the *Dead End Kids.* The 1930s became a decade filled with the images of sweet-faced young film stars. Consistent with the middle-class family ideal that had been promoted by child-welfare reformers since the Progressive Era, most roles for young actors emphasized that childhood and adolescence should be a time free from adult worries and responsibilities.[31]

The *Little Rascals* shorts supported this viewpoint by putting the series' pre-adolescent actors in various adult situations where they inevitably behaved in comedic and childish ways. Their antics were funny because the effort to imitate grownups looked so out of place, thus reinforcing the modern childhood ideal suggesting that the lives of children should be distinct from those of adults. Hal Roach began filming the first *Little Rascals* shorts in 1922. In the 1920s some communities sponsored Little Rascals look-alike contests, and a few even made their own copycat films. By the 1930s Metro-Goldwyn-Mayer (MGM) distributed the *Little Rascals* films, bringing them to an even wider audience. In 1938 Roach sold the series to the studio, which released the last *Little Rascals* films in 1944. Over the years Roach and MGM produced 221 individual episodes, each lasting approximately 10 to 20 minutes. When the original cast grew too old for the series' story lines, the individual child actors changed, but the basic characters continued to fit the predictable social and cultural stereotypes outlined in the first *Little Rascals* episodes: the fat kid, the freckle-faced redhead, the skinny kid with the bow tie and cowlick, the black boy with big eyes and a toothy grin, and several cute girls complete with curls, dimples, and frilly dresses. The *Little Rascals* shorts portrayed childhood as a time of mini-adventures, largely separate from the world of adults, where no one was ever seriously hurt or emotionally harmed.[32]

The *Dead End Kids* series was a slightly darker depiction of American childhood that centered on the lives of troubled adolescents in a poor New York City neighborhood. The idea for the series came from a 1935 Broadway production entitled *Dead End*, written by the Pulitzer Prize–winning playwright Sidney Kingsley. The play was a social commentary on the problems of poor families living near the affluent Sutton Place neighborhood. The play's characters included a gang of young toughs that hung around the docks, got into various forms of mischief, stole, fought, and tried to emulate their hero, a local gangster. In 1937 United Artists turned the play into a film that incorporated the ensemble of young actors from Broadway: Billy Halop, Leo Gorcey, Bobby Jordan, and Bernard Punsley. The film was popular with audiences, so Warner Bros. quickly signed the ensemble of young actors for six more movies, released from 1938 to 1939: *Crime School, Angels with Dirty Faces, They Made Me a Criminal, Hell's Kitchen, Angels Wash Their Faces*, and *On Dress Parade*. The series also included adult box office stars such as Humphrey Bogart, James Cagney, Pat O'Brien, and Ann Sheridan. The scripts remained true to Kingsley's original message that poverty and hopelessness could turn good kids into bad—a theme also familiar to audiences who had seen William Wellman's 1933 *Wild Boys of the Road*. Still, in the end, the *Dead End Kids* films were consistent with the themes prescribed by the Hays Code and part of the modern childhood ideal. In other words, even juvenile delinquents could be saved if given the chance for a more protected and idealized childhood spent in school, without abuse, as part of a supportive family. The 1938 film *Boys Town* starring a very young-looking seventeen-year-old Mickey Rooney, suggested that even orphans could have lives closer to the ideal if the adults gave them the support of a homelike environment modeled on the modern ideal of a protected American childhood.[33]

A young Mickey Rooney also contributed to the proliferation of this image through the highly successful *Andy Hardy* series. These films provided strong visual images of idyllic modern American childhood, especially during adolescence. Andy Hardy and his high school friends lived in happy and stable middle-class families in small-town America. The teens spent their time going to school and enjoying social lives overseen, but not controlled, by parents and teachers. The series' story lines followed Andy and his pals, both boys and girls, with their families, in school, and at the local soda shop. The young people experienced joy and sadness as they struggled to mature into adults, but their lives were dress rehearsals for adult realities. Mickey Rooney first appeared as Andy Hardy in the MGM film *A Family Affair* (1937). It was about the entire Hardy family, but Rooney stole the show. By the series' fourth movie, *Love Finds Andy Hardy* (1938), Rooney's character dominated the scripts. The depression and the social problems associated with poverty and disrupted families, portrayed in the *Dead End Kids* series, did not existent in *Andy Hardy* films. Crises provided drama but were always solved by the close of each film. Warner Bros. produced sixteen *Andy Hardy* films, the last released in 1958. Rooney's small stature and boyish looks helped him remain a teen longer than anyone else in movie history. His young female co-stars included Judy Garland and Lana Turner.[34]

Film series like the *Little Rascals* and *Andy Hardy* did not ask audiences to evaluate the emotional complexities of growing up. Instead they presented heartwarming stories of cartoonish cuteness, avoiding what Steven Mintz has called "the otherness of childhood" later addressed in some post–World War II movies. Films released in the 1930s generally do not deal with the emotional consequences of child abuse, sexuality, or even the difficulties of coming of age during the depression. Perhaps audiences did not wish to be confronted

Judy Garland and Mickey Rooney, in the 1938 film *Love Finds Andy Hardy*, personified the model of idyllic American adolescence centered on high school and teenaged peers. *(Academy of Motion Picture Arts and Sciences)*

with images of life's harsh realities during a decade when they could easily find such reminders outside a theater's doors.

But everything young people saw in films reflected the virtues of idyllic childhood and family life. Fantasy and adventure films emphasized escapism over the promotion of all-American values, especially in the early 1930s. In the pre-Code days of 1931, children as well as adults thrilled at being frightened by Frankenstein's monster (played by Boris Karloff) and Dracula (played by Bela Lugosi). Viewers of all ages flocked to see a scantily clad and screaming Fay Wray carried off by the giant ape King Kong in 1933. Hollywood also produced a wave of gangster movies during pre-Code days that paralleled the public's fascination with the crime wave covered in the nation's press. Better sound technology fueled the gangster genre for filmmakers. Critics, however, worried that movies like *Little Caesar* (1930), *Public Enemy* (1931), and *Scarface* (1932) celebrated the lives of unethical, violent, and self-destructive criminals. But such films glorified individuals who operated outside the system, and thereby turned social evil into personal evil. Some adults also charged Hollywood with increasingly using sex to sell films. Comedies that appealed to audiences of all ages, such as the Marx Brothers' *Animal Crackers* (1930) and *Horse Feathers* (1932), contained sexual innuendo as well as slapstick. Elaborately staged musicals such as *42nd Street* (1933) and the romantic films of Ginger Rogers and Fred Astaire presented images consistent with films released after the enforcement of the Hays Production Code. The enforcement of the Code after 1934 curbed the more controversial themes in all films.[35] It is difficult to measure what role the studios self-imposed censorship played in attracting audiences to movie theaters. It is logical to assume, however, that producing more films that featured young actors was an easy way to attract children and teens to theaters. Young actors provided a special connection to Hollywood among young moviegoers, and the images of children and teens portrayed in films grew similar over the decade.

While movies generally depicted an ideal of American youth, the young actors were real people—and their lives were often very far from the images they portrayed in films. In 1935 Jackie Coogan became the poster boy for the problems young actors could face when he engaged in a very public fight over access to the trust fund that held his childhood earnings. Coogan sued his mother and stepfather for what he believed was his right to an estimated $4 million. Restricted by laws that favored parental rights over those of children, a California court awarded Coogan a miserly $126,000. The case received extensive national exposure, and the resulting public outcry led legislators to enact the California Child Actors Law, sometimes referred to as the Coogan Act. The legislation did little to help Coogan, but it set a new standard for the legal rights of child film stars in a decade when a growing number of young actors appeared on America's movie screens.[36]

The New Juvenile Literature and American Realities

Classic children's literature often served as story lines for popular films. Filmmakers also turned to new books published for young readers in the 1930s. At first glance many of these works followed the same themes in classic children's literature. Upon closer examination, however, several authors created more realistic young protagonists and placed them in less romanticized settings than past writers had done. In some ways children's literature took more risks than radio and the movies. As Gail Murray explains in her book tracing the history of American children's literature, in the 1930s authors "strove for exacting physical detail and attempted to realistically portray children's abilities and emotions." Juvenile literature had been around since the late nineteenth century and in the 1920s was legitimized by professionals. The American Booksellers Association created Children's Book Week to encourage the publication and reading of books aimed at younger readers, and the American Library Association (ALA) established the Newbery Medal for the year's best work in children's literature. In 1938 the ALA added the Caldecott Award for the best children's picture book.[37]

In the 1930s authors like Laura Ingalls Wilder, Carol Ryrie Brink, and Marjorie Rawlings turned to nineteenth-century settings to show young readers examples of children who overcame difficult challenges. Wilder wrote eight books based on her memories of growing up on the Great Plains during the late nineteenth century. Her first, *The Little House in the Big Woods*, was published in 1932; the last appeared in 1953. Wilder used her stories to uphold ideals of self-sufficiency, individualism, and reliance on family. Her daughter, Rose Wilder Lane, was a great influence on Wilder's stories. The conservative politics advanced in Wilder's book reflected her daughter's thinking as well. Lane was a professional journalist who quit the Democratic party over her objections to Franklin Roosevelt's New Deal. The *Little House* characters experienced hardship and sadness but always succeeded by relying on family and a community of friends—never the government—to overcome problems. Wilder's stories also featured strong female characters, but she was careful to make sure they never rejected traditional gender stereotypes grounded in marriage, motherhood, and the recognition of men as society's primary breadwinners.[38]

Carol Ryrie Brink took a similar view with her popular book *Caddie Woodlawn* (1935), a Newberry Award winner. Caddie is an eleven-year-old tomboy living in late-nineteenth-century Wisconsin. At first her father encourages her adventurous spirit, but eventually he reprimands his daughter's boyish behavior. He explains that the time has come for Caddie to act more ladylike because it's the important job of females to tame men and ensure beauty in the world.

In 1938 Marjorie Rawlings took a slightly different approach in her book *The Yearling*, which features a boy, Jody, as the main character. Like Wilder and Brink, Rawlings uses an historical setting to emphasize how family can help young people overcome difficulties. Her story is set in the northern Florida swamps of the 1870s and openly discusses the family's financial difficulties. That *The Yearling* won the Pulitzer Prize and was selected by the Book-of-the-Month Club suggests some recognition of children's emotional maturity and willingness to deal with family difficulties during hard times. Critics applauded Rawlings and other juvenile authors, but as one reviewer noted in the *New York Times*, emphasis on America's past seemed "bent on ruthlessly undermining the superior glories of city life."[39]

Young readers were even more strongly attracted to books ignored by literary professionals and critics. Millions of elementary- and middle-school youngsters enjoyed the adventure and mystery series books produced by companies like the Stratemeyer Syndicate. Edward Stratemeyer had founded the company in 1905 as a packager of inexpensive books for younger readers. He hired a pool of ghostwriters to produce new publications packaged as part of series allegedly written by a single author. One of the most successful was the *Hardy Boys* mystery collection, which began publication in 1927 under the author's name of Franklin W. Dixon. The books detailed the exploits of teenage detectives Frank and Joe Hardy. Marketed primarily to fourth-through-sixth-grade boys, the books were profitable for the company and popular among young readers. Thinking that a female protagonist might also attract girls to such stories, in 1930 Stratemeyer introduced the *Nancy Drew* mystery series. The eighteen-year-old Drew was strong, smart, quick, clever, and capable, but like the girls in other popular books of the 1930s she did not threaten traditional gender roles. She had a boyfriend and lived in a very feminine world where scarlet slippers, women's diaries, and ivory charms could reveal the next important clue necessary for solving the story's mystery. Harriet Wirt Benson wrote all but seven of the first thirty *Nancy Drew* books (published from 1930 through 1953). By 1934 the *Nancy Drew* collection was the most popular series in juvenile literature. As intended, it appealed almost exclusively to girls.

Girls might read books about boys, but most males did not read stories that featured female characters. The Stratemeyer Syndicate tried to duplicate the success of Nancy Drew with similar books featuring female characters, but *Judy Bolton* (1932), the *Dana Girls* (1934), and *Kay Tracey* (1934) never reached the same level of popular appeal.[40] The Nancy Drew character combined just the right amounts of independence and femininity that appealed to many girls growing up during an era that challenged traditional gender stereotypes but did not alter them. Overall, series literature for young readers mirrored the values included in other forms of commercial popular culture directed at young consumers. Not surprisingly, this included racial and ethnic stereotypes that could also be heard on radio and seen in the movies. New books contained few ethnic or racial minorities, usually only in peripheral roles as criminals or people of questionable moral character.[41]

Reading could offer hours of entertainment and escapism, but many youngsters could not afford to purchase even the most inexpensive books. Some borrowed materials from local libraries or shared with friends. Others simply went without or turned to a new form of children's literature invented during the 1930s, comic books.

Creating the Comic Book Generation

The new comic books of the 1930s also had their roots in the late nineteenth century. Newspaper publishers had used the funnies (comic strips) as part of an overall strategy to sell their product to adults. Adult readers shared the funnies with children, but few youngsters bought newspapers for themselves. Early funnies such as *The Happy Hooligan* (1899), *Buster Brown* (1902), and *Mutt and Jeff* (1907) emphasized the comedic aspect of the funnies. *Blondie*, introduced in 1930, portrayed the mundane yet comic side of everyday married family life. Another popular newspaper comic strip, *Li'l Abner* (1934), appealed to a generation of increasingly savvy and modern teens who laughed at the script's backward hillbilly stereotypes. Newspapers added fantasy strips such as *Tarzan* (1929), *Buck Rogers* (1929), and *Dick Tracy* (1931) in the 1930s, but the characters remained quite human.[42] Children and adolescents whose parents could not afford a newspaper were nevertheless familiar with the story lines in the newspaper funnies. Young Robert Hastings understood that his parents were too poor to buy a Sunday paper, but he was still able to see the comics. A sympathetic neighbor always shared a copy.[43]

In 1933 M. C. Gaines and two associates asked and received permission to reprint some of the newspaper comic strips in book form, entitled *Funnies on Parade*. Gaines and his associates distributed ten thousand copies to Procter and Gamble Company customers. Gaines noted the success of the idea and decided to print a second collection he called *Famous Funnies*. This time he sold it on newsstands for ten cents apiece and in 1934 turned the project into a bimonthly publication. Major Malcolm Wheeler-Nicholson established the first distinct comic book publication in 1935 with *New Fun Comics*. Wheeler-Nicholson's publication was unique because it included comic strips not available in newspapers. In addition, many of the New Fun Comics were darker and more mysterious than the comedic strips featured in newspapers and reprinted in *Famous Funnies*. In 1937 Wheeler-Nicholson took his effort a step further when he teamed with publisher Harry Donenfeld to form D.C. Comics.

In June 1938 D.C. Comics introduced Superman, the first major comic book character with superhuman powers. In 1939 D.C. Comics sold over one million copies per issue of *Superman*. From 1940 to 1945 comic book publishers released more than four hundred different superhero characters. Many of them had been orphaned by a tragic event in their childhoods. Superman's parents, for example, were presumed dead after the explosion of their home planet. Batman's alter ego, Bruce Wayne, had witnessed as a child the murder of his parents by an evil villain. Comic book writers used these stories of childhood tragedy to explain the inner strength their heroes had developed to fight for freedom and democracy. Readers learned that they could overcome almost any difficulty by emulating the values of their favorite heroes.[44]

Comic books drew young readers into a fantasy world that had a distinct look and language they could share with peers. Boys bought most comic books. Even the most famous female character, Wonder Woman, introduced in 1941, was designed to appeal to young male readers. Boys often read comic books alone, but enthusiasts also built a subculture similar to what would develop among video game fans more than fifty years later. Comic books' inexpensive price, ten cents, added to their popularity among young customers. Small change scavenged from collecting returnable bottles, cutting a neighbor's grass, selling newspapers, or shining a pair of shoes could buy a comic book. In 1940 publishers produced 150 different titles that generated more than $20 million in sales. The market doubled during the next decade, and, at least for a time, the industry escaped the calls for censorship directed at radio and movies. That situation changed during the 1950s when educators, child psychiatrists, social conservatives, and politicians targeted comic books as a source of juvenile delinquency.[45] But in the 1930s few adults paid much attention to comic books, which strengthened the growth of a distinct consumer culture for children and teens.

Working at Play

Even the cheapest forms of commercial entertainment were out of reach for some American children in the 1930s. Many people who grew up during the Great Depression remember a childhood where they found ways to fill their free time with activities that did not cost much money. Robert Hastings put it this way in his memoir, *A Nickel's Worth of Skim Milk*: "The Depression may have denied me some of the frills of growing up, but it didn't rob me of the fun of just being a boy with my friends."[46]

Some games could be played with no special equipment or toys. Many of them had been passed down by generations of American children. By the 1930s radio, movies, and current events influenced children to alter the rules of some traditional games. Players updated

Despite the decade's hard times, most adults agreed that laughter and play were essential to a healthy childhood. These youngsters in Washington, D.C., were having a good time with a small wooden horse. Playing with neighborhood children was an important rite of childhood. *(Library of Congress)*

Hide 'n' Go Seek by assuming the role of cowboys and Indians, cops and robbers, or G-Men and gangsters. Boys and girls often played such games together, especially during the elementary-school years. Girls were more likely to play games like cowboys and Indians if boys were also included. But girls usually did not join pickup games of football, basketball, baseball, or stickball unless there were not enough boys around to field a team. Most boys and girls considered playing with dolls, jumping rope, or playing hopscotch girls-only games. Girls played house, but most boys did so only under duress.

Dolls, especially homemade paper dolls, filled hours of playtime for many girls. Shirley Temple dolls were also highly popular with girls whose parents found a way to afford them. Most doll play involved dressing and undressing dolls in clothing the girls made themselves or was sewn by older family friends or relatives. Fantasies tended to focus on believing that the dolls were models, movie stars, or, of course, mothers.[47]

Children's games could be complex or simple. Players enforced the rules through cooperation and intimidation. Disagreements often resulted in fights and it was important to be able to defend yourself. Floyd Salas had his first fight when his older brother bet another boy, "My brother can whip yours!" The six-year-old Salas was quickly overwhelmed by his larger competitor and he ended up with a bloody nose before his brother intervened to stop the beating. Floyd learned that the fight was just one of many he would have as a child growing up in rural California. He was proud of his reputation as a "scrapper," and found that other boys wanted to be friends because he was "handy with his fists."[48]

Some child experts worried that more affluent parents were overregulating their children's time, but the majority encouraged adults to take a larger interest in their children's play. They maintained that entertaining play was necessary for a healthy childhood but required the careful guidance of adults. Magazine and newspaper articles urged parents to abandon harsh discipline and instead offer companionship to their children. Some argued that the depression offered the opportunity to spend more time together at home. Philadelphia's Wanamaker Department Store and New York's F.A.O. Schwarz began selling Monopoly in 1934; the next year the toy manufacturer Parker Brothers signed an agreement with the game's designer that launched it as the most successful board game in history. Even poor parents who could not afford board games could play cards with their children. Jigsaw puzzles were a popular pastime by 1932, and in 1934 manufacturers introduced inexpensive die-cut jigsaw puzzles that were often given away as promotions. Franklin Roosevelt, a stamp collector himself, helped spur an interest in the hobby that could be shared by children and adults.[49]

Of course it took money to buy toys and hobby supplies, but the emphasis on play as important for children's development put new pressure on many parents to give their children more free time and autonomy. For youngsters who did not have to work at a job or help their families, it was not unusual on nonschool days to leave home after breakfast and not return until the evening dinner hour, or even after dark. City children took the subway and streetcars to travel far from their neighborhoods. Most long-distance excursions also involved an older sibling or cousin. The details of what happened to fifteen-year-old Edward Posluzny in a Baltimore theater are unusual, but the fact that he was there without an adult was not out of step with the times. Edward and his fourteen-year-old brother and a sixteen-year-old cousin went to Baltimore's State Theater for a Sunday matinee. Sitting near the front row, the boys suddenly found a three-year-old lion in their laps. Edward later told a newspaper reporter that he first thought the animal was a dog, but he realized his mistake when he heard people in the audience yelling "Lion, lion!" A policeman shot the lion in the shoulder. Fortunately, Edward suffered only a laceration to his knee, and his two companions were unharmed.[50] Other children and teens could be seen at baseball games, amusement parks, skating rinks, and other public venues common in America's cities. The availability of inexpensive public transportation in urban areas offered children and adolescents mobility without a car.

Children from the city and the country played outside during all kinds of weather. Sledding and ice skating were popular in places with cold winters. Swimming was a great relief from summer heat, though the high number of young drowning victims is a sad testament to the dangers that were also part of enjoying the nation's ponds, lakes, rivers, and beaches. In 1934, approximately

In an era before air conditioning, swimming was a popular pastime and helped children endure the summer heat—as in this homemade pool near a Pittsburgh steel plant in July 1938. *(Library of Congress)*

450 children drowned in New York City waterways alone.[51] Mark A. McCloskey, director of recreation for the New York City Board of Education, appealed to parents to help adult-monitored recreation programs "compete with the thrill and excitement of so many forbidden pleasures—playing along the waterfront, hitching onto trucks, scrambling into vacant buildings"—that threatened children's safety.[52]

Even traditional children's games could be dangerous. Mumblety-peg, for example, was a very popular game among boys. The rules may have differed by neighborhood, but the game always involved throwing the blade of a pocket knife into a circle drawn on the ground. Homemade guns and slingshots constructed from sticks, pieces of wood, inner-tube scraps, and rubber bands could efficiently launch potentially eye-damaging pebbles, rocks, marbles, and other small objects. Children rode bicycles, homemade scooters, and roller skates without wearing a helmet or other safety gear. In rural America it was not uncommon for children as young as twelve to drive tractors, cars, or other motorized vehicles. In general, children had a lot of autonomy and often played at games and engaged in activities that would send shivers down the spines of many parents today, not to mention the adults in their own time. Ride the Donkey (also called Ride the Pony) involved children jumping on each other's backs while standing on a precarious location such as the top of a concrete wall.[53] Advice columns in parents' magazines largely ignored children's safety, concentrating instead on the growing commercialization of childhood and advice about health care, diet, and schools.

Swing Kids

As more American adolescents remained in school longer than ever before, their leisure activities became progressively distinct from those of children and adults. The image of American adolescence portrayed in *Andy Hardy* films was far from reality for many teens. The expansion of high school attendance, however, reinforced an image in popular culture of late adolescence and early youth as a unique period of life that centered on socializing with peers. The sound that came to be known as swing served as the background music for a generation coming of age in the 1930s. The combination of radio and teens fueled the phenomenal popularity of swing.

Radio listeners in the thirties had a wide range of musical choices. Nothing attracted teens and youth more than swing. Popular memory tends to associate swing music with the World War II years, but the genre was first popularized during the depression. Big bands led by musicians like Charlie Barnet, Count Basie, Tommy and Jimmy Dorsey, Duke Ellington, Benny Goodman, Fletcher Henderson, Harry James, Artie Shaw, Chick Webb, and many others carried swing music to radio airwaves and local dance halls across the United States. Swing music had its roots in a combination of New Orleans–style jazz, Southern blues, and the Charleston sound popularized during the 1920s by black musicians like Louis Armstrong and Eubie Blake. In 1932 the elegant African-American Duke Ellington coined one of his most popular tunes, "It Don't Mean a Thing (If It Ain't Got That Swing)." Ellington did not invent swing, but his song provided the label.[54]

The clarinetist and bandleader Benny Goodman is often given credit for turning the swing sound into a national phenomenon. In 1934 Goodman was the twenty-five-year-old leader of a twelve-piece band working in New York City when the group joined NBC's Saturday night broadcast from 10:30 p.m. to 1:30 a.m., *Let's Dance*. The Goodman band's segment did not air until the program's last hour, so the audience in the East Coast time zone was fairly small. The West Coast, on the other hand, drew a much larger pool of listeners. Goodman's band offered a repertory of jazz and blues songs arranged by Fletcher Henderson, the most successful African-American jazz bandleader of the 1920s.

In 1935 the Goodman band went on a road tour across the United States. Most people who came to the shows during the early days of the tour offered only a lukewarm reception to the band's unfamiliar musical style. The story was different when the band reached Los Angeles' Palomar Ballroom on August 25, 1935. There Goodman and his fellow musicians received an enthusiastic welcome from young fans very familiar with the band's broadcasts on *Let's Dance*. The band got a similar response when it played in Goodman's hometown of Chicago on the way back to New York.

In Chicago young fans labeled the new sound "swing," and the music's syncopated rhythms set the tone for youth music during the depression and World War II. In June 1936 the CBS network aired a radio program called "Saturday Night Swing Session" which featured Goodman and his band. The next March, young swing fans at the Paramount Theater in New York City got up and danced in the aisles during a Benny Goodman concert. Goodman understood the connection between radio and the movies in America's popular culture directed at young audiences. In 1936 and 1937 he and his band made two films, *The Big Broadcast of 1937* and *Hollywood Hotel*.[55]

Bands that identified with the swing sound most often consisted of a piano player, clarinets, and various brass and percussion instruments. Swing music always had a strong four-four beat that encouraged audiences to tap their toes, snap their fingers, and move their hips. The genre built a strong link between dance and popular music for America's teens and youth. Dances such as the Lindy Hop, the Suzy Q, and the Big Peach were part of a dance style popularly known as "jitterbug." Dancers could improvise moves, but many spent hours practicing jitterbug's fast steps, body throws, and spins. As couples became more proficient at the new style, swing dance contests spread across the country. Many took place in commercial amusement parks or publicly owned recreation areas. Cincinnati's Coney Island Amusement Park included an open-air dance venue called Moonlight Gardens. During the 1930s Moonlight Gardens featured big bands that attracted teens and youth from the entire Ohio Valley region. The city of Cincinnati also sponsored dance contests in local public parks. They attracted the most talented jitterbug dance fans as well as those who came only to watch.[56]

Harlem's Savoy Ballroom became the mecca for young swing dance fans. The Savoy's audiences were somewhat unusual because they included blacks and whites. Teens listened to swing music on radios and jukeboxes, and bought records produced by both black and white musicians. While swing music's popularity crossed racial, regional, and class lines, most public dance venues did not include mixed-race audiences. In 1936 Benny Goodman, then known as the King of Swing, took an important step when he made several recordings with the black musician Lionel Hampton. In 1938 Goodman performed in concerts at New York City's Carnegie Hall with both black and white musicians.[57] Such advances did not end racial segregation or the refusal by most radio stations to play "race records" (recordings by black musicians), but they marked an important shift toward the racial integration of commercial music that would become more commonly associated with rock 'n' roll.[58]

Some teens combined the fun they had listening and dancing to swing music with making money. Marathon dance contests drew teenage dancers as well as unemployed youth in their twenties. The fad began as fun promotions in the early 1920s but took on a darker image in the 1930s, with some participants risking their health in grueling marathons that dragged on for weeks. Ann "Susie" Witt's story shows the more positive side of teens' relationship to swing and public dance contests. Ann was only four years old in 1924 when her Polish immigrant father abandoned his family. Ann quit school at age nine in order to take a job as a seamstress in a Baltimore garment factory. As she grew older, she spent much of her free time learning to dance. She did not have money for formal dance lessons, but they were not necessary. Like many cities and towns throughout the United States, Baltimore held dances for teens and youth in public parks and other venues. By the time Ann reached her teens she had won several local dance contests. She was so good by age seventeen that she landed a job as a professional dancer in *The Baltimore Follies*, a Broadway-style musical. She also worked as a tap dancer in the 1938 Busby Berkeley–inspired *Stardust Revue*, performed in Baltimore's glamorous Hippodrome Theater. Ann described her years as a young dancer as "exciting in capital letters."[59]

Even though she did not go to high school, Ann Witt shared the music and dance of her generation.

A Generation Apart

Swing music appealed to teens and youth partly because it was their own. Generational disagreements over musical tastes and standards of acceptable behavior preceded the 1930s. But the growing age segregation and proliferation of popular culture often added to such tensions within families. A woman from California wrote the U.S. Children's Bureau asking for parenting advice. "We are elderly parents (50 & 65)," she explained. Her daughters, age thirteen and sixteen, were popular and had many friends. "However," the mother lamented, "we feel ignorant of how best to control their good times. We want to allow them all the liberty we can—but it is quite plain that youngsters are 'different'—the boys do not seem gentlemanly— the girls have little reserve of manner—if any. Perhaps living in the age of bathing suits has a lot to do with it." The Children's Bureau's Ella Oppenheimer sympathized and replied, "You are not alone in your difficulty in knowing how best to handle your girls. I wonder if your girls belong to the *Girl Scouts*. The influence of this organization during adolescence, especially, is salutary."[60]

Experts like Oppenheimer had promoted the advantages of adult-directed clubs, playgrounds, athletic teams, and other social activities for children and adolescents since at least the Progressive Era. Clubs such as the Girl Scouts, Boy Scouts, Camp Fire Girls, the Department of Agriculture's 4-H, and groups associated with the YMCA, YWCA, and similar character-building recreational organizations gained new members in the 1930s. Thousands of boys attended weekly summer camp at Ten Mile River, a Boy Scout facility outside New York City that could handle up to two thousand youngsters at a time. Franklin Roosevelt helped the group acquire the ten-thousand-acre facility in 1927 while he was president of the Boy Scout Federation. The Boy Scouts and Girl Scouts, along with charitable organizations scattered throughout the United States, sent millions of boys and girls to summer camps. Sports teams and hobby clubs also attracted young members. In 1938 Carl E. Stortz organized the first boys' Little League Baseball team in Williamsburg, Pennsylvania. The Jimmie Allen Club attracted aspiring aviators who also heard about building model airplanes on the club's radio program. The American Legion organized the Air Cadets in 1933, and the Hearst newspapers established the Junior Birdmen of America club in response to many young people's fascination with aviation. The female pilot Amelia Earhart promoted a trophy with her name for girls interested in model airplanes.[61] After dance halls, amusement parks, and pool halls had drawn the ire of many adults during the early decades of the twentieth century, religious organizations and groups such as the YMCA and YWCA formed private clubs to attract children and teens. By the 1920s reformers, politicians, and parents increasingly turned to high schools as the primary monitor of the social lives of teens. Schools sponsored clubs based on hobbies, vocational interests, and self-improvement activities. Athletic teams for both boys and girls were also popular. Chaperoned dances were standard at most high schools by the 1920s, and in the late years of the depression decade, senior proms became a fixture in a growing number of American high schools.[62]

Group activities dominated the free time of most adolescents. Having fun with a group lowered social pressure between the sexes and was generally more inexpensive than dating. Dating could present problems for boys who had little money to spend on entertainment. Social practice dictated that males pay the evening's expenses while on a date. "Going Dutch" meant that girls would pay their own way during an evening of co-ed socializing. The practice was not unique to the 1930s, but it became increasingly popular among adolescents during hard times. It also took some of the pressure off a girl to provide sexual favors in exchange for a boy paying for entertainment or food.[63]

"Going steady" was another popular dating practice. The announcement that a boy and girl were going steady meant that the two had agreed to an exclusive relationship but were not serious enough to proceed with formal engagement and marriage. In 1938 Sally Jackson was "going steady with Bill Young." Bill lived near the Jackson family farm, about four miles southeast of Chapel Hill, North Carolina. Sally's father explained that Bill "sometimes got the use of his father's car," and the couple used it "to go 'gallavanting' around the country to churches, fairs, ball-games, and movies." Sally Jackson was lucky to have a boyfriend with access to a car because, as her father realized, she lived "too far from Chapel Hill to take part in the social life of the high school and must leave for home in the school bus promptly after school is out." Her father's tolerance for his daughter's dating behavior reflected a very modern attitude shared by many parents. It also mirrored the growing social acceptance of going steady as part of adolescence. A girl who went steady could enjoy consistent male companionship and still maintain a respectable reputation. She needed to avoid kissing and necking in public, but doing so in private with her steady beau was less perilous to a girl's reputation than dating several boys at the same time. During the 1930s adolescent boys and girls spent a lot of time together outside the watchful eyes of adults. Going steady was one way teens devised to self-regulate the new freedoms surrounding dating and social activities.

Charles Champlin "went steady for the first time, in an intense but chaste way, at sixteen." The relationship was only a rehearsal because Champlin "moved on" and eventually married another girl. A woman who grew up in Oakland, California, in the 1930s married her high school boyfriend. Several years later the woman told researchers that she and her boyfriend had used his car to neck when he brought her home at the end of a date. The girl's mother would flick the porch light on and off to signal that it was time for the girl to come in. If she did not respond right away, the girl's mother "would come out and yell and stamp her foot." The couple had a strong physical attraction for each other but waited until they married to have intercourse.[64]

But some teens did "go all the way." About one-fourth of female teens in a California study acknowledged that they had sex in high school, or at least before marriage. Janice Rice remembered that she "only went to high school because I had to . . . I didn't like it, wasn't happy there at all." She felt rejected by her peers and began hanging out in dance halls where she met older men and felt "popular." Asked whether she engaged in sexual intercourse, Rice replied,

> Most of the time I'd go all the way, and I got in trouble. Then my mother bought me a diaphragm and made me wear it—even if I went to the movies with a girl friend, because "you never can tell." That's what I'd do with a daughter, get her a diaphragm. . . . Once you've gone all the way, it's hard to stop. . . . I didn't want to stop. . . . If they don't get it from you, they will from someone else, and you don't want that to happen.

Janice Rice had an illegal abortion while still in high school and married for the first time at age nineteen. Between then and age thirty-eight she married and divorced five times. Janice was a rebellious teen and continued to resist mainstream conventions throughout her life.[65] She was an extreme example of teen sexual experience in the 1930s, but the increase in unsupervised social activities did foster opportunities for sexual activity among adolescents. Since most did not have good access to information about birth control, it is likely that the traditional condemnation of birth outside of marriage discouraged many young couples from engaging in intercourse. Like birthrates, teen pregnancy rates declined in the 1930s and doubled in the years after World War II. As with successive generations, it appears that in the 1930s most adolescents curbed their sexual behavior to fit what they perceived to be in their best interest.

Boy-meets-girl dating, club activities, and athletic events popularized in the 1930s "kleen teen" films became the model of modern adolescent dating and social behavior perpetuated in America's high schools. Young people also adopted the era's social taboos that prohibited the recognition of homosexuality. The strong emphasis on teen heterosexuality contributed to a growing social condemnation of even the camp culture introduced by Mae West and other avant-garde performers in the 1920s.[66] The 1930s model of heterosexuality and middle-class ideals, however, did not end tensions between generations. "The hardest thing for me to do is to obey my parents," a fifteen-year-old unwed mother in New York told a researcher in 1935. "They love me but they don't understand what girls ought to be doing these days. I guess they forget when they were young. Besides, things are different now."[67] Of course the girl's parents may have expressed the same complaint when they were growing up.

Time, Money, and Self-improvement

Glamorous images of movie stars and models in films and popular magazines combined with the growing emphasis on clubs and high-school-based social activities in the 1930s to foster a culture of competition among teens. Gender influenced most of the parameters in this peer culture, but both boys and girls in their teens spent more of their time and money on self-improvement schemes. The growing emphasis on self-improvement also paralleled a refusal to believe that the American system had failed. Instead the trend suggested that individual improvement would help guarantee success.

Since the late nineteenth century, rising industrialization and urbanization had paralleled a stronger link between American manhood and athletics. In the 1930s the growth of high schools provided new fuel for this connection. Team sports, boys were told, simulated the competitive world of work they would encounter as adults. Success on the field or the court provided important character-building experiences that would ensure a more secure future. Girls also learned that high school was a dress rehearsal for their adult lives. Adolescent females should develop skills that would help them earn a living if necessary, but, most important, a girl's success relied on her ability to attract a successful husband. Girls learned that meeting standards of femininity as defined in popular culture would help them find a good husband. Hoping to get a jump on their competition, or at least to fit in among their peers, many adolescents turned their own bodies into projects that consumed more and more time, money, and attention.

By the 1930s Charles Atlas was a familiar icon of the masculine ideal. Born Angelo Siciliano in Italy in 1893, he had immigrated to the United States in 1903 with his father. Harassed by bigger and stronger boys in his working-class New York neighborhood, as a teen Siciliano devised a fitness program that he claimed changed him from a ninety-seven-pound weakling into a strongman. In 1912 admirers began to call him Charles Atlas, and in 1915 he legally adopted the name. Atlas earned the title of the "The World's Most Perfectly Developed Man" at bodybuilding contests held in New York City; in 1929 he joined forces with advertising man Charles P. Roman. Roman named Atlas's fitness program "Dynamic Tension" and created a comic-strip-style advertisement that has been called the "single greatest mail order ad of all time." By the mid-1930s the Charles Atlas image was a regular feature in the ad sections of most popular comic books. Entitled "The Insult That Changed Mac," the ad pictures a "97 lb. weakling" and his date sitting on a beach. A muscular bully torments the couple by kicking sand in their direction. "Hey, quit kicking that sand in our faces!" is Mac's only response. Embarrassed that he is so much smaller and weaker than the bully, Mac decides to gamble on the Atlas program and in no time develops bulging muscles. When he has another encounter with the beach bully, his girlfriend admiringly looks on while the new Mac knocks the bully to the ground with one powerful punch.

The message was clear: just like the comic book superheroes, Mac is a good guy who has gotten his revenge on an evil bully. Being able to buy the program via mail order ensured young customers' privacy, and the isometric exercises and diet were easy to follow. The Dynamic Tension program appealed to adolescent boys anxious about their popularity, masculinity, and the physical changes taking place in their bodies. Letters to the Atlas Company from satisfied customers claimed that the program had produced the promised results. "Nobody calls me bird chest anymore and I got my girlfriend through you too. . . . My Mom and Dad are proud of me."[68]

Like boys, adolescent girls also paid increasing attention to the physical changes happening to their bodies and looked for new ways to improve their appearance so as to meet the popular ideal. Magazines told girls that fashion and cosmetics would help to make them popular. Home Economics teachers reinforced notions about the value of traditional female skills to attract a good husband. As a consequence, the feminine ideal of the 1930s combined new images of female beauty with very traditional gender roles. Girls compared themselves to the perfect female bodies and glamorous faces they saw on the movie screen and in magazines. The images were of white females, but girls from American ethnic and racial minorities also spent a lot of energy trying to match the mainstream standards of beauty. Some African-American girls used hair-straightening chemicals. (Ironically, at the same time permanent waves were popular among girls with naturally straight hair.) The long-running "Breck Girl" advertising campaign for Breck shampoo was first released in beauty salons in 1936. All of the first nineteen females in the company's advertisements released between 1936 and 1940 were "ordinary women" made to look like models. The suggestion, of course, was that any girl could meet the standards of idealized beauty by using the right shampoo. Advertisements like those for Marvelous Make-Up in *True Story* magazine included the headline, "Nice . . . But Lonely." Obviously the right makeup would bring popularity and male companionship. Ads for Amolin Powder and DEW warned that maturing female bodies produced offensive odors that could be controlled with the right deodorant.[69]

It was more socially acceptable for girls than boys to worry openly about their appearance, so adolescent females typically shared information about beauty products, fashion, and diets among their friends. Five-and-ten-cent stores carried the most inexpensive cosmetics and beauty aids, but many girls did not even have that much money, so homemade cosmetics—such as using egg whites to make hair shine or beauty masks made from vegetables or household products—were also common. Girls tried to copy the latest hairstyles they saw worn by their favorite film stars.[70]

"Healthy" skin also became important for teens. Skin blemishes had been considered a relatively unimportant problem, more common in girls than boys. The twentieth century's new standards of cleanliness and physical appearance encouraged a change in thinking. Pimples and acne appeared to be the result of unclean habits, or worse, morally suspect behavior such as masturbation and/or sexual promiscuity. A 1938 study of unemployment in Chicago reported that employers often discriminated against young male jobseekers whose faces were pitted with pimples or acne scars. Doctors warned that teens with poor skin might become social outcasts at risk for economic and emotional problems. By the 1930s acne had become "the plague of youth" for both boys and girls. Seventeen-year-old Frances Storck took a train each week from suburban New Rochelle to New York City to see a dermatologist who treated the pimples on her forehead. Storck's parents were not wealthy enough to send their beautiful and academically talented daughter to college, but they somehow found the money to pay for her weekly appointments at the dermatologist. In fact at the time there was little that teens or the medical community could do about acne.[71]

Some of the most private aspects of the adolescent maturation process became public in the 1930s. The shift underscored the importance many teens now placed on their physical appearance. Dieting had become common practice among middle- and upper-class teens in the 1920s, but the ideal female body shape changed during the 1930s, and brassieres based on cup size entered the fashion market. The teenager Malvis Helmi was embarrassed by her growing breasts and wanted a bra, as brassieres became known. After consulting with her mother, Malvis tried to order one of the new bras from the Sears, Roebuck catalogue. Her father canceled the request, angrily telling his daughter, "Our kind of people can't afford to spend money on such nonsense." Many girls like Malvis wanted bras, but limited family incomes made such purchases seem like unnecessary luxuries. In response, some high school Home Economics teachers added instructions for making homemade bras to their curriculum. Sewing helped girls on small budgets use their free time to make less expensive versions of the new undergarment as well as other items reflecting the latest fashions.

Boys' underwear also changed when Jockey briefs entered the market in 1935, but boys generally did not sew, and mothers were more likely to spend their time making new outfits or resizing hand-me-down clothes for their children than sewing the male undergarments.[72]

The makers of sanitary napkins and tampons established educational divisions that supplied schools, parent-teacher organizations, and the Girl Scouts with pamphlets about what they called "menstrual health." The corporate-sponsored documentary film "Marjorie May's Twelfth Birthday," first released in 1932 and shown to single-sex audiences in schools throughout the United States, taught adolescent girls that the changes in their bodies were natural—but also something best understood by listening to the advice of experts.

The companies, of course, were selling their products, but this cooperation between corporations, schools, and girls' organizations was also a very public recognition of girls' sexual maturity. This was very different from the private discussions between mothers and daughters in earlier generations that had been the source of information for most girls. Not all mothers had been good at helping their adolescent daughters learn about the important changes in their bodies, but the move to schools as a source of such information was another expression of the increasingly separate world of adolescents.[73] Wearing the right clothes, using beauty products, having the right body shape, and adopting the right hairstyle consumed much of the time, money, and energy of teens growing up in the 1930s.

Many of the letters Eleanor Roosevelt received from adolescents pleaded with the first lady to help them get the clothes they felt were necessary to be accepted among their high school peers. Most letters asked for castoff or secondhand clothes. Some of the most desperate came from teens who had fallen out of the middle class and may have felt a special anguish at their inability to compete with their peers. One fifteen-year-old girl from New Jersey asked for a new coat, explaining, "We were once the richest people our town but now, we are the lowest, considered the worst people of Port Morris. For Easter some friends of mine are thinking of getting new out-fits and I just have to listen to them. How I wish I could have at least a coat."[74] The growing teen culture centered in America's high schools offered new opportunities for leisure and entertainment. It also created problems linked to an emphasis on consumerism and competition among adolescent peers.

John McKee's body was racked by cerebral palsy, but he wanted to join in activities with his peers. He adapted to the situation and did everything he could to feel part of his peer group.

When we played basketball, I had always to pass to my teammates when I was in position to make a shot because I did not have the combination of balance and arm strength to shoot quickly or while I was in motion. When I joined the gym class in the high school pool, I did not swim. I clung to the side of the pool and kicked my feet or walked slowly up and down across the shallow end of the pool while the others were swimming and diving and playing the water games I could not play. . . . I couldn't have been a normal boy if I had not wanted to be at least as good as some of my friends were at basketball or swimming or gymnastics. So I gradually let it go. Like a rat in a maze I bounced off the walls made by things that I could not do, and I went along the paths that were open to me.[75]

The Right to Play and Leisure

Like other aspects of their lives, region, gender, ethnicity, and class influenced children's and adolescents' experiences surrounding play and leisure. Parental tolerance of popular culture and changing social behaviors also affected individual experiences. Hardships fostered by the depression forced some youngsters to take on adult responsibilities before fully growing up themselves. Despite obstacles of class, race, and ethnicity, the 1930s generation shared an increasingly standardized commercial culture directed specifically at children and teens. They learned that consumerism and growing up were as American as apple pie. The Great Depression restricted the ability of many children and adolescents to take advantage of this popular culture, but young Americans found ways to "belong," especially through the images and sounds of radio and the movies. In 1937 sixty-seven-year-old Booth Tarkington, author of many books including the 1916 children's classic *Penrod and Sam*, told a *Milwaukee Sentinel* reporter that radio and movies had fostered "more sophistication among the children of today. It is inevitable."[76]

Children were not simply clay in the hands of advertisers and movie studios. As individuals they absorbed and rejected what they saw and heard according to their own tastes and personal experiences. On the other hand, the proliferation of radio and movies in the 1930s made those who grew up during the decade part of the first generation to share the same sounds and images on so large a scale. The experience helped produce a shared identification in a generation that grew up in a decade of uncertainty. It counteracted the hard times that had the potential to widen traditional social and economic divisions in America.

CHAPTER SIX

Uncle Sam's Children

🖋 THE GENERATION that shared the new youth-centered popular culture also witnessed the birth of federal policies designed to help equalize access to education and economic security for young Americans. The Roosevelt administration's selling of the New Deal complemented the shift in popular culture, emphasizing traditional American values of democracy, freedom, and continual progress. For young Americans, federal law by 1940 included a clear definition of childhood dependency from birth to age eighteen. The Roosevelt administration also initiated federal programs that enhanced access to school-based education, improved the quality of life for many young people, created a Social Security safety net for the nation's most vulnerable children and adolescents, provided new means to help older adolescents and youth achieve adult independence, and established the first federal prohibitions against the most abusive forms of exploitative child labor. This New Deal for America's youth provided the framework for what the depression generation understood as the parameters of modern American childhood.

In 1930 the Parkinson children—Dan (age twelve), Thom (ten), Jacob (eight), Ruth (three), and Frank (one month)—lived with their parents Bill and Hazel on a 205-acre dairy farm near

St. Clairsville, Ohio. Like most farm families in the 1930s United States, the Parkinsons worked from dawn to dusk. They had a woodstove, depended on kerosene lanterns for light after the sun went down, had no running water or electricity, and used an outhouse. Milking was done each morning and evening by hand. Wood had to be chopped for the woodstove to heat the house and cook food, and water was hand-pumped from a well. The Parkinsons' lives were not unlike those of generations of farmers who had lived in the area, but lower farm prices during the depression made times especially hard. The family raised most of the food they needed, but cash income was short because milk prices hit rock bottom during the early years of the depression. The lack of electricity also meant that milk often spoiled during the summer months and could not be sold to the local dairy.

The Parkinsons' lives changed in 1940 when the Rural Electrification Administration brought electricity to their farm and offered government loans to bring the family into the twentieth century. The dairy market had improved too, and the federal government now offered subsidies to guarantee minimum prices for the products the Parkinsons sold to the local dairy. Electric milking machines and a new refrigeration system made the family's milk production more efficient and profitable. Additional income enabled the Parkinsons to add electric lights to the home, brightening the house in winter and extending everyone's day. The family also installed running water, and an electric water heater provided hot showers and baths for everyone. A new electric stove helped improve the family's diet and reduced kitchen chores, including the daily necessity to chop wood. Electricity was also a reliable source of power for the family's radio, which provided hours of entertainment and access to news.

A documentary film produced for the Rural Electrification Administration in 1940, entitled "Power and the Land," told the Parkinsons' story, arguing that federally funded electricity programs had brought the family and others like them a better life. Rose Dudley Scearce, another REA beneficiary, would have agreed. She described the changes that electricity had brought to her family in rural Kentucky. "I am thoroughly enjoying the many things that electricity has made possible, and I am enjoying life more because I have more time to spend visiting my friends, studying and reading, doing the things that make life richer." Such comments were just what "Dr. New Deal" (Franklin Roosevelt) had ordered.[1]

Frank Capra's 1939 film *Mr. Smith Goes to Washington* is an excellent example of the connections between young Americans, government, and traditional values that became a significant part of mainstream society by the close of the 1930s. In this popular movie Jefferson Smith, an everyman character played by a boyish-looking thirty-year-old Jimmy Stewart, is an honest, simple, but wise youth who is the publisher of a popular boys' magazine. Throughout the film Smith and a cast of fresh-faced boys explain the importance of fundamental American values and provide insightful and honest comments. In a scene near the beginning of the film, one of the governor's sons offers sympathy to his father who is being pressured by a powerful and corrupt businessman named Jim Taylor to appoint a political hack to a dead senator's seat, "You're in a deuce of a pickle, aren't you, Pop?" A second son interrupts, "Looks like Henry Hill, huh Pop?" A third chimes in, "Naw, it's Horace Miller or else!" The first son quickly adds, "I wouldn't appoint an old twerp like Horace Miller. Taylor or no Taylor!" When the governor tries to camouflage his predicament by asking what Taylor has to do with things, the first son responds, "Well, he's running the show, ain't he, Dad?" Angered by his children's honest insights, the governor yells at his wife, "Emma, I will not have conversations of this sort carried on by the children at dinner!" She fires back, "Nonsense. Why don't you listen to your children for a change? You might actually learn something." The boys then tell their father that Jefferson Smith, "head of the Boy Rangers" and publisher of the organization's popular newspaper, should be the next senator. "Right now he's the greatest hero we've ever had," one son explains. Smith and a group of Boy Rangers had put out a serious fire, saving "hundreds of people and millions of dollars." In the scene's final moments, the governor's sons convince their father that naming Jeff Smith to the post is not only wise but politically savvy.

After a few days in Washington, Senator Smith is betrayed by the man he trusts and respects most, the senior senator from his own state, Joseph Paine. Smith finds that the only people he can really trust to tell the truth and give him unfailing support are his mother, the young boy pages who work in the Senate chamber, his army of Boy Rangers, and a street-smart Senate aide played by a sarcastic and youthful Jean Arthur. Unwittingly Smith uncovers a corrupt political deal between Paine, the governor, and Taylor when he proposes that Congress loan seed money to the Boy Rangers for a summer camp. Seeking support for his idea, Smith explains, "Funny thing about men, you know. They all started life being boys. I wouldn't be a bit surprised if some of these Senators were boys once. Yes, it seemed like a pretty good idea, boys coming together—of all nationalities and ways of living—finding out what makes different people tick the way they do." It seemed "like a good idea to get boys out of crowded cities and stuffy basements for a couple of months out of the year. And build their bodies and minds for a man-sized job, because those boys are gonna be behind these desks some of these days."[2]

While some members of Congress may have been upset by the unflattering stereotypes of Washington politicians in the film, Smith's words summed up the major point behind the New Deal's programs for children, especially boys. Washington needed to offer a helping hand to America's youngest citizens so that they could carry on the country's heritage of democracy, freedom, and opportunity. In the face of the Great Depression's economic emergency, young people and their families would not be able to go it alone.

The Success of the CCC

One of the most important accomplishments of the New Deal was the attention it brought to the effects of poverty on access to school-based education. New Deal programs did not concentrate exclusively on education, but money funneled through federal work-relief programs provided new avenues of access for American youth. On the seventeenth day of his presidency, March 21, 1933, Franklin Roosevelt asked Congress for enabling legislation to implement one of the New Deal's first work-relief efforts. The president told Congress he wanted to establish "a civilian construction corps to be used in simple work, not interfering with normal employment, and confining itself to forestry, the prevention of soil erosion, flood control, and similar projects."[3] On March 30 legislators approved a bill, and the selection of enrollees for the president's Civilian Conservation Corps began on April 7. The first CCC facility opened ten days later at Camp Roosevelt, Virginia, outside Washington, D.C. In May 1933 Congress authorized a half-billion dollars in relief funds for the new Federal Emergency Relief Administration, to be headed by Harry Hopkins. The CCC became part of this larger federal effort. No other New Deal program was more quickly organized or drew greater public support than the CCC. By July 1 more than 275,000 older adolescents and youth had enrolled in over 1,300 CCC sites scattered throughout the United States.

It took several months after its establishment for the CCC to include educational benefits in its program. Immediately the CCC functioned as work-relief for unemployed, unmarried veterans and young males aged eighteen through twenty-five from families already on relief. In 1935 the program expanded to include seventeen-year-olds and added funding for an educational program. Education never replaced or even became a serious competitor with the CCC's work program, but even the minimal provisions offered new educational opportunities to many enrollees. By the end of 1935 the CCC was operating 2,650 camps located in every state of the union. Before the program ended in 1942, the CCC also established camps in Hawaii, Alaska, Puerto Rico, and the Virgin Islands. During its duration, some 3 million Americans spent time as "Soil Soldiers" in "Roosevelt's Tree Army."[4]

The average CCC enrollee was a boy who had just reached his eighteenth birthday. He had completed the eighth grade but read at only a sixth-grade level and had been unable to find permanent employment since leaving school. His health was good, but he was probably "significantly underweight." He was more likely to be a country boy than an urban youth since 60 percent of enrollees came from rural areas, and he was probably a native-born white. By design, blacks constituted only 10 percent of CCC recruits. This matched the proportion of African Americans in the general population but was much less than their share of the nation's poor, especially in the South. The CCC also initially overlooked needy American Indians but quickly added special units for recruits from Indian reservations. About eighty thousand American Indians served in the CCC over the course of its existence.[5]

The CCC limited eligibility to males. In 1934 FERA established a similar program for females from families on relief, but the effort that became known as the "She-She-She" was much smaller and short-lived. Only eight thousand to ten thousand adolescent girls and young women took part, and the program ended in 1937.[6] The CCC's focus on older adolescent boys and young men coincided with gender stereotypes that identified males as the nation's future breadwinners and females as its homemakers.

Despite its popularity, it took depression era conditions to gain support for the idea of a government-funded CCC. More than thirty years earlier, the philosopher William James had called for the establishment of a private national youth conservation corps. After World War I, several European countries had implemented such government-sponsored programs. But nothing happened in the

United States until Franklin Roosevelt took office, three years into the Great Depression.

Beliefs among many Americans that disaffected young males contributed to rising crime rates, and concerns that they were vulnerable to revolutionary ideas contributed to the CCC's initial popularity. And by 1933 many Americans knew an older boy who was unable to find a job, so this personal connection put a human face on the issue. Such feelings combined with romantic notions about America's historical tradition of sending young men into the wilderness in order to build their manhood (similar to the arguments later made by the fictional Jeff Smith in Frank Capra's film).[7] The CCC's initial strategies also added to its popularity. CCC enrollees lived in military-style camps usually located far from urban centers. The only exceptions were American Indians who lived and worked on reservation lands. Each recruit received $30 per month, of which between $22 and $25 went directly home to the enrollee's family. This left $5 to $8 for a CCC recruit to spend on personal expenses, use for recreation, or put into savings. The low pay might have stirred opposition from unions, which had always feared the influence of low-wage employment on the job market. To placate organized labor, Roosevelt named Robert Fechner, vice president of the International Order of Machinists, to head the CCC. Fechner had also served as an army officer and was a white Southerner who enthusiastically embraced Jim Crow.[8] Fechner's appointment put a military stamp on the CCC that emphasized discipline and orderly behavior. His Southern background and personal politics eased the fears of some critics who suggested that the CCC was socialistic and potentially disruptive to the nation's racial hierarchy. Fechner headed the CCC from its founding until his sudden death in 1939. His successor continued his policies until the program ended in 1942.

Luther C. Wandall reported for enlistment in the CCC at Pier I in New York City at 8 a.m. on Monday, April 15, 1935. A young African American, Luther soon discovered that racial segregation would be the order of the day in the CCC. As he explained in an article published in *Crisis* magazine in August 1935, "When my record was taken at Pier I, a 'C' was placed on it. When the busloads were made up at Whitehall street an officer reported as follows: '35, 8 colored.'" The buses took the enrollees to their muster facilities at Fort Dix, New Jersey. "Before we left the bus," Luther recalled, "the officer shouted emphatically: 'Colored boys fall out in the rear.' The colored from several buses were herded together, and stood in line until after the white boys had been registered and taken to their tents." Black recruits were finally sent to their tents after the whites had been given their assignments. "And such tents!" Wandall complained. "They were the worst in Camp Dix. Old, patched, without floors or electric lights. It was dark already, so we went to bed immediately, by candlelight. And since it was cold, we slept in most, and in some cases all, of our clothes."

Throughout his tenure, Robert Fechner ignored or defied efforts by some members of the Roosevelt administration to correct some of the blatant aspects of racial inequality in the CCC. Although he was never a champion of black civil rights, Roosevelt personally asked Fechner to give qualified black recruits supervisory positions within the CCC's segregated units. Fechner resisted even small gestures of equality, but sometimes the pressure to change was too strong even for the CCC director. In one incident, Eddie Simmons, a black enrollee from New York City with a good CCC record, received a dishonorable discharge after refusing to brush flies off a white supervisor. Reportedly Simmons said that brushing flies was not part of his job. The white CCC officer in charge angrily dismissed Simmons and ordered the withholding of his last month's pay allotment. The NAACP took up Simmons's case and lodged a protest. Three weeks later, in a letter to the NAACP, Fechner stated that Simmons would be awarded an honorable discharge, "free from any charge of insubordination," and "paid all cash allowances and allotments due." Yet the CCC's policy limiting black enrollment to 10 percent of the program's total did not change and remained an important indication of its racist policies.

Most enrollees, no matter their race or ethnicity, seemed convinced that holding a job in the CCC was better than being unemployed. Luther Wandall explained that things improved for him when he arrived at his CCC work assignment. Located in the upper South where Jim Crow segregation was a daily fact of life, Luther found that "this camp was a dream compared to Camp Dix . . . with plenty to eat, and we slept in barracks instead of tents." He noted that the food was often poorly cooked and tasteless, but very filling. Recruits gained an average of ten pounds during their service. Recruits like Luther worked on conservation and construction projects eight hours a day, five days a week, but that left them with several hours of free time. They were generally required to stay on camp grounds. "At the 'rec' we have a radio, a piano, a store called a 'canteen,' a rack of the leading New York papers, white and colored, as well as some from elsewhere. There is a little library with a variety of books and magazines. All sports are encouraged. We have a baseball team, boxing squad etc.," Luther reported. "An orchestra has been formed and classes in various arts and crafts." Perhaps because his expectations had been so low when he enlisted, he was "gratified rather than disappointed with the CCC. I had expected the worst. Of course it reflects, to some extent, all the practices and prejudices of the U. S. Army. But as a job and an experience, for a man who has no work, I can heartily recommend it."[9]

CCC discipline countered some of the concerns held by communities located near the camps. Luther noted, "There are colored people living on farms on all sides of this camp. . . . But they are not very friendly toward CCC boys in general, and toward the northerners in particular."[10] But politicians clamored for the location of CCC camps within their states and congressional districts and local businessmen argued that communities directly benefited from the purchases of camp officials and enrollees.

As part of the continuing effort to keep recruits busy and out of trouble, by the close of 1934 some CCC camps had added academic and vocational classes to the list of activities available to recruits during their free time. The CCC never prioritized education over work assignments, but some recruits benefited from the rudimentary schooling offered in CCC camps. In 1935 Congress mandated that the CCC operate an educational program but allowed it to be limited to evenings and weekends. More than forty thousand of the enrollees who had entered the CCC as illiterate learned to read and write. Some gained vocational skills and a few even a high school diploma. The camps also exposed enrollees from poor families to middle-class standards of cleanliness and behavior. They became healthier and learned how to work with others in a society based on middle-class models. Many enrollees also gained a sense of pride since the money they earned helped family members back home. On a personal level and for the long term, CCC experience seemed to help enrollees gain better opportunities for their own future. A survey conducted with CCC alumni twenty years after the program ended showed that their incomes outpaced the national average for the same age cohort.[11] For states and communities, federal money filtered through the CCC helped ease pressure on already strained or nonexistent budgets.[12]

CCC recruits made both short- and long-term contributions to the quality of life in the United States. They completed thousands of conservation and land improvement projects that benefited Americans in the 1930s and beyond. They built thousands of park facilities, including the construction of 800 state parks. They established firebreaks, erected 3,470 fire towers, and opened 97,000 miles of access roads on national forest land. They reinvigorated fish stocks and counted wildlife as part of conservation efforts. CCC recruits planted millions of trees and implemented efforts to curb flood damage. They also helped during emergencies such as the 1937 flood that devastated communities in middle America. Even in its earliest days of operation, the CCC served as a model for what New Deal work-relief programs could accomplish.[13]

The large number of websites and memoirs by former CCC participants are testimony to the program's popularity among recruits and the general public. A 1938 survey conducted among enrollees by researchers at Case Western Reserve University uncovered highly positive feelings about the program. Of course these results reflected the attitudes of young men who stuck with the program.[14] But there were dissenters. In the spring of 1933, Gilbert Dick was an unemployed recent high school graduate living in Lipsic, Ohio, the youngest of six and the only boy in a very poor family. During especially hard times his father, a railroad worker who was often laid off more than he was employed, and his mother sent some of their children to live with other relatives. The onset of the depression only worsened the family's precarious situation. An athlete who was used to hard work and sparse living conditions, Gilbert spent only three days in an Ohio CCC camp. He remembered being turned off by the program's military-style regimentation. He decided to hit the road in search of work rather than stay in the CCC. Another young transient interviewed during the early days of the CCC expressed a similar opinion. "I've been in jail twice, and three years in a reformatory . . . and I've lived three months at Sally's [Salvation Army shelter] in Chicago, but that army chain gang was worse than any."

A mother interviewed for the Federal Writers' Project in 1939 told a similar tale about her son. Seventeen-year-old Charlie Harrell went to the CCC Camp at King's Mountain, South Carolina, but stayed only four months. He "quit and come home—just didn't like it," his mother reported. Charlie's mother was especially unhappy with her son's behavior because local officials had forced her to give up her FERA relief-job when they found out that Charlie had joined the CCC. Making matters worse, Charlie's mother claimed that the CCC money never reached her. "You know, while that boy was in the C.C.C. Camp, I never got a dollar of his money," Agnes Harrell explained. "He'd spend his part soon as he got it and [by the] time the other part come home to me, he'd be here to grab it."[15] So everything about the CCC did not work out the way Roosevelt and his officers planned. Despite such problems, most young recruits were happy and proud of their CCC experience.[16]

The roots of another popular New Deal program directed at young Americans began in 1933 when the FERA diverted some of its funds to universities and colleges to provide relief payments for up to 10 percent of enrolled students. Needy students received an average allotment of $15 per month in exchange for part-time work. The program was so successful that FERA officials increased the quota to 12 percent of campus enrollments in 1934, or 100,000 college students that received FERA stipends. The American Youth Congress (AYC) enthusiastically supported the program and organized a drive calling for its expansion and the inclusion of high school students. AYC leaders enlisted Eleanor Roosevelt's support to help promote their plan to the president. Growing public attention to high unemployment rates among teens and youth, and rising fears about the potentially dangerous effects of the depression on young Americans also helped. The problem of educational opportunities for the poor, and the desire among many to keep young people out of the full-time labor force, added leverage to an expansion of the FERA's program.

In June 1935 President Roosevelt signaled his agreement by signing Executive Order 7086, thereby adding the National Youth Administration to New Deal efforts for America's older teens and youth. Unlike the CCC, the NYA from the outset included girls and boys. It lowered the age of eligibility to sixteen and emphasized education over work. The president's executive order simply stated that the NYA should "initiate and administer a program of approved projects to . . . provide relief, work relief, and employment for persons between the ages of sixteen and twenty-five years who are no longer in regular attendance at a school requiring full time, and who are not regularly engaged in remunerative employment." In his remarks attached to the announcement, Roosevelt explained, "I have determined that we shall do something for the Nation's un-employed youth because we can ill afford to lose the skill and en-ergy of young men and women. They must have their chance in school, their turn as apprentices and their opportunity for jobs—a chance to work and earn for themselves."[17]

The president named Aubrey Williams as NYA director. Like Robert Fechner, Williams was a white Southerner, but unlike the CCC director, his politics leaned left of center. Williams planned to use the NYA as a tool to gain social justice for underprivileged youth across the United States. He wanted to help erase inequities of class and race that hindered progress for many young Americans. Under his leadership the NYA served as an educational program, but it also acted as a window to middle-class values, behaviors, and aspirations for youth who had never experienced them. NYA coun-selors taught enrollees how to look for a job, what to wear to an in-terview, how to present themselves, and what employers expected from workers. The NYA program also addressed issues of racial in-equality. Williams established a special division for the education of blacks, headed by the African-American educator Mary McCloud Bethune. Although both were interested in social reform, at least during the New Deal years, neither Williams nor Bethune used the NYA to challenge gender stereotypes. Williams's racial politics were controversial, but he understood that keeping youth out of the labor market and in school was a major selling point for the new agency. Thus the NYA aimed to keep teens in school at least through high school graduation. Williams believed his agency should help young Americans acquire skills that would enhance their opportunities for economic self-sufficiency throughout their lives.[18]

Whatever Williams's long-term goals, the agency's establish-ment within the WPA rather than the Office of Education or the

U.S. Children's Bureau signaled that it was only a temporary measure during the economic emergency. The NYA was never intended to be a permanent educational program for needy young Americans. The New Deal agenda did not include permanent work-relief, even for programs in education. The NYA did, however, provide a strong example of how a combined program of school-based education and part-time work could help students from poor families remain in school. High schools, colleges, and universities throughout the United States retained control over administration of the program. The effort also included educational training and relief work for teens and youth who had already left school. This effort required a more difficult administrative setup which included up to two-week stays at residence camps. At the camps, enrollees were exposed to middle-class values, habits, and behaviors. Girls learned "family-life" skills such as the cooking of "American foods," good nutritional habits, modern child care techniques, and the entertaining of dinner guests. They also attended classes where instructors talked about how to wear their hair and makeup to fit middle-class fashions. Boys learned about middle-class standards of behavior and how to enhance a home with simple furniture such as shelves and small tables they could build themselves. Other topics included lessons on modern farming techniques and job skills. As one NYA representative explained, youth in the resident camps "constantly see contrasts in diets, cleanliness, and general household management [and] they often tell me of applying what they have learned here at home."[19]

During its existence from 1935 to 1943, the NYA enrolled 1.5 million high school students and 600,000 college students. Another 2.6 million unemployed teens and youth who were no longer in school full-time registered in the agency's training programs. Aubrey Williams's commitment to greater equality of educational opportunity helped highlight the inequities in America's schools, especially for black Americans. Critics labeled Williams "a nigger

New Deal programs helped improve the diets of many young Americans by providing relief funds to families and up-to-date information about healthy eating and food preparation. *(Library of Congress)*

lover," but he stuck to his principles. Mary McCloud Bethune also deserves credit for the agency's accomplishments on behalf of black youth. Describing her experience, Bethune said the NYA "tunneled its way into the rural and urban conditions of our country, awakening and inspiring thousands and thousands of youths, opening doors of opportunity. . . . I have worked and fought with my sleeves rolled up night and day." The principal of a black high school in Atlanta explained the importance of the NYA to his students: "The grants have created confidence and hope in the hearts of these youth and brought success where failure threatened. . . . It is to be hoped that NYA aid may be continued [so] that the door of opportunity may continue to open to thousands of American youth who, otherwise, would not be able to continue their preparation in school."[20]

Glen Van Gundy, an eleventh-grader from Des Moines, Iowa, believed that the NYA was the reason he had stayed in school. The money he earned helped him buy "many things that have made life more pleasant."

> When I started school in September, I did not know whether I was going to continue to go or not. . . . When I got my first check I was so tickled I could have shouted. I went to town that evening and got some bread for my brothers' and sisters' and my own lunches. We had been taking home-made bread. It was good, but I always thought people made fun of it, so sometimes I went to school without lunch. Next I got some shoes. Even if they weren't high priced, I was proud of them, because I had bought them with my own money. With next month's pay I had my teeth fixed.[21]

An enrollee from Pittsburgh wrote Eleanor Roosevelt in 1937 to express his gratitude for the NYA program for youth who had already left school. Under the NYA, he explained, he attended welding classes at night and worked for the WPA during the day. "Words cannot express my gratitude to our President who has made this possible for me and the thousands of others. . . . I trust that you and the President will continue your good work and remain at the White House for a 'long time.' "[22]

Sarah Elizabeth Bundy, a girls' vice principal at a large urban high school, supported the NYA's efforts but admitted to having reservations, especially when the NYA bulletin first arrived on her desk. "I felt like jumping out my office window and calling it a day. The burden of my job as girls' vice-principal in a cosmopolitan high school was sufficiently heavy and varied without additions." After two years experience with the NYA she outlined some of the problems the program presented. For example, Bundy believed that a sixteen-year-old girl "who carries the physical result of having broken child labor laws in her earlier years" was too weak to go to school and also work. Bundy thought the girl "should not be an NYA worker, and yet her overwhelming need prompted me to assign her to after-school desk work which would be as little drain as possible upon her physical strength." Bundy thought the NYA's work and study requirements made it difficult to meet the specific needs of individual students. She was also reluctant to give high-achieving needy students NYA appointments because the dual responsibilities of part-time employment and schoolwork might lower their academic performance. And she worried that the NYA set a precedent in suggesting that students should be paid for service they provided the school; she feared this would lessen the spirit of volunteerism.

In the end, however, Bundy concluded that even with these negatives, the NYA's advantages far outweighed its liabilities. She noted that participation in the program reduced truancy. "I have seen a listless, apparently incompetent girl transformed within three brief months into an alert, dependable worker, eager to begin her assignment and reluctant to stop when it was time to go home." Another girl, "awkward and oversized . . . who previously made minor ailments the excuse for staying home, was assigned to serve ice water at noon in the cafeteria. She has scarcely missed a day and is far more agile and decidedly neater in appearance than when I doubtfully assigned her."[23]

While the NYA was clearly a popular program, it did not elicit the feelings of nostalgia shared by many CCC alumni. The NYA's emphasis on education and stipends, intended to keep teens and youth at home with their parents, led participants to identify with their schools and communities rather than with the agency. The sentiment is comparable to that held today by students who receive financial aid from federal work-study programs. This lack of celebratory nostalgia, however, does not diminish the NYA's impact on

As this National Youth Administration poster suggests, the New Deal promoted the idea that the federal government could help level the playing field for a generation of young Americans hurt by the Great Depression. *(Library of Congress)*

many young Americans in the 1930s. By 1942 President Roosevelt liked the agency so much that he fought for its retention as a permanent program. But the NYA, like the CCC, fell victim to wartime budget cuts, a national focus on the war effort, and the end of the depression's high unemployment.

Neither the CCC nor the NYA solved the problems of all homeless, hopeless, needy, or unemployed youth. Both agencies excluded adolescents under their mandated qualifying ages, no matter how desperate the individual circumstance. The CCC's requirement that the majority of money earned by enrollees be sent to parents excluded many transient teens and youth who had been separated from their parents for a variety of reasons. Too, CCC racial discrimination and quotas hindered the program's effectiveness for blacks and members of other American minority groups. On an even larger scale, the CCC's exclusion of girls and young women ignored the plight of needy young females and strengthened gender stereotypes that limited their educational and work opportunities. The NYA also adhered to gender stereotypes in its vocational training, academic education, and work-relief opportunities. Finally, early on, the American Youth Congress complained that the NYA's enrollment quota was too low and that student stipends were so miserly that many of the neediest teens and youth could not take advantage of the program.[24]

Despite such weaknesses, the creation of the CCC and the NYA recognized, at least temporarily, a new role for the federal government in helping American youth transition to the world of working adults. The agencies also deserve credit for providing immediate help and hope to millions of young Americans. The NYA's age range of sixteen through twenty-five defined education as a legitimate and wise full-time pursuit for all young people in this age group. This was clearly a departure from the belief that school-based education was not a critical tool for ensuring self-sufficiency in adulthood. For teens, the NYA encouraged their self-identification as a generation where high school was the normative experience of American adolescence. Where only 54.9 percent of fourteen-through-seventeen-year-olds were in school in 1930, ten years later 70 percent went to school full-time. The percentage dropped slightly during World War II but proved to be only a short-term reversal in the trend toward universal high school attendance. In 1950, 76.6 percent of all adolescents in the same age cohort were in school, and in 1960 the proportion rose to 89 percent. By the close of the twentieth century, 90 percent of seventeen-year-olds remained in school.

Despite such progress, the national dropout rate showed that inequalities highlighted by the depression continued in the nation's schools. In 1940 a little over 13 percent of adolescents still left school each year before finishing their high school requirements. Within that group, black students were more likely to leave school than whites, and Hispanic students failed to complete high school at a rate almost three times that of white teens from other ethnic groups. Today schools continue to struggle to provide equal access to quality education. Education for students with limited English-language skills and those with physical and mental disabilities have persistently challenged efforts to equalize opportunity for all young Americans.[25] New Deal efforts like the NYA did not create the level playing field some reformers envisioned. And the CCC's mission was work-relief, not education. Nevertheless these agencies did support the modern definition of childhood and adolescence as a time for education and distinct from full adult responsibilities. And they provided access to schools for some children and adolescents who would not have had such opportunities without federal intervention.

At the low end of the age range, in 1933 the federal government established Emergency Day Nurseries (EDN) that brought high-quality preschool education to children from needy families. EDN gave jobs to unemployed teachers, but it also expanded access to preschool education for thousands of American children. The concept of preschool education had begun in Europe in the late nineteenth century and spread to the United States. A few nursery schools based on European models had been operating in the United States since the turn of the century, but they reached only a limited pool of American children from upper-middle-class and wealthy families. Nursery schools never became popular among the general public. According to the National Society for the Study of Education, in 1928 there were only eighty-four nursery schools spread between twenty-three states and Washington, D.C. In 1930 the U.S. Office of Education counted 262 nursery schools, still a paltry show of support for school-based education for toddlers. Day-care facilities for poor children were more plentiful than nursery schools. One estimate in 1930 counted slightly more than 800 municipal facilities that cared for thousands of infants and toddlers. Money problems during the Great Depression forced many of these centers to close. By 1933 fewer than 500 nursery schools and day-care facilities operated in the United States.[26]

Advocates of nursery schools promoted their model as part of modern scientific parenting and denounced day-care facilities as unprofessional and harmful warehouses for America's poor children. Experts in the burgeoning field of child guidance, such as Helen Woolley, advised parents that a few hours in a quality nursery school each day could improve a child's IQ and success in later life. Preschoolers needed the attention of experts because keeping a child "profitably busy involves more knowledge of stages of development than most mothers possess." Woolley and other child guidance experts promoted the idea that nursery schools should be a part of the overall expansion of school-based education for American children. The child guidance movement suggested that the very name for this age group, "preschooler," was an outmoded anomaly in modern America.[27]

When the Roosevelt administration began planning its initial relief programs, Secretary of Labor Frances Perkins urged the president and the head of the newly established FERA, Harry Hopkins, to include nursery schools, public health projects, and school lunch programs in federal relief efforts, in order to ensure the inclusion of children. Roosevelt and Hopkins agreed and made EDN a part of the early FERA. Hopkins explained in a 1933 press release why he believed nursery schools should be part of the federal government's relief programs: "Young children of pre-school age in the homes of needy and unemployed parents are suffering from the conditions . . . incident to current economic and social difficulties. The education and health programs of nursery schools can aid as nothing else in combating the physical and mental handicaps being imposed upon these young children." Hopkins and other officials assured Americans that the new institutions would not simply be day-care facilities and that only children who had reached at least their second birth-day would be admitted. The U.S. Children's Bureau strongly ob-jected to enrolling children younger than two, arguing that it was healthiest for these children to be kept at home with their mothers. The agency also worried that any federal support for preschools might encourage mothers of toddlers to work outside the home. From the early days of industrialization in the United States, most Americans, both male and female, had objected to married women, especially the mothers of young children, working outside the home. High unemployment rates among men during the 1930s in-creased public objections to married women working for wages. A 1936 Gallup poll found that 82 percent of respondents believed a wife should not work outside the home if her husband had a job.[28]

Partly because of these popular sentiments, Emergency Day Nurseries were not designed to serve the children of working moth-ers. At least in the 1930s, children spent only a few hours at the schools, and the Emergency Day Nurseries served children whose families were on relief, not in the workforce. By the end of 1934 the federal government operated 3,000 Emergency Day Nurseries that provided care for 64,000 children. Most were housed in public school buildings or other government-owned facilities. By 1936 the EDN program had been fully transferred to the Works Progress Ad-ministration, which paid the salaries of teachers, janitors, and cooks. To help lower operating costs, local WPA workshops made toys and basic supplies for the schools. Parents contributed a small fee that helped pay some expenses, but local school districts or other government agencies were responsible for rent and utilities.

The educational programs involved the application of princi-ples advocated by child guidance experts. Specially shaped building blocks, games, drawing and painting activities, and other aspects of children's "play" received the same attention given to the children of more affluent parents at private nurseries like Detroit's presti-gious Merrill-Palmer School or others run by college-trained child guidance experts. EDNs were open to both blacks and whites, and the WPA also contributed to the operation of a few nurseries for Indian children like the Penick Indian School for Choctaw children in Trout, Louisiana.[29]

At WPA nursery schools both parents and children received educational instruction. For example, WPA nurseries in Philadelphia offered mothers presentations on topics ranging from childhood illnesses and healthy diets to "How to Buy a Dress." Children learned about colors, shapes, music, games, and how to count. Public health nurses offered diagnostic advice and weighed and measured enrollees. Photographs from WPA nurseries show happy as well as distraught children, but overall the records reveal consistently high-quality care. Parents appreciated the WPA nurseries' educational aspects, but contrary to federal officials' public statements, many adults also used the facilities as day-care centers. In 1942 the federal government recognized the positive aspects of WPA nurseries as day-care facilities for the children of working mothers when the need for women in war industries outweighed old arguments about the harm of all-day nursery care for young children. Many mothers were disappointed when federal nursery funds ended at the close of World War II and the business of providing high-quality nursery care for the children of working mothers was left to private enterprise.[30]

As Frances Perkins had suggested, during the Roosevelt years the federal government initiated relief efforts that directly affected the lives of children, especially in areas that touched education. In 1933–1934 alone, the early version of the FERA (the Civil Works Administration) built or improved 40,000 schools and 3,500 playgrounds and athletic fields, often located near or on school grounds. It paid the salaries of more than 50,000 teachers who would otherwise have lost their jobs. It established self-help projects, experimented with the establishment of entire new communities, and made loans to farmers.[31] On a fundamental level for children and adolescents, the FERA helped parents buy food for their children and helped many young Americans remain in their homes and schools. It was difficult for a homeless and hungry child to learn, or for those children whose local school had closed due to a lack of funding.

In January 1935 Congress provided more money for federal relief programs and initiated the creation of the WPA. The agency continued many of the early programs and implemented a school lunch program as well as paying the salaries of staff working in many local libraries. Many Americans, like the people in Gee's Bend, Alabama, witnessed the important role the federal government could play in the lives of children when WPA funding came to their area. Gee's Bend's first "real school" was a WPA construction project. Educational opportunities had been so poor in the community that the first-grade class included "children" in their early twenties. The situation in Gee's Bend was extreme, but many other places also saw federal funds pay for the construction of the first modern school buildings in their communities. New schools became centers of local pride and social activity for children and their families left behind by traditional means of school funding in America.[32]

In 1931 Herbert Hoover's National Advisory Committee on Education had praised the U.S. approach to education because it placed control and funding responsibilities at the state and local levels rather than with the federal government. Hoover's committee cautioned against what it saw as a "growing trend toward federal centralization" in laws such as the 1862 Morrill Act (granting the states public land for colleges) and the 1917 Smith-Hughes Act (providing federal funds to support the teaching of agriculture).[33] The later New Deal's efforts did not co-opt traditional state and local controls over schools, they simply provided needed federal money and a national focus on education. The primary goal was to put unemployed adults, especially men, back to work. The specifics of this effort had the added benefit of providing better school-based educational opportunities for America's youngest citizens.[34]

Having Fun at Uncle Sam's Expense

As already noted, the New Deal encouraged Americans to think about ways the federal government could contribute to safer and more accessible recreational facilities for America's youngest citizens. Adults employed in WPA workshops built children's toys and established toy-lending programs. Children and teens learned to swim, ski, dance, and play sports from teachers and coaches sponsored with WPA funds. Organizations such as the American Legion, YMCA, and YWCA also sponsored social activities and athletic teams as well as "educational" programs enhanced with WPA funding. Some young Americans participated in the Federal Theater Project and special NYA-directed social activities.[35]

In the 1930s people of all ages grew more dependent on public recreational facilities, and young Americans especially benefited from the change. The WPA is known for its work on improving the nation's infrastructure, but many WPA dollars went toward the construction of recreational facilities and funded social activities for children, adolescents, and youth. The federal government alone spent $750 million over the decade on new recreational projects, and many communities added their own venues for enhancing the quality of life among citizens. Throughout the United States the WPA built 770 swimming pools and 5,898 athletic fields. Participants in Resettlement Administration experiments such as Maryland's Greenbelt neighborhood considered recreational facilities essential to their model neighborhood. The WPA also built recreational facilities in rural areas like Carbon Hill, Alabama. The number of cities with public recreation programs doubled to over 2,100, and public expenditures for recreation increased from $27 million at the start of the New Deal to $57 million in 1940.[36]

New recreational facilities provided safer play places for many children and adolescents. Drowning deaths in New York City fell from over 450 in 1934 to less than 300 in 1936 when the city opened

Recreational programs in local community centers that received New Deal funds had the dual purpose of providing education as well as fun for area children, like this girl in San Francisco. *(National Archives)*

11 WPA-funded municipal swimming pools. New York City's pools stayed open during the summer from 10 a.m. to 10:30 p.m. Entry was free until 1 p.m., and thereafter 10 cents for children under 14 and 20 cents for everyone else. McCarren Pool, built on New York's Lower East Side, was the largest with a capacity of 6,300 swimmers. An estimated 75,000 people showed up on a hot Friday night in July 1936 to celebrate the giant swimming pool's grand opening.[37]

Alan Kniberg was born in 1927 and grew up in the Lower East Side neighborhood where officials located McCarren Pool. Kniberg was the youngest of eight children. His family lived in a crowded tenement several decades before air conditioning became common in most homes and apartments; Kniberg and many other city dwellers sometimes slept on the fire escape during summer heat. For Kniberg and the other children and teens in his community, the WPA pool "was the center of all the action. . . . It was our Hamptons." He spent as many hours as possible at the pool. McCarren and the other ten WPA pools located throughout New York City were expensive to operate, but the small fees from patrons earned a $70,000 profit when the pools were open for a full season. During the colder months the drained pools served as basketball courts or for other games devised by creative children and teens.[38]

WPA workers also made play safer by helping supervise young people at recreational facilities and on city streets. In Los Angeles, seven hundred WPA "white collar" workers served as crossing guards and supervisors at municipal playgrounds.[39] WPA jobs often had the reputation of being little more than busywork, but the recreational facilities built, maintained, and sometimes supervised through this important New Deal program are testament to the value of how federal work-relief dollars could be directed at programs that brightened the lives of millions of American youth.

Economic and Social Security for America's Children

At the 1930 White House Conference on Child Health and Protection, U.S. Children's Bureau Chief Grace Abbott warned that America's youngest citizens were suffering too. Rising adult unemployment and dwindling resources meant that many children could no longer depend on parents, states, local governments, and charity for economic support or basic services. Privately Abbott complained about President Hoover's failure to act to help meet children's growing needs. Abbott and other members of the Children's Bureau were happy to see Franklin Roosevelt elected in 1932. The Children's Bureau began an aggressive push for New Deal programs that would directly assist needy children and adolescents. Addressing the question of the depression's effect on young Americans, Abbott noted that in 1930 six million undernourished children lived in the United States. She estimated that during 1932 the worsening economy had doubled that number. "One-fifth of . . . preschool and school children," Abbott declared, were "showing the effects of poor nutrition, inadequate housing, and of the lack of medical care." Providing security for children should be one of the most important tasks of government, she pleaded, because it would help ensure the future of the United States. The nation's children were "showing the effects of the anxiety and the sense of insecurity that prevails when the father is unemployed for long periods. . . . The strain of living in a state of uncertainty week after week, month after month, and year after year deepens and intensifies the serious effects on the children in the family group." Abbott and many of her supporters believed that only the federal government had the resources to make a difference. She argued that the twenty-year-old Children's Bureau was the best federal agency to oversee New Deal efforts to help America's children weather the nation's economic crisis. Abbott and her supporters also saw Roosevelt's New Deal as an opportunity to secure permanent policy changes they had been advocating for children since the Progressive Era.[40]

The first Children's Bureau efforts under the New Deal involved children's health. In October 1933 the agency, now overseen by Secretary of Labor Frances Perkins, held a Child Health and Recovery Conference in Washington, D.C. There participants outlined plans "to stimulate a movement for the recovery of ground lost, during the Depression, in conditions affecting the health and vitality of children." Afterward, with the help of the FERA's Harry Hopkins, the Children's Bureau implemented the Child Health and Recovery Program (CHRP). The new program followed the same basic formula the Bureau had used to administer the Sheppard-Towner Maternity and Infancy Act from 1921 to 1929. During 1933–1934, CHRP directed efforts to provide emergency food and

medical care to the six million families with children on federal relief rolls. CHRP had potential, but its effectiveness was severely handicapped by a lack of staff and funds at a time of overwhelming need.
This weakness revealed the need for a program that could provide
comprehensive medical care for children.[41]

The Children's Bureau also led the effort to include financial
assistance for children who depended on the state for support. The
agency worried that the depression was reversing progress that had
been made during the 1920s in the expansion of state-administered
mothers' pension programs, designed to provide income for children living at home but whose fathers were dead, had deserted, or
were in jail. From its founding, the Children's Bureau had argued
that children had a right to mothers' pension payments. In other
words, mothers' pensions were not charity or relief for short-term
economic emergencies. Rather, the state had an interest in providing families with mothers' pensions because having a mother at
home to care for their needs was a natural right for all children,
even those without a father. In the March 1934 edition of the *Survey* magazine, Abbott told readers that "300,000 children, most of
them fatherless and all of them dependents, [were] supported by
mothers' pensions." All but two states had established mothers'
pension systems, but most were in danger of defaulting on their
programs. States were turning to federal emergency relief for needy
families. That situation, Abbott argued, jeopardized the idea that
children who depended on the state for support had a right to
mothers' pensions and a full-time mother at home. The needs of
dependent children, she maintained, should not be met with emergency relief but "with the same kind of security . . . as is now being
sought for the aged in old age pensions." Abbott warned that "in
the long future, our democracy will have to pay in perhaps arith-
metical or even geometrical progression for our failure to bring security and stability to the care of these especially disadvantaged
children."[42]

In June 1934 Abbott and the Children's Bureau had an opportunity to include dependent children and adolescents in the New Deal's most significant social welfare program, Social Security. Franklin Roosevelt's Committee on Economic Security (CES) oversaw the design of the president's Social Security bill. The CES asked Grace Abbott, by then retired from the Children's Bureau; Katharine Lenroot, the Bureau's new interim chief; and Martha May Eliot, a physician and head of the Bureau's health division, to devise a set of children's programs for inclusion in the Social Security bill to be sent to Congress. The three women came up with a plan emphasizing that "children are not merely pocket editions of adults." They needed "special health and protective services."[43] Three major provisions were proposed: Title IV, Aid to Dependent Children; Title V, Maternal and Child Health for needy mothers and children; and Title VII, Aid for Children with Special Needs. All three programs provided for a combination of federal and state funding.

Title VII went through hearings without attracting much attention. The program provided funds to children with "special needs" described as minors living in "situations of neglect in homes, feeblemindedness in parents or children, cruel and abusive parents, illegitimate children without competent guardians, children who are delinquent, truant, or wayward, or who suffer from mental disturbances or handicaps." In 1935 only one-fourth of the states operated statewide welfare boards to look after the interests of an estimated 575,000 "special needs" children living in the United States. Approximately 180,000 children under eighteen lived in foster homes, 200,000 in facilities overseen by the state and federal juvenile courts, and another 120,000 in other institutions. Title VII implemented a federal program to deal with the needs of these vulnerable children, but it depended on the states to identify the children who needed protection. During the depression many state officials overlooked such parental neglect since so many new families were falling below the poverty line.

Title V provided funding to states for new and improved maternal and infant health-care programs. It also established special services for "crippled" children and paid for the health care of young children from very poor families. State health departments could use Title V funds to provide a wide variety of health-care services for needy children and mothers: prenatal and child health clinics, medical examinations for school-age children, dental health services, and the salaries of public health nurses. The Roosevelt administration had originally intended to include national health insurance in the Social Security bill but dropped the idea when opposition from the American Medical Association and the insurance industry threatened the entire proposal.[44]

Removing national health insurance as a potential lightning rod in the Social Security bill shifted political debate in Congress and the press to the old-age pension and unemployment compensation proposals. Most politicians and journalists paid little attention to the children's programs; only Title IV's Aid to Dependent Children attracted objections during congressional debates. Modeled after the mothers' pension systems that already existed in all but two states, the ADC proposal provided federal funding to supplement state allocations. The Children's Bureau estimated that in 1935, 700,000 of the 7.4 million American children living in families on federal emergency relief qualified for mothers' pensions. States turned to federal relief because they ran out of money. Abbott, Lenroot, and Eliot argued that ADC should not be an aid "to mothers but defense measures for children." Instead it would "release from the wage-earning role the person whose natural function is to give her children the physical and affectionate guardianship necessary . . . to rear them into citizens capable of contributing to society." ADC defined the "natural" caregiver more broadly than the state mothers' pension programs, but it continued to rely on the idea that the adult who cared for a dependent child should not work outside the home. The ADC proposal defined a dependent child as an individual

under the age of sixteen who has been deprived of parental support or care by reason of the death, continued absence from
home, or physical or mental incapacity of a parent, and who is
living with his father, mother, grandmother, brother, sister,
stepfather, stepmother, stepsister, uncle, or aunt, in a place of
residence maintained by one or more of such relatives as his or
their own home.[45]

Congress set the maximum federal contribution for ADC benefits at $18 per month for the first child and $12 for each additional
child. This was the same standard allowable under the veterans'
pension acts paid to the children of servicemen killed during World
War I, but Congress ignored the separate $30 benefit paid to veter-
ans' widows on top of allowances for children. Besides this important shortcoming, as the CES chairman remarked, the ADC
amount was "utterly inadequate and completely out of line with
pensions of $30 per month to individual old people." Congress fur-
ther underscored the second-class status of ADC by limiting federal
matching funds to the states to one-third while agreeing to contribute one-half to the old-age pension and unemployment compensation programs. By the time ADC was ready for inclusion in
the final Social Security bill, it had become a public assistance program that more closely resembled charity than the social insurance
provisions for elderly Americans or unemployed adults.[46]

Congress passed the legislation and President Roosevelt signed
the Social Security Act into law on August 14, 1935. Despite the in-
credibly low allowances included under ADC, the average benefit to
dependent children increased from $22.31 per month to $32.12, and
the number of recipients rose from 300,000 to 700,000. In 1939
amendments to the Social Security Act expanded the definition of
"dependent child" to sixteen- and seventeen-year-olds but added a
"suitable home" provision that in fact allowed open discrimination
against minorities and other applicants deemed "unworthy" by local

standards. Another change moved the sympathetic category of widows and children into the Old Age and Survivors Insurance program, further contributing to the image of ADC families as those on public assistance due to desertion, divorce, or unwed motherhood. In 1940 Congress raised the federal contribution to ADC to one-half, but benefits varied widely since they were set by each individual state. Many children from poor families were also left outside the program. A report in 1940 claimed that 13 million American children lived in families that earned less than $800 a year.

Despite these significant weaknesses, ADC marked an important affirmation of the idea that the federal government had a responsibility for helping the nation's needy children. By 1940 approximately 3 percent of American children received benefits under ADC, more than three times the number that had benefited from mothers' pensions in 1931. In 1941 Mississippi became the final state to implement the ADC program.[47] Perhaps most important for all American children, for the first time in its history the federal government had defined childhood dependency from birth through age seventeen.

The Fair Labor Standards Act

The New Deal also set forth federal child labor regulations for the first time in American history. Upon entering the White House, President Roosevelt consistently called for the "elimination of child labor." He praised the inclusion of prohibitions against child labor in the National Recovery Administration labor codes and lamented their loss in 1935 when the Supreme Court declared the NRA unconstitutional. Roosevelt declared passage of the Fair Labor Standards Act in 1938 a law that finally "ends child labor."[48] The FLSA was the first federal law prohibiting the employment of individuals under age sixteen in industries engaged in interstate commerce or those deemed hazardous by the Department of Labor. It limited working hours and prohibited work past 10 p.m. on school nights for anyone under eighteen. The law emphasized the importance of school over paid labor by limiting the work hours of sixteen- and seventeen-year-olds, something that many states did not do at the time. The abusive working conditions noted in the Children's Bureau's 1935 study of sugar beet workers had led to the inclusion of child labor regulations in the 1937 Sugar Beet Act. The FLSA also included restrictions for that industry, requiring that sugar beet field workers be at least fourteen years of age, and that fourteen- and fifteen-year-olds could not work in the fields more than eight hours a day.

Most important, the FLSA provided the first federal regulation of children's wage labor, even though the law contained important exemptions. For example, the FLSA provided for exemptions in agricultural labor outside the sugar beet industry, and the law made no mention of domestic service. It also waived regulations for children working in a business owned by their parents other than manufacturing or mining. The rules did not apply to young people working as actors or performers, or those engaged in the delivery of newspapers directly to consumers. Another exemption allowed fourteen- and fifteen-year-olds to apply for special work certificates that provided exemptions to the FLSA's general prohibition against employment under age sixteen. Fourteen- and fifteen-year-olds could still engage "in work (other than manufacturing or mining) that does not interfere with their schooling, health, or well being." This was an important loophole since the language was rather vague and the design and enforcement of mandatory school attendance laws rested with the states.[49] Roosevelt's claim that the FLSA "ends child labor" was clearly an overstatement, but the law did help eliminate the most exploitative forms of child labor in industrial production. More important, the FLSA's inclusion of sixteen- and seventeen-year-olds under federal authority underscored the definition of modern childhood dependency as the period up to age eighteen.

The rise in adolescent employment during World War II highlighted the weaknesses in the FLSA's child labor regulations, but this proved to be only a temporary blip. During the late 1940s and 1950s the numbers of adolescents who stayed out of the full-time labor force until after high school graduation rose. By 1948, according to the Department of Labor, children under sixteen had been virtually eliminated from the paid labor force. Still, adolescents and children continued to make important contributions to the American economy. Even in formal wage-labor employment at the end of the twentieth century, American sixteen- and seventeen-year-olds worked more hours than the comparable age group in other industrialized nations.[50] The fact that teenagers in the United States can earn a driver's license at sixteen (two years earlier than most young people in other countries), and the American dependence on automobiles, helps explain this circumstance. In a broader context, by the end of the 1930s federal law defined all Americans through age seventeen as a special group apart from adults. They were now Uncle Sam's children.

CHAPTER SEVEN

Modern Childhood and the New Deal Generation

✒ FRANKLIN AND ELEANOR ROOSEVELT, along with an army of New Deal colleagues, sold the federal government's programs to adults and to the generation that came of age during hard times. Although help did not reach everyone who needed it, the long arm of the federal government touched the lives of the vast majority of Americans who grew up in the 1930s. At a minimum, children and teens throughout the United States witnessed the construction of schools, parks, roads, bridges, post offices, government buildings, and recreational facilities funded with new federal dollars. Others understood that federal relief assistance had paid for the food they ate and the clothes they wore. Millions of older teens and youth received monthly stipends from the CCC or the NYA. Either to their relief, or over their objection, new FLSA regulations removed almost all children under fourteen from the wage-labor force in businesses outside agriculture. Roosevelt sometimes seesawed over how far in debt the federal government should go to provide economic help to Americans, but he and other members of his administration never backed off from New Deal rhetoric suggesting that the federal government had a direct interest in protecting the nation's youngest citizens.

As a consequence, many children and adolescents felt a direct connection to the federal government. Thousands of letters expressing admiration for the president and the first lady arrived at the White House. A letter from a girl in Minnesota to Eleanor Roosevelt in March 1934 expressed sentiments similar to many the president and his wife received during the depression: "I have been very interested in you because I read in the papers how much you are doing for the poor children and crippled children I want to thank you for doing so much for those little children cause I know how tough it is now." Sometimes letters reflected the New Deal's limitations. Two days after Christmas in 1934, a sixteen-year-old from Double Springs, Alabama, noted, "we want to thank your Husband Mr. Roosevelt for his good plan he has planned for us poor people. . . . But it seems it hasn't reached us yet much."[1] A boy living in Chicago in 1936 summed up many of the difficulties that continued to face young people and their families as the depression dragged on year after year.

Dear President and Mrs. Roosevelt,

I'm a boy of 12 years. I want to tell you about my family. My father hasn't worked for 5 months. He went plenty times to relief, he filled out application. They won't give us anything. I don't know why. Please you do something. We haven't paid 4 months rent. Everyday the landlord rings the door bell, we don't open the door for him. We are afraid that will be put out, been put out before, and don't want to happen again. We haven't paid the gas bill, and the electric bill, haven't paid grocery bill for 3 months. My brother goes to Lane Tech. High School. He's eighteen years old, hasn't gone to school for two weeks because he got no car fare. I have a sister she's twenty years, she can't find work. My father he staying home. All the time he's crying because he can't find work. I told him why are you crying daddy, and daddy said why shouldn't I cry when there is nothing in the house. I feel sorry for him. That night I couldn't sleep. The next morning I wrote this letter to you in my room. Were American citizens and were born in Chicago, Ill. And I don't know why they don't help us. Please answer right away because we need it. will starve. Thank you. God bless you.[2]

Other children and teens seemed confused and frustrated by an America that promoted democracy and equality while so many policies appeared blatantly unfair. In November 1934 a thirteen-year-old boy from Cleveland asked President Roosevelt, "What I would like to know is this: how can a bank take our money and get by while an old couple have to let their houses go." Many others demanded that the Roosevelts "do something" to help.[3]

The Roosevelt administration may not have done enough, but it did do something. Franklin Roosevelt's willingness to experiment and his ability to connect with ordinary people, especially children and youth, helped make him very popular among members of the depression generation. For many children and youth, Eleanor Roosevelt seemed like someone who understood and cared about their personal situations. In a radio address to a gathering of Young Democrat Clubs of America in 1935, the president spoke directly to the depression generation. The clubs had first met in March 1932 in Washington, D.C., then a year later in Kansas City. Members had seen the fortunes of their organization rise along with the Roosevelt administration. They applauded enactment of the first New Deal and looked to the president for further leadership. Roosevelt told his young audience that he believed the Great Depression had changed "the very objectives of young people. . . . You place emphasis on sufficiency of life, rather than on a plethora of riches." Building support for his New Deal, the president said he believed that most Americans had "come to an understanding of . . . new ways of protecting people." He cautioned, however, that "a paternalistic system which tries to provide for security for everyone from above calls for an impossible task and a regimentation utterly uncongenial to the spirit of our people."

Asking for his young audience's support, Roosevelt continued, "I say from my heart that no man of my generation has any business to address youth unless he comes to that task not in a spirit of exultation, but in a spirit of humility." His generation may have had good intentions, "but we have certainly not been adequate in results." The younger generation of Americans should "not only . . . maintain the best in your heritage, but . . . labor to lift from the shoulders of the American people some of the burdens that the mistakes of the past generation have placed there."[4]

Jim Mitchell's story expresses the positive feelings many young Americans held toward Franklin Roosevelt and his New Deal philosophy. The onset of the depression broke Jim's fragile family. Abused at home, he ran away in 1933 at age thirteen and spent the next four years on the road doing whatever he could to survive. In 1937 he turned seventeen and joined the CCC. The experience, Jim believed, changed his life for the better. "On the road you lived for yourself and to hell with everyone else. In the CCC you not only learned to live with other guys. . . . You learned to work as a team." Before enrolling in the CCC Jim felt that his life "had no direction. Back home I'd had no role models to measure my life against. In the corps there were well-educated fellows whose goals had been interrupted. I wanted to be like them and I knew that I had to get an education to do so." Jim worked to better himself and also got "a big boost" from the first letter he received from his mother after joining the CCC.

Dear Son,

I want you to know how grateful we are to you and proud too. The $25 we get each month goes a long way in holding us together. It's good to look Dimitri in the eye and plunk down cash for groceries, and not be obliged to Merriweather for rent.

Jim Mitchell stayed in the CCC for two years. Like many CCC recruits and those who enrolled in the NYA, he felt proud to be doing something meaningful and a step to a better future. He said he encountered two types of young homeless wanderers during the time he spent on the road. One type firmly believed in the American system: "By God, this is gonna work." The second type consisted of "Marxist revolutionaries" who "wanted to start the revolution now." In the early 1930s Jim had also believed that the country was "on the brink of hell." But joining Roosevelt's Soil Soldiers tempered his radical and despondent views. He credited Franklin Roosevelt's positive attitude as being a major factor in preventing the social and political turmoil among young people that hit other countries during the depression decade. "Despite all the horrors of the Depression, we didn't live in terror but looked ahead. We knew that down the road things were going to get better."[5]

Jim Mitchell's memory may be colored by his distance from the difficulties he faced during the Great Depression, but many individuals of his generation echo his sentiments. The federal government seemed to offer the possibility of leveling the playing field for young Americans, even if they did not need the assistance themselves. Most shared an identity as Uncle Sam's children that helped to temper a generation vulnerable to feelings of distrust and disillusionment. It is impossible to know what would have happened if the depression had continued into another decade, but by 1940 the groundwork had been laid for ties that further united a generation of young Americans against a common enemy during World War II. And their experiences in the 1930s helped seal a belief in a model of modern American childhood that they believed could be possible for all Americans during "normal" times. They embraced the model as a right for their own children after the two decades of turmoil that shaped their own lives.

Many Americans who grew up during the Great Depression hold fond memories of their childhood, despite the decade's hard times. Polls show that Franklin Roosevelt is still cited as one of the public's favorite presidents and Eleanor as one of the greatest first ladies. As Mary Caliguri remembers, "We thought Roosevelt was a god."[6] The Roosevelt New Deal promoted a modern childhood ideal embraced by Caliguri and most members of her generation. At the same time, the Roosevelt administration's strategy in selling many of its programs as essential antidotes to the nation's economic emergency may have unwittingly muted the public's memory of how important such federal efforts were in the lives of American youth. Trying to thwart accusations that the New Deal was socialism, the Roosevelt administration emphasized the need for such efforts during the economic emergency. The more permanent programs, like old-age pensions in Social Security, became entitlements based on returns for individual independent initiative. ADC was charity and not a right for dependent children.

After the end of the Great Depression and the Allied victory in World War II, many Americans forgot that inequities highlighted by the 1930s crisis continued to exist for many young people. Instead they remembered the Roosevelt administration's infectious optimism and the "all-American" values promoted by childhood icons like Jack Armstrong. These images fit the hyper-patriotism of the early cold war years and its more prosperous times. The 1930s model of childhood became the standard of modern American life—but still unattainable for too many to make the dream a reality.

Notes

Introduction

1. Tom Brokaw, *The Greatest Generation* (New York: Random House, 1998), introduction and jacket flap; Howard Zinn, "The Greatest Generation?" *Progressive,* 65 (October 2001), http://www.progressive.org/0901/zinn1001.html, accessed February 23, 2005.

2. A few examples include Paula Fass and Mary Ann Mason, eds., *Childhood in America* (New York: New York University Press, 2000); N. Ray Hiner and Joseph M. Hawes, *Growing Up in America: Children in Historical Perspective* (Urbana: University of Illinois Press, 1985); Joseph E. Illick, *American Childhoods* (Philadelphia: University of Pennsylvania Press, 2002); Joseph Kett, *Rites of Passage: Adolescence in America, 1790 to the Present* (New York: Basic Books, 1978); Steven Mintz, *Huck's Raft: A History of American Childhood* (Cambridge, Mass.: Harvard University Press, 2004); Elliott West and Paula Petrik, eds., *Small Worlds: Children and Adolescents in America, 1850–1950* (Lawrence: University Press of Kansas, 1992); and Judith Sealander, *The Failed Century of the Child: Governing America's Young in the Twentieth Century* (New York: Cambridge University Press, 2003).

3. Frank Hobbs and Nicole Stoops, U.S. Census Bureau, "Demographic Trends in the Twentieth Century, Census 2000 Special Reports" (Washington, D.C.: Government Printing Office, 2002); http://www.census.gov/prod/2002pubs/censr-4.pdf, accessed February 20, 2004.

4. Robert Cohen, ed., *Dear Mrs. Roosevelt: Letters from Children of the Great Depression* (Chapel Hill: University of North Carolina Press, 2002); Glen H. Elder, Jr., *Children of the Great Depression: Social Change in Life Experience* (Chicago: University of Chicago Press, 1974); John A. Clausen, *American Lives: Looking Back at the Children of the Great Depression* (New York: Free Press, 1993).

Chapter 1. Stable and Fragile Families in Hard Times

1. "Documenting America: Farm Security Administration Photographs," American Memory Project, Library of Congress, http://memory.loc.gov/ammem/ fsahtml/fachap05.html, accessed November 15, 2004; Debbie Elliot interview with Kathryn Tucker Windham, "The Women of Gee's Bend," broadcast on NPR "All Things Considered," November 28, 2004, http://www.npr.org/ templates/story/story.php?storyId=4184856, accessed November 30, 2004; B. J. Sommers, "Black Families of Alabama's Black Belt," http://www .prairiebluff.com/blackbelt/geesbend.html, accessed March 17, 2005; Jeanette Keith, *The South: A Concise History* (Upper Saddle River, N.J.: Pearson Education, 2002), II, 109; it appears that the entire community of blacks in Gee's Bend, Wilcox County, is missing from the 1930 Census, a fact that underscores their invisibility to the outside world before the New Deal.

2. Clausen, *American Lives*, 210–217; Robert S. Lynd and Helen Merritt Lynd, *Middletown in Transition: A Study in Cultural Conflicts* (New York: Harcourt, Brace, 1937), 145.

3. Elder, *Children of the Great Depression*, 87; Cohen, *Dear Mrs. Roosevelt*, 1–31, 35.

4. Hobbs and Stoops, "Demographic Trends"; http://www.census.gov/prod/ 2002pubs/censr-4.pdf, accessed February 20, 2004.

5. Elder, *Children of the Great Depression*, 87.

6. *Children in a Democracy: General Report Adopted by the White House Conference on Children in a Democracy* (Washington, D.C.: Government Printing office, 1940), 11–14; John W. Jeffries, *Wartime America: The World War II Homefront* (Chicago: Ivan R. Dee, 1997), 3–15.

7. Elder, *Children of the Great Depression*, 283.

8. Robert J. Hastings, *A Nickel's Worth of Skim Milk: A Boy's View of the Great Depression* (Carbondale: Southern Illinois University Press, 1972; 2nd ed. 1986), xiii, 1–15, 70; Hastings appears in the 1930 Census as "Bobbie Hasting," living with his parents and two older brothers, LaVerne (fourteen) and Champ (seventeen), in Williamson County, sheet no. 1A.

9. Hastings, *A Nickel's Worth of Skim Milk,* 4–7; U.S. Census Bureau, "Food Consumption and Food Per Capita Expenditures, 1929–2001, No. HS-19," *Mini Historical Statistics, Statistical Abstract* (Washington, D.C.: Government Printing Office, 2003), 31, http://www.census.gov/statab/hist/HS-19.pdf, accessed February 17, 2005.

10. Hastings, *A Nickel's Worth of Skim Milk,* xiii, 4–7; Elmus Wicker, "The Banking Panics (1930–1933)," in Robert S. McElvaine, ed., *Encyclopedia of the Great Depression* (New York: Macmillan Reference, 2004), I, 88–93.

11. Hastings, *A Nickel's Worth of Skim Milk*, xiii, 1–15, 70.

12. Interview with Mary Caliguri Caputo, conducted by the author in Owings Mills, Md., July 20, 2004, audiotape in author's possession; Robert S. McElvaine, ed., *Down and Out in the Great Depression: Letters from the Forgotten Man* (Chapel Hill: University of North Carolina Press, 1983), 124–142.

13. Caliguri interview; Lisa Krissoff Boehm, "Women, Impact of the Great Depression On," in McElvaine, *Encyclopedia of the Great Depression*, I, 1050–1053; U.S. Census Bureau, "Marital Status of Women in the Civilian Labor Force, 1900–2002, No. HS-30," *Mini Historical Statistics, Statistical Abstract* (Washington, D.C.: Government Printing Office, 2003), 30, http://www.census.gov/statab/hist/HS-30.pdf, accessed February 18, 2005.

14. Caliguri interview.

15. Ibid.; U.S. Census Bureau, *Mini Historical Statistics, Statistical Abstract*, "Expectation of Life at Birth by Race and Sex, 1900–1901, No. HS-16" (Washington, D.C.: Government Printing Office, 2003), 27, http://www.census.gov/statab/hist/HS-16.pdf, accessed February 18, 2005.

16. Katrina M. Leitkowski, "Public Enemy Number One," unpublished paper completed at University of Maryland, Baltimore County, May 6, 2004, paper in author's possession. Leitkowski's grandmother is the daughter of Ruehl James Dalhover; she was born shortly after his execution. Federal Bureau of Investigation, "Famous Cases: The Brady Gang," http://www.fbi.gov/libref/historic/famcases/bradygang/bradygang.htm, accessed April 12, 2004.

17. Russell Baker, *Growing Up* (New York: Congdon Weed, 1982), 21–22, 80–84.

18. Jeane Westin, *Making Do: How Women Survived the '30s* (Chicago: Follett, 1976), 120–130.

19. Clausen, *American Lives*, 70–72.

20. "Proceedings of the Conference on the Care of Dependent Children, Held at Washington, D.C., January 25, 26, 1909," Senate Document 721, 60th Cong., 2d sess., 1909; Julia Lathrop, "Seventh Annual Report of the Chief," U.S. Children's Bureau (Washington, D.C.: Government Printing Office, 1919).

21. Herbert Hoover, "Address of President Hoover at the Opening Session of the White House Conference on Child Health and Protection," November 19, 1930 (Washington, D.C.: Government Printing Office, 1930), copy in Herbert Hoover Presidential Papers, box 97, file "Child Health Conference," 1–2, Hoover Presidential Library, West Bend, Iowa.

22. "The White House Conference," *Nation*, 131 (December 3, 1930), 595.

23. William E. Leuchtenburg, *Franklin D. Roosevelt and the New Deal* (New York: Harper and Row, 1963), 1–3; Anthony Badger, *The New Deal: The De-*

pression Years, 1933–1940 (Chicago: Ivan R. Dee, 2002), 11–29; Robert S. McElvaine, *The Great Depression: America, 1929–1941* (Pittsburgh: Three Rivers Press, 1993); T. H. Watkins, *The Hungry Years: A Narrative History of the Great Depression in America* (New York: Owl Books, 2000); Francisco E. Balderrama and Raymond Rodríguez, *Decade of Betrayal: Mexican Repatriation in the 1930s* (Albuquerque: University of New Mexico Press, 1995), 77.

24. Mintz, *Huck's Raft,* 236–237; Steven Mintz and Susan Kellogg, *Domestic Revolutions: A Social History of American Family Life* (New York: Free Press, 1988), 136.

25. U.S. Census Bureau, *Statistical Abstract of the United States,* "Births, Deaths, Marriages, and Divorce Rates per 1,000 Population, 1900–1940" (Washington, D.C.: Government Printing Office, 1951), 57–58, http://www2.census .gov/prod2/statcomp/documents/1951-02.pdf, accessed February 1, 2004.

26. Interview with "Charles E. Banister, Oregon Folklore Studies, Federal Writers' Project, 1936–1940," May 25, 1939, included in "American Life Histories: Manuscripts from the Federal Writers Project," Library of Congress, Washington, D.C., http://memory.loc.gov/ammem/wpaintro/wpahome.html, accessed June 7, 2004.

27. Hastings, *A Nickel's Worth of Skim Milk,* 46–47.

28. Letter to Eleanor Roosevelt from M.G., The Bronx, N.Y., December 28, 1934, included in Cohen, *Dear Mrs. Roosevelt,* 170.

29. Duval Edwards, *The Great Depression and a Teenager's Fight to Survive* (Seattle, Wash.: Red Apple Publishing, 1992), 19; Clyde Edwards was counted in the 1930 Census as living with his parents and four siblings (two brothers and two sisters) in Pineville, Rapides Parish, La., sheet no. 7A.

30. Interview with "Glenn Knapie Brent Cochrane, North Carolina, Federal Writers' Project, 1936–1940," September 19, 1939, included in "American Life Histories," accessed June 6, 2004.

31. John D. McKee, *Two Legs to Stand On* (New York: Appleton-Century-Crofts, 1955), 11–18.

32. Kriste Lindenmeyer, *"A Right to Childhood": The U.S. Children's Bureau and Child Welfare, 1912–1946* (Urbana: University of Illinois Press, 1997), 104–107; U.S. Census Bureau, "Live Births, Infant Deaths, Maternal Deaths: 1900–2001, No. HS-13," *Mini Historical Statistics, Statistical Abstract* (Washington, D.C.: Government Printing Office, 2003), 21, http://www.census.gov/statab/ hist/HS-13.pdf, accessed February 17, 2005.

33. Andrew J. Dunbar and Dennis McBride, *Building Hoover Dam: An Oral History of the Great Depression* (New York: Maxwell Macmillan International, 1993), 131.

34. William C. Pryor, "A New Deal for Carbon Hill, Alabama, Mrs. Nelson Greene and Baby," New Deal Network, http://newdeal.feri.org/carbonhill/k93.htm, accessed March 15, 2004.

35. Interview with "Mrs. B, Bridgeport, Connecticut," Federal Writers' Project, 1936–1940, March 13, 1939, Clinton Avenue Survey, included in "American Life Histories," accessed June 5, 2004.

36. Kriste Lindenmeyer, "Expanding Birth Control to the Hinterland: Cincinnati's First Contraceptive Clinic as a Case Study, 1929–1931," *Mid-America*, 77 (Spring/Summer 1995), 145–173; Westin, *Making Do*, 159–160.

37. Interview with "Mrs. A, Bridgeport, Connecticut," Federal Writers' Project, 1936–1940, no date, 1939, included in "American Life Histories," accessed June 6, 2004.

38. Gerald Markowitz, "Health and Nutrition," in McElvaine, *Encyclopedia of the Great Depression*, I, 428–431; Michael Grey, *New Deal Medicine: The Rural Health Programs of the Farm Security Administration* (Baltimore: Johns Hopkins University Press, 2002), 41–129; Jeffrey Allen Smith, "Indian Children and Nurses: Native American Health and Field Nurses in Southern California, 1928–1948," *Native Studies Review,* 15 (2004), 21–35.

39. Letter from A. M. Waldrop to E. W. Kelley, September 4, 1937, reprinted in *New Deal Network*, http://newdeal.feri.org/carbonhill/01.htm, accessed June 23, 2004.

40. Keith, *The South*, II, 65; Grey, *New Deal Medicine*, 98–99.

41. U.S. Census Bureau, "Specified Reportable Diseases, Cases per 100,000 Population, 1912 to 1921, No. HS-18," *Mini Historical Statistics, Statistical Abstract* (Washington, D.C.: Government Printing Office, 2003), 29, http://www.census.gov/statab/hist/HS-18.pdf, accessed February 20, 2005; "Students Suspended as Health Measure," *Milwaukee Sentinel*, May 16, 1936, reprinted in *Children in Urban American Project,* Marquette University, Milwaukee, Wisc., http://xserver1.its.mu.edu/index.html, accessed July 15, 2004.

42. "Richard Waskins, An Oral History," *Michigan History Magazine,* 66 (January–February 1982), http://www.michigan.gov/hal/0.1607.7-160-17451_18670_18793-535-,00.html, accessed November 10, 2004.

43. U.S. Bureau of the Census, "Specified Reportable Diseases," 29; Terra Ziporyn, *Disease in the Popular Press: The Case of Diphtheria, Typhoid Fever, and Syphilis, 1870–1920* (Westport, Conn.: Greenwood Press, 1988), 35.

44. Leroy Ashby, *Endangered Children: Dependency, Neglect, and Abuse in American History* (New York: Twayne Publishers, 1997), 108–112.

45. Ibid.; Kenneth Cmiel, *A Home of Another Kind: One Chicago Orphanage and the Tangle of Welfare* (Chicago: University of Chicago Press, 1995), 105–112;

Ira A. Greenberg et al., eds., *The Hebrew National Orphan Home: Memories of Orphanage Life* (Westport, Conn.: Bergin & Garvey, 2001), 141–143.

46. Julie Berebitsky, *Like Our Very Own: Adoption and the Changing Culture of Motherhood, 1851–1950* (Lawrence: University Press of Kansas, 2000), 75–101.

47. Child Welfare League of America, "Minimum Safeguards in Adoption," November 5, 1938, included in the Adoption History Project, http://darkwing .uoregon.edu/~adoption/archive/CwlaMSA.htm, accessed July 10, 2004; Linda Tollett Austin, *Babies for Sale: The Tennessee Children's Home Adoption Scandal* (Westport, Conn.: Praeger, 1993), 1–76.

48. Paul K. Conkin, *Tomorrow a New World: The New Deal Community Program* (Ithaca: Cornell University Press, 1959), 230; M. G. Trend and W. L. Lett, "Government Capital and Minority Enterprise: An Evaluation of a Depression-Era Social Program," *American Anthropologist*, 88 (September 1986), 595–609; "Documenting America: Farm Security Administration Photographs," American Memory Project, Library of Congress, http://memory .loc.gov/ammem/fsahtml/fachap05.html, accessed November 15, 2004; Elliot interview with Kathryn Tucker Windham, accessed November 30, 2004; Sommers, "Black Families of Alabama's Black Belt."

Chapter 2: Work, If You Could Find It

1. Studs Terkel interviewed Slim Collier for the book *Hard Times: An Oral History of the Great Depression* (New York: Pocket Books, 1970), 119–122; an audio excerpt of the Slim Collier interview is available online at Studs Terkel, "Conversations with America, *Hard Times*," Chicago: Chicago Historical Society, http://www.studsterkel.org/htimes.php, accessed April 19, 2004. Terkel often used pseudonyms, but there are several Collier families living in Iowa at the time of the 1930 Census that fit the description in his book.

2. Daniel Scott Smith, " 'The Number and Quality of Children': Education and Marital Fertility in Early Twentieth Century Iowa," *Journal of Social History*, Winter 1996, 368.

3. Terkel, *Hard Times*, 119–122.

4. Jeremy Felt, *Hostages of Fortune: Child Labor Reform in New York State* (Syracuse: Syracuse University Press, 1965); Stephen B. Wood, *Constitutional Politics in the Progressive Era* (Chicago: University of Chicago Press, 1968); Walter I. Trattner, *Crusade for the Children: A History of the National Child Labor Committee and Child Labor Reform in America* (Chicago: Quadrangle Books,

1970); Joseph M. Hawes, *The Children's Rights Movement: A History of Advocacy and Protection* (Boston: Twayne Publishers, 1991), 39–53.

5. Shelley Sallee, *The Whiteness of Child Labor Reform in the New South* (Athens: University of Georgia Press, 2004); Robert Willard McAhren, "Making the Nation Safe for Childhood: A History of the Movement for Federal Regulation of Child Labor, 1900–1938," Ph.D. dissertation, University of Texas at Austin, 1967; Andrew John Fish, "The Children's Crusade: The Effect of Culture and Ideology on the Movement to Ratify the Federal Child Labor Amendment, 1924–1937," Ph.D. dissertation, State University of New York at Stony Brook, 2001.

6. Elder, *Children of the Great Depression*, 65–66.

7. U.S. Census Bureau, "School Retention Rates—Fifth Grade Through College Entrance: 1924–1932 to 1962–1970," in *Historical Statistics of the United States, Bicentennial Edition* (Washington, D.C.: Government Printing Office, 1976), 379; "School Attendance for Persons 5 to 24 Years of Age, by Single Years of Age, Color and Sex, for the United States, Rural and Urban, 1940," Table 1, in "Educational Characteristics of the Population of the United States by Age, 1940," report Series P-19, December 27, 1943, U.S. Census Bureau, http://www.census.gov/population/socdemo/education/p19-4/tab-01.pdf accessed January 20, 2004.

8. Katharine F. Lenroot, "Child Welfare, 1930–1940," *Annals of the American Academy of Political and Social Science,* 212 (November 1940), 5.

9. Trattner, *Crusade for the Children,* 189; Sealander, *Failed Century,* 138.

10. Press Release, U.S. Department of Labor, Children's Bureau, December 22, 1937, RG 102, CBP, Box 929, file 6-1-0-3(0). The communities in the study were located in Alabama, Georgia, Indiana, Massachusetts, Missouri, and New Hampshire. Helen Wood, "Young Workers and Their Jobs in 1936: A Survey in Six States" (Washington, D.C.: Government Printing Office, 1940), CB pub. no. 249, 3–5.

11. Ibid.

12. Ibid.; Wood, "Young Workers," 17; Sealander, *Failed Century,* 138.

13. Sealander, *Failed Century,* 137–183.

14. Letter from V.B.F. to Eleanor Roosevelt, November 10, 1940, reprinted in Cohen, *Dear Mrs. Roosevelt,* 72–73.

15. The Library of Congress's *American Memory Project* includes a searchable database of Farm Security Administration photographs from this period, "America from the Great Depression to World War II, Photographs from the FSA–OWI, 1935–1945," online collection in the LOC's *American Memory*

Project, http://memory.loc.gov/ammem/fsowhome.html, 2004; John Stein-beck, *The Grapes of Wrath* (New York: Viking Press, 1939); *The Grapes of Wrath,* film, John Ford, director (Twentieth Century Fox, 1940); Brad D. Lookingbill, *Dust Bowl, USA: Depression America and the Ecological Imagination, 1929–1941* (Athens: Ohio University Press, 2001), 89–125.

16. Cesar Chavez and his family are included in the 1930 Census for Yuma, Ariz., Sheet 1A; Susan Ferriss and Ricardo Sandoval, *The Fight in the Fields: Cesar Chavez and the Farmworkers Movement* (New York: Harcourt Brace, 1997), 12–30.

17. Elizabeth S. Johnson, "Welfare of Families of Sugar-Beet Laborers: A Study of Child Labor and Its Relation to Family Work, Income, and Living Conditions in 1935" (Washington, D.C.: Government Printing Office, 1939), CB pub. no. 247, 3–5. Mexican Americans continue to make up the largest proportion of migrant farm families.

18. Balderrama and Rodríguez, *Decade of Betrayal,* 34–35.

19. U.S. Census Bureau, "Urban and Rural Population, 1790–1990," Table 1, http://www.census.gov/population/censusdata/urpop0090.txt, accessed April 24, 2004.

20. U.S. Census Bureau, "Agriculture—Farms, Acreage, Income, and Foreign Trade: 1900–2002," No. HS-44, http://www.census.gov/statab/hist/HS-44.pdf, accessed March 11, 2004.

21. Interview with Dorothy Skinner and Virginia Skinner Harris, conducted by Melissa Walker, included in Melissa Walker, ed., *Country Women Cope with Hard Times: A Collection of Oral Histories* (Columbia: University of South Carolina Press, 2004), 160–88.

22. George W. Zorsch, "1932 Report Covering Street Trades Enforcement," Rochester, New York Child Labor Committee, box 3, folder 9, 1 cited in Vincent DiGiorlamo, "The Newsboys' New Deal: Child Labor Reform and Imagery in the Great Depression," paper presented at the Society for the History of Children and Youth Conference, June 27, 2003, Baltimore, Md. For an overview of newsboys' history, see Vincent DiGiorlamo, "Crying the News: Children, Street Work and the American Press, 1830s–1920s," Ph.D. dissertation, Princeton University, 1997.

23. DiGiorlamo, "Newsboys' New Deal."

24. Frank DeMarco, "Being a Newsie," *Good Old Days* (November 1992), 35; T. Earl Sullenger, "The Newsboy as Juvenile Delinquent," *Journal of Juvenile Research,* vol. 15 (1931); all cited in DiGiorlamo, "Newsboys' New Deal," 3–4.

25. Ibid.

26. Edwin Emery and Michael Emery, *The Press and America* (Englewood Cliffs, N.J.: Prentice Hall, 1954; 6th ed. 1992), 535–536; William H. Young with Nancy K. Young, *The 1930s* (Westport, Conn.: Greenwood Press, 2002), 160.

27. U.S. Children's Bureau, "Children Engaged in Newspaper Selling and Delivery" (Washington, D.C.: Government Printing Office, 1935), CB pub. no. 227, 30–34; Todd Postal, "Creating the American Newspaper Boy: Middle-Class Route Service and Juvenile Salesmanship in the Great Depression," *Journal of Social History*, vol. 31, no. 2 (Winter 1997), 327–336.

28. "Report on the Bronx Home News Hearing" (November 13, 1933), New York Child Labor Committee Papers, box 33, folder 20, cited in DiGiorlamo, "Newsboys' New Deal," 12.

29. DiGiorlamo, "Newsboys' New Deal," 4–7.

30. Children's Bureau, "Children Engaged in Newspaper Selling and Delivery."

31. The National Child Labor Committee collected newspaper clippings on the strike: National Child Labor Committee Papers (NCLC Papers), box 64, Library of Congress, Manuscript Division, Washington, D.C. Data on the 1933 strike was gleaned from the 1933–1934 Minute Books compiled for the Pennsylvania Department of Labor and Industry, RG 16, box 2, Pennsylvania State Archives, Harrisburg, Pa.

32. Elliot Gorn, *Mother Jones: The Most Dangerous Woman in America* (New York: Hill and Wang, 2001), 131–138; C. K. McFarland, "Crusade for Child Laborers: Mother Jones and the March of the Mill Children," *Pennsylvania History*, 38 (July 1971), 283–296; Russell E. Smith, "The March of the Mill Children," *Social Science Review*, 41 (September 1967), 300–310; Stephen Currie, *We Have Marched Together: The Working Children's Crusade* (Minneapolis: Lerner Publications, 1997). Mary Harris Jones described the July 1903 march in *The Autobiography of Mother Jones,* chapter 10, first published by Charles Kerr in 1925 and available on the Internet at http://www.angelfire.com/nj3/RonMBaseman/mojones1.htm, accessed January 20, 2003. Kenneth C. Wolensky, "Child Labor in Pennsylvania" (Harrisburg: Pennsylvania Historical Museum Commission, 1998), Historic Leaflet No. 43. Pennsylvania State Library, Harrisburg, Pa.

33. Letter from Mary Harris Jones to Theodore Roosevelt, July 15, 1903, included in Philip Foner, ed., *Mother Jones Speaks* (New York: Monad Press, 1983), 555–556; Gorn, *Mother Jones*, 135.

34. McAhren, "Making the Nation Safe for Childhood," 5–6; U.S. Children's Bureau, "Child Labor Facts and Figures," Children's Bureau pub. no. 197 (Washington, D.C.: Government Printing Office, 1930). Gorn, *Mother Jones*, 139.

35. Currie, *We Have Marched Together*, 37; Gorn, *Mother Jones*, 132–134; Smith, "March of the Mill Children," 301–302; *New York Times*, July 10, 1903, 1, and July 12, 1903, 1; Trattner, *Crusade for the Children*, 171–172; Nettie P. McGill, "Children in Street Work," U.S. Children's Bureau pub. no. 183 (Washington, D.C.: Government Printing Office, 1928).

36. The Pennsylvania State Code includes specifics about each of these laws: Pennsylvania State Law Library, Harrisburg, Pa.; Wolensky, "Child Labor in Pennsylvania," 4.

37. Mac Parker, "Sweatshop Probe Hears of Hardships of 'Baby Strikers,'" *Philadelphia Record*, April 28, 1933, newspaper clipping in NCLC Papers, container 64, Library of Congress, Manuscript Collection, Washington, D.C.

38. "Doak Says Children Should Not Be Employed," *New York Times*, December (no date), 1932, NCLC Papers, box 64; U.S. Children's Bureau memorandum, "Effect of NRA codes on Child Labor," June 5, 1935, Children's Bureau Papers (CBP), RG 102, box 6, file 6; and "NRA Summary," typed report, CBP, RG 102, box 10, file 3.

39. Ibid.

40. Paul Comly French, "Children on Strike," *The Nation*, May 31, 1931, reprinted in New Deal Network, http://newdeal.feri.org/texts/238.htm, accessed July 26, 2004.

41. Parker, "Sweatshop Probe"; Dorothy Roe, "Forlorn Parade of Sweat-Shop Children Protests $1 Week Wages," *Winston-Salem Sentinel*, no date (but probably April 28 or 29, 1933), NCLC Papers, box 64; Mildred Sweeney is listed in the 1930 Census for Lehigh County, Pa., Sheet no. 29B; French, "Children on Strike."

42. Budd L. McKillips, "Sweatshop Conditions Force Children's Strike," *Toledo Leader*, April 28, 1933, NCLC Papers, box 64.

43. French, "Children on Strike."

44. French, "Children on Strike"; Parker, "Sweatshop Probe."

45. Minutes of the Industrial Board, Department of Labor and Industry, RG 16, "Meeting of the Industrial Board Meeting, Harrisburg, Pennsylvania, April 21, 1933," 75–76.

46. "Speeches," Cornelia Pinchot Papers, typed transcript of speech, no date, but probably delivered several times in April and May 1933, box 271, file "Speeches, 1933," Library of Congress, Manuscript Division, Washington, D.C.; "Mrs. Pinchot Joins March of Strikers," *Lorain Journal-Times Herald*, May 12, 1933, NCLC Papers, box 64.

47. Minutes of the Industrial Board, June 22, 1933, and July 12, 1933, "Employment of Minor under sixteen years of age where strikes are in progress,"

89–92, 109–110. The full regulation states: "The employment of minors under 16 years of age in an establishment where a strike or lockout is in progress is prohibited, except that this prohibition shall not apply to minors who were legally certificated to work in such establishment before the strike or lockout was declared." Rule M-38 of the Regulations Affecting the Employment of Minors.

48. "Allentown Strikers Given Wage Increase," *Philadelphia Inquirer,* April 25, 1933, microfilm, Library of Congress, Washington, D.C.

49. Hugh D. Hindman, *Child Labor: An American History* (New York: M. E. Sharpe, 2002), 6; Hawes, *Children's Rights Movement,* 39–53; Lindenmeyer, *"A Right to Childhood,"* 10–11, 111–118, 135–137; Sealander, *Failed Century,* 137–183.

50. "Labor Force by Age and Sex: 1890–1970," Series D 29–41, in *Historical Statistics of the United States,* 132; for a summary examining the economic and social reasons for the decline in child labor, see Carolyn Moehling, "State Child Labor Laws and the Decline of Child Labor," *Explorations in Economic History,* 36 (1999), 72–106.

51. Gertrude Folks Zimand, "The Changing Picture of Child Labor," in James H. S. Bossard and Eleanor S. Boll, eds., "Adolescents in Wartime," special issue of *Annals of the American Academy of Political and Social Science,* 236 (November 1944), 86.

Chapter 3. Transient Youth: On the Road to Nowhere?

1. Excerpts from an interview with Clarence Lee conducted in 1994 by Errol Lincoln Uys, cited in Errol Lincoln Uys, *Riding the Rails: Teenagers on the Move During the Great Depression* (New York: TV Books, 1999), 53–54; 132–135 and video excerpts of the interview with Lee are in *Riding the Rails,* by Michael Uys and Lexy Lovell (WGBH, Boston, 1998, American Experience Series); short video clip available at http://www.ridingtherails-themovie.com/video/clip22.html, accessed June 19, 2004. I was unable to find Clarence Lee in the 1930 Census.

2. Grace Palladino, *Teenagers: An American History* (New York: Basic Books, 1996), 16; Uys, *Riding the Rails,* 136.

3. Smith, "Number and Quality of Children," 368.

4. U.S. Census Bureau, "Educational Attainment by Sex: 1910–2002," *Statistical Abstract of the United States,* Mini Historical Statistic (Washington, D.C.:

Government Printing Office, 2003), 37, http://www.census.gov/statab/hist/ HS-22.pdf, accessed April 10, 2004; as noted in the preceding chapter, the Department of Labor did not calculate unemployment rates for the age cohort under sixteen.

5. Edwards, *Teenager's Fight to Survive,* 31.

6. Paul Popenoe, "When Youth Goes Radical," *Parents Magazine,* 15 (November 1940), 118, and Maxine Davis, *The Lost Generation* (New York: Macmillan, 1936), 4, both quoted in Olaf Stieglitz, " 'We may be losing this generation': Talking About Youth and the Nation's Future During the New Deal Era," in Norbert Finzsch and Hermann Wellenreuther, eds., *Visions of the Future in Germany and America* (New York: Oxford University Press, 2001), 403, 408–412.

7. Uys, *Riding the Rails,* 27–30; Thomas P. Minehan, *Boy and Girl Tramps of America* (New York: Farrar and Rinehart, 1934), 37–53; Palladino, *Teenagers,* 36.

8. I wish to thank Errol Lincoln Uys for generously sharing the letter he received from Harold Hoopes in 1994; Uys mentions Hoopes in *Riding the Rails,* 148; Hoopes is listed in the 1930 Census as living with his parents and five siblings in Paradise, Russell County, Kansas, on April 8, 1930; Hoopes's father's occupation is recorded as "general farmer," 1930 Census, page for Russell County, Kansas, Paradise County, sheet 4A.

9. Uys, *Riding the Rails,* 9–30; A. Wayne McMillen, "An Army of Boys on the Loose," *Survey Graphic* (September 1933), 389–392, 59; the 1930 Census lists eight-year-old Ina B. Máki living with her parents, three sisters, and two brothers in Atkin County, Minnesota, sheet 1A (April 11, 1930). Minehan, *Boy and Girl Tramps,* 37–53; Palladino, *Teenagers,* 36.

10. Errol Lincoln Uys, "Gene Wadsworth, Sequim, Washington," Interview, "Riding the Rails" website, http://ww.erroluys.com/GeneWadsworth.htm, accessed June 22, 2004; Uys, *Riding the Rails,* 32.

11. Edwards, *Teenager's Fight to Survive,* 42, 47; Westin, *Making Do,* 155; Stieglitz, "Youth During the New Deal Era," 411.

12. "Patrolman Ward Shot by Gang Dies," *New York Times,* May 7, 1934, 1, 3; "Gun on Parole Trapped by a Boy as Police Killers," *New York Times,* May 21, 1934, 1, 3.

13. Adam C. Richetti, "Kansas City Massacre—Charles Arthur 'Pretty Boy' Floyd" (Washington, D.C.: Federal Bureau of Investigation), http://www.fbi .gov/libref/historic/famcases/floyd/floyd.htm, accessed July 29, 2004; Bryan Burough, *Public Enemies: America's Greatest Crime Wave and the Birth of the*

FBI, 1933–34 (New York: Penguin Books, 2004). The nation's prison incarceration rate rose each year during the Great Depression, from 98 per 100,000 population in 1929 to 137 in 1939: U.S. Census Bureau, "Uncle Sam's Mini Historical Statistics, Federal and State Prisoners by Jurisdiction and Sex, 1925 to 2001," No. HS-24, http://www. census.gov/statab/hist/HS-24.pdf, accessed July 21, 2004. Rape is a very difficult crime to document since so many cases went unreported during the 1930s; the U.S. Justice Department reported only 79 rape convictions of juveniles in 1933; U.S. Census Bureau, "Juvenile Delinquents Received from Courts, 1933," No. 71, *Statistical Abstracts, 1940,* 80, http://www2.census.gov/prod2/statcomp/documents/1940-02.pdf, accessed July 21, 2004. The nation's homicide rate rose from 8.4 deaths per 100,000 residents in 1929 to 9.7 in 1933, but it is not clear if the fear of rising juvenile delinquency expressed in the popular press during the early 1930s was simply perception or reality: U.S. Census Bureau, "Homicides and Suicides: 1900–1970," *Historical Statistics of the United States, Bicentennial Edition* (Washington, D.C.: Government Printing Office, 1976), 414.

14. U.S. Bureau of Justice, "Bureau of Justice Statistics at a Glance, 2003: Number of Persons Executed in the United States, 1930–2004" (Washington, D.C.: Government Printing Office, 2004).

15. Stieglitz, "Youth During the New Deal Era," 408–411.

16. "White House Conference on Child Health and Protection Held in Washington, D.C., November 19–22, 1930," program, included in Herbert Hoover Presidential Papers, "Child Health Conference," box 97, Hoover Presidential Library (HPL), West Branch, Iowa; Maxine Davis, "200,000 Vagabond Children," *Ladies' Home Journal,* September 1932, 8–9, 46–48; "Wandering Boys Become a Social Problem in America," *New York Times Sunday Magazine,* October 23, 1932, 2.

17. Uys, *Riding the* Rails, 136.

18. Robert Francis Saxe, "Scottsboro Case," in McElvaine, *Encyclopedia of the Great Depression,* 870–872; Douglas O. Linder, "The Trials of the Scottsboro Boys," University of Missouri, Kansas City, Law School, http://www.law.umkc.edu/faculty/projects/FTrials/scottsboro/SB_acct.html, accessed March 3, 2003; biographies of each defendant are available on Linder's website: http://www.law.umkc.edu/faculty/projects/FTrials/scottsboro/scottsb.htm, accessed March 3, 2004.

19. Ibid.; for an overview of the media coverage of the case, see Dan T. Carter, *Scottsboro: A Tragedy of the American South* (Delanco, N.J.: Notable Trials Library, 2000).

20. *New York Times,* July 27, 1937, reprinted in Robert H. Bremner, et al., *Children and Youth in America: A Documentary History* (Cambridge, Mass.: Harvard University Press, 1971), III, 1007–1008. Despite the happy occasion upon their release in 1937, tragedy continued to follow two of these young men: Olen Montgomery was convicted of raping a black woman at knifepoint in 1940; Roy Wright killed his wife and committed suicide in 1959. Bremner, *Children and Youth,* 1008.

21. Saxe, "Scottsboro Case," 870–872; Linder, "Trials of the Scottsboro Boys," and Linder website.

22. Richard Reiman, *The New Deal and American Youth: Ideas and Ideals in a Depression Decade* (Athens: University of Georgia Press, 1992), 29.

23. A. Wayne McMillen, University of Chicago, "Relief for Unemployed Transients," cited in Uys, *Riding the Rails,* 13–16.

24. Kingsley Davis, *Youth in the Depression* (Chicago: University of Chicago Press, 1935), 8, 29.

25. John R. Burkhart, "Cleveland Studies Its Transient Boys," *Transient* (January 1936), 16, included in Bremner, *Children and Youth,* III, 1933–1973, Parts 1–4, 31.

26. A. Wayne McMillen, "An Army of Boys on the Loose," *Survey Graphic* (September 1933), 389–392; Lowell Ames Norris, "America's Homeless Army," *Scribner's Magazine* (May 1933), 316–317; Herman J. P. Schubert, *Twenty Thousand Transients—A One Year's Sample of Those Who Apply for Aid in a Northern City* (Buffalo, N.Y.: Emergency Relief Bureau, 1935), cited in Uys, *Riding the Rails,* 15–16.

27. Uys, *Riding the Rails,* 13–14.

28. Grace Abbott, "Relief for Unemployed Transients," Hearings held before a Subcommittee of the Committee on Manufacturers on S. 5121, United States Senate, 72nd Cong., 2d. sess. (Washington, D.C.: Government Printing Office, 1933), 23–35.

29. "Youth in the Depression," *Survey,* 1933, 67.

30. H. A. P. Smith to Frances Perkins, no date, ca. June 1934, U.S. Children's Bureau Papers, RG 102, National Archives, College Park, Md., cited in Palladino, *Teenagers,* 36.

31. Letter from J. Newton Cole to Herbert Hoover, February 13, 1933, and copy of Hoover's reply February 16, 1933, Presidential Papers of Herbert Hoover, box 99, folder "Children's Correspondence, 1931 June–Dec," HPL; 1930 Census, page for Campbell County, Kentucky, 3rd Ward, sheet 10-A.

32. *Wild Boys of the Road,* William Wellman, Director (Warner Bros., 1933); Stieglitz, "Youth During the New Deal Era," 415.

33. F.S.N., "America's Young Hobos," *New York Times,* September 22, 1933; interview with Robert Symmonds included in Uys, *Riding the Rails,* 265–266, Symmonds never lost his love of "hoboing," 268–269.

34. Born February 8, 1903, in Bird Island, Minn., Minehan grew up in the region and earned his B.A. from the University of Minnesota in 1924. In 1924–1925 he worked as a teacher in North Carolina. His graduate school records indicate that during the balance of the twenties he worked as "a freelance journalist." The 1930 Census shows that twenty-eight-year-old Minehan lived in St. Paul, Minn., with his Irish-born mother and "roomers." Minehan's occupation was listed as "author." He completed his M.A. in sociology in 1933, worked as an instructor at the university, and ran the school's federal student work-relief program funded through FERA. I want to thank archivist Karen Klinkenberg, University of Minnesota Archives, for sending me the biographical information on Minehan in an email message, June 18, 2004. Thomas Minehan is listed in the 1930 Census, St. Paul, Ramsey County, Minn., sheet No. 6B; in 1935 Minehan was named director of reeducation in the Minnesota State Department of Education. From 1945 to 1946 he was secretary to Democratic Congressman Frank Starkey of Minnesota. Minehan died of a heart attack in 1948 at his brother's home in Minneapolis, Donald Whisenhunt, "Introduction" to 1976 reprint of *Boy and Girl Tramps of America* (Seattle: University of Washington Press, 1976), xvi.

35. Minehan, *Boy and Girl Tramps,* xv; John Chamberlin, "America's Wild Children," *New York Times,* June 18, 1934; other reviews included *Books,* the *Survey,* the *New Republic,* and the *Christian Century.* See Whisenhunt, "Introduction," xi–xx.

36. Minehan, *Boy and Girl Tramps,* xii–xiii.

37. Ibid., Appendix, 253–262.

38. Ibid., 35, 49, 51.

39. Ibid., 49–53.

40. Ibid., 77–78.

41. Ibid., 141–142, 169.

42. Ibid., 162, 170.

43. Ibid., 245.

44. Ibid., 172; Davis, *Lost Generation,* 4, quoted in Stieglitz, "Youth During the New Deal Era," 414.

45. "Boy Held in Theft Wins Aid of Court," *New York Times,* May 7, 1934, 4.

46. Franklin Roosevelt, *The Public Papers and Addresses of Franklin Roosevelt, Volume II, The Year of Crisis: 1933* (New York: Random House, 1938), 80.

47. Traditionally high schools in the United States had eleven grades, so seventeen was accepted as the usual age at graduation; high schools increasingly added the twelfth year during the 1930s; Sealander, *Failed Century*, 158–161.

48. Leroy Donelley, ed., *The Donelley Collection of Presidential Executive Orders, Executive Orders, Proclamations, Memoranda Issued by President Franklin D. Roosevelt, 1933–1945,* http://www.conservativeusa.org/eo/fdroosevelt.htm.

49. American Youth Congress, "The Declaration of the Rights of Youth," July 4, 1936, Robert Cohen Personal Collection, reprinted on New Deal Network, New York University, http://newdeal.feri. org/students/ayc.htm, accessed December 5, 2004.

50. Ibid.

51. Robert Cohen, "Activist Impulses: Campus Radicalism in the 1930s," New Deal Network, New York University, http://newdeal.feri.org/students/essay03 .htm, accessed December 5, 2004.

52. U.S. Children's Bureau, "Statistics on Unemployed Youth," internal memo dated April 5, 1940, CBP, RG 102, box 929, file 6-1-3-0 (o).

Chapter 4. The Importance of Being Educated

1. Interview with Joe Penniger, Huntsville, North Carolina, Federal Writers' Project, 1936–1940, July 5, 1939, included in "American Life Histories: Manuscripts from the Federal Writers Project," Library of Congress, Washington, D.C., http://memory.loc.gov/ammem/wpaintro/wpahome.html, accessed July 6, 2004.

2. Before the late 1920s most public high schools ended with the eleventh grade, so the U.S. Census Bureau traditionally used age seventeen for counting the number of Americans earning high school diplomas; U.S. Census Bureau, "Educational Summary—Enrollment, Graduates, and Degrees: 1900 to 1998, and Projections 1999 and 2000, No. 1425" in *Statistical Abstract of the United States, 1999, Section 31, 20th Century Statistics* (Washington, D.C.: Government Printing Office, 1999), 876; "Educational Attainment by Sex, 1910–2002, No. HS-22" (Washington, D.C.: Government Printing Office, 2002), http://www.census.gov/statab/hist/HS-22.pdf, accessed July 23, 2004; "Summary Measures of the Educational Attainment of the Population 25 Years and Over, 2003, Table A" in *Educational Attainment in the United States, 2003* (Washington, D.C.: Government Printing Office, June 2004), 3, http://www.census.gov/prod/2004pubs/p20-550.pdf, accessed July 23, 2004; U.S. Census Bureau, "High School Graduates by Sex, 1870–1970," *Historical*

Statistics of the United States, Bicentennial Edition (Washington, D.C.: Government Printing Office, 1976), 379. As evidence of the continuing trend toward higher education, in 2003, 84.6 percent of Americans age 25 and over had earned at least a high school diploma and 27.2 percent of Americans held at least a four-year college degree.

3. On the shift in public attitudes toward schools, see Lynd, *Middletown in Transition*, 204–207. By the 1950s a teen who left school before receiving a high school diploma earned the negatively charged label "dropout." Sherman Dorn, *Creating the Dropout: An Institutional and Social History of School Failure* (Westport, Conn.: Praeger, 1996); John W. Harrington, "Survey Shows Rise of 'Consolidateds,'" *New York Times,* March 28, 1937.

4. Samuel Prince, "Grade School and Junior High at the 'H,'" included in Greenberg, *Hebrew National Orphan Home*, 181–182.

5. Interview conducted by the author with Hiroko Kamikawa Omata at her home in Millersville, Md., June 25, 2004, audiotape in author's possession; Omata also shared a typed autobiography of her memories. Hiroko Kamikawa Omata is recorded in the 1930 Census as living in Fresno, Calif., with her parents and six siblings, though she is incorrectly identified on the Census as a "son," Fresno County, sheet No. 23A.

6. The incident Schmitt recalls likely occurred in the 1920s, but some teachers still used this tactic during the 1930s. "Interview with Walter Schmitt," *Wessels Living History Farm,* http://www. livinghistoryfarm.org/movies/WalterSchmitt .htm, accessed January 30, 2005; Lawrence A. Cremin, *American Education: The Metropolitan Experience, 1876–1980* (New York: HarperCollins, 1988).

7. Sealander, *Failed Century*, 204–208.

8. Patrick Joseph Ryan, "Shaping Modern Youth: Social Policies and Growing Up Working Class in Industrial America, 1890–1945," Ph.D. dissertation, Case Western Reserve University, 1998, 256–327; Joseph F. Kett, *The Pursuit of Knowledge Under Difficulties: From Self-Improvement to Adult Education in America, 1750–1990* (Stanford: Stanford University Press, 1994), 248; Paula S. Fass, *Outside In: Minorities and the Transformation of American Education* (New York: Oxford University Press, 1989), 199; Jessica I. Elfenbein, *The Making of a Modern City: Philanthropy, Civic Culture, and the Baltimore YMCA* (Gainesville: University of Florida Press, 2001), 104.

9. Hiroko Kamikawa Omata interview.

10. Ibid. Hiroko Kamikawa Omata went on to Fresno State College in the fall of 1939, but the start of World War II interrupted her education when the War Relocation Authority ordered her entire family's incarceration in 1942.

11. Joseph F. Kett, *Rites of Passage: Adolescence in America, 1790 to the Present* (New York: Basic Books, 1977), 184–187; Fass, *Outside In,* 76–78.

12. Eleanor Roosevelt, "Good Citizenship: The Purpose of Education," *Pictorial Review,* April 1930, 94, 97, reprinted in "Selected Writings of Eleanor Roosevelt," *New Deal Network,* http://newdeal.feri.org/er/er19.htm, accessed February 23, 2004.

13. Joel Spring, *Educating the Consumer-Citizen: A History of the Marriage of Schools, Advertising, and the Media* (Mahwah, N.J.: Lawrence Erlbaum Associates, 2004), 80–94, 125–135; Thomas Hine, *The Rise and Fall of the American Teenager* (New York: Perennial Books, 2000), 197–219.

14. Joan Jacobs Brumberg, *The Body Project: An Intimate History of American Girls* (New York: Vintage Books, 1997), 47–48.

15. Roger Daniels, *Asian America: Chinese and Japanese in the United States Since 1850* (Seattle: University of Washington Press, 1988), 173–177.

16. Franklin Odo, *No Sword to Bury: Japanese Americans in Hawaii During World War II* (Philadelphia: Temple University Press, 2004), 75–90; Valerie Matsumoto, "Redefining Expectations: Nisei Women in the 1930s," *California History,* 73 (1994), 44–53.

17. Elfenbein, *Making of a Modern City,* 177.

18. Selma Berrol, "Immigrant Children at School, 1880–1940," included in Elliott West and Paula Petrik, *Small Worlds: Children and Adolescents in America, 1850–1950,* (Lawrence: University Press of Kansas, 1992), 42–60; Kamikawa interview.

19. "The Children's Charter," President Hoover's White House Conference on Child Health and Protection, November 19–21, 1930 (Washington, D.C.: Government Printing Office, 1930); Committee on the School Children, "Addresses and Abstracts of Committee Reports on the White House Conference on Child Health and Protection" (Washington, D.C.: Government Printing Office, 1930), both reprinted in Sol Cohen, ed., *Education in the United States: A Documentary History* (New York: Random House, 1974), IV, 2551–2555; Lindenmeyer, *"A Right to Childhood,"* 151–152.

20. In 1920, 22 percent of Americans had spent less than five years in school, and only 16.4 percent had completed at least four years of high school. In 1940 only 13.7 percent of Americans had spent less than five years in school, and 24.5 percent had completed at least four years of high school—approximately a 50 percent change over the span of a single generation. U.S. Census Bureau, "Educational Attainment by Sex, 1910–2002, No. HS-22," *Mini Historical*

Statistics (Washington, D.C.: Government Printing Office, 2003), http://www.census.gov/statab/hist/HS-22.pdf, accessed August 4, 2004.

21. "Chicago Teachers Demonstrate for Payment of Salaries, 1933," *New York Times,* April 16, 1933, reprinted in Bremner, *Children and Youth,* III, 1579–1582; U.S. Senate, "Federal Corporation in Unemployment Relief. Hearing Before a Subcommittee of the Committee on Manufacturers," 72nd Cong., 1st sess., May 9, 1932 (Washington, D.C.: Government Printing Office, 1932), 48–51, reprinted in Cohen, *Education in the United States,* IV, 2531–2534; "Teachers Stage Huge Parade to Protest Plight," *Chicago Tribune,* April 16, 1933, 4.

22. Sealander, *Failed Century,* 187–259.

23. Interview with Margaret Newton, Miami, Fla., December 14, 1938, and interview with " 'Mrs. Bennett,' wife of a shrimper," St. Augustine, Fla., Federal Writers' Project, 1936–1940, February 28, 1939, included in "American Life Histories," accessed June 2, 2004.

24. Fass, *Outside In,* 73–75; Lynd, *Middletown in Transition,* 204–207; and Sherman Dorn, *Creating the Dropout: An Institutional and Social History of School Failure* (Westport, Conn.: Praeger, 1996). It should be noted that the word "dropout" did not become popular until the 1950s.

25. At thirty-two years of age, Tilda Guy Kemplen entered a program designed for adults who had never earned a high school diploma but wanted to attend college. Over the next several years, the mother of two continued to take classes and at age thirty-seven earned a teaching degree from Cumberland College. Throughout her life Guy worked to expand educational opportunities for children in her rural community; Tilda Guy Kemplen, *From Roots to Roses: The Autobiography of Tilda Kemplen,* transcribed and edited by Nancy Herzberg (Athens: University of Georgia Press, 1992), 1, 4, 7–9, 11–15. Kemplen wrote that it took ten years for her to pay off the student loans she accumulated earning her teaching degree. In 1930, Campbell County, Tennessee, had only 25,827 residents, a population density of 584 persons per square mile; 1,289 sixteen- and seventeen-year-olds lived in the county, but only 616 reported that they were still attending school. Campbell County had only two high schools, one in La Follette and a smaller facility in Jacksboro; in 1940, 703 sixteen- and seventeen-year-olds were in school, and in 1950 there were 755 attending school (57 percent of the cohort); school graduation and attendance rates remain behind the national average in rural Tennessee to this day; U.S. Census Bureau, "U.S. Census Data for the Years 1930, 1940, and

1950: Sorted by County—Tennessee," Inter-University Consortium for Political and Social Research, http://fisher.lib.virginia.edu/cgi-local/censusbin/census/ cen.pl?year=930, accessed April 2, 2004.

26. Interview with Eve Hardison, East Durham, N.C., Federal Writers' Project, 1936–1940, August 23, 1938, included in "American Life Histories," accessed June 2, 2004.

27. Interview with Lusette Smith, East Durham, N.C., Federal Writers' Project, 1936–1940, August 23, 1938, included in "American Life Histories," accessed June 2, 2004.

28. A number of works discuss the transformation of ideas about poverty from a family circumstance to the sole responsibility of parents by the 1930s; for a concise and insightful summary see Ryan, "Shaping Modern Youth," 172–178.

29. Baker, *Growing Up,* 168, 181.

30. "Baltimore City College, 1839–1989," original document, Baltimore City College 150th Anniversary Collection, MSA SC 2067, Maryland State Archives, Annapolis, Md.; "Baltimore City College: A Capsule History," Baltimore City College website: http://baltimorecitycollege.org/cityhistory/history.htm, accessed, May 3, 2004.

31. Bremner, "Education," *Children and Youth,* 575.

32. *La Mesa Scout,* 1926 cited in Robert R. Alvarez, Jr., "The Lemon Grove Incident: The Nation's First Successful Desegregation Court Case," *Journal of San Diego History,* 32 (Spring 1986), 116–135, available online without page numbers at http://www.sandiegohistory.org/journal/86spring/lemongrove.htm, accessed May 2, 2004.

33. Alvarez, "Lemon Grove Incident," 1–2; interviews with some of the adults who were students at the time are included in the documentary film *The Lemon Grove Incident,* KPBS Television, San Diego, 1986, producer and writer Paul Espinosa, director Frank Christopher.

34. Marilyn Holt, *Indian Orphanages* (Lawrence: University Press of Kansas, 2001); Daniels, *Asian America.*

35. Alvarez, "Lemon Grove Incident"; Balderrama and Rodríguez, *Decade of Betrayal,* 32.

36. Alvarez, "Lemon Grove Incident"; Abraham Hoffman, *Unwanted Mexican-Americans in the Great Depression* (Tucson: University of Arizona Press, 1974), 39.

37. Superior Court of the State of California, San Diego County, Writ of Mandate, February 13, 1931, cited in Alvarez, "Lemon Grove Incident."

38. Alvarez, "Lemon Grove Incident," and interview included in *The Lemon Grove Incident* documentary.

39. Alvarez, "Lemon Grove Incident."

40. *Murray v. Pearson* cited in W. Edward Orser, "Neither Separate Nor Equal: Foreshadowing *Brown* in Baltimore County, 1935–1937," *Maryland Historical Magazine,* 92 (Spring 1997), 9.

41. U.S. Census Bureau, "U.S. Census Data for the Year 1930: Sorted by County—Maryland," Inter-University Consortium for Political and Social Research, http://fisher.lib.virginia.edu/cgi-local/censusbin/census/cen.pl?year=930, accessed April 2, 2004. I wish to thank my colleague Edward Orser for sharing his insights about this case; Orser, "Neither Separate Nor Equal," 5–35. Margaret Williams's words are taken from an interview conducted by Louis Diggs and transcribed in Louis S. Diggs, *In Our Voices* (Baltimore: Uptown Press, 1998), 61–63. Orser notes that during the early 1930s the city of Baltimore extended high school education to include a twelfth year at all of its secondary schools while the county operated only eleven grades. In response to the city's changed policy, in 1934 the county agreed to pay an additional senior-year tuition for black students attending high school in the city; but it did not provide a twelfth year for white students in all county high schools.

42. Orser, "Neither Separate Nor Equal," 11–12.

43. Louis Azrael, *Baltimore News-Post,* March 3, 1936, as cited in Orser, "Neither Separate Nor Equal," 18–19.

44. Orser, "Neither Separate Nor Equal," 20–23; Diggs, *In Our Voices,* 62; "Bars School to Negro," *New York Times,* May 27, 1937, 25. After graduation Lucille Scott worked in a white beauty shop, waited tables, and then took a job with Western Electric; Williams went on to nursing school and worked in various hospitals and public health facilities throughout her life.

45. Ibid.

46. Robert A. Tennert, Jr., *The Phoenix Indian School: Forced Assimilation in Arizona, 1891–1935* (Norman: University of Oklahoma Press, 1988), 112–205.

47. Transcript of joint interview with Lorenzo Mattwaoshshe and James Wabaunsee conducted by Marilyn Holt, included in Marilyn Holt, ed., *Model Ts, Pep Chapels, and a Wolf at the Door: Kansas Teenagers, 1900–1941* (Lawrence: University of Kansas Division of Continuing Education, 1994), 167–171; Lloyd New, "The Failure of National Policy: A Historical Analysis," in U.S. Congress, Senate, Committee on Labor and Public Welfare, Special Subcommittee on Indian Education, *Indian Education: A National Tragedy—A National Challenge,* 91st

Cong., 1st sess. (1969), Report No. 91–501 (Washington, D.C.: Government Printing Office, 1969), 152–156, reprinted in Bremner, *Children and Youth*, 1711–1714. See also in Bremner, "Educational Provision of the Indian Reorganization Act, 1934," 1714; and "The Johnson-O'Malley Act, 1934," 1715–1717.

48. I examined approximately 75 different school yearbooks in order to get a sense of the major topics featured in school publications; most of the volumes were published by schools located in either the Baltimore area or near Washington, D.C. I also accessed materials from Milwaukee area schools reprinted on the "Children in Urban America" website. This is not meant to be a scientific study, but the repetition of topics and formats observed in the books indicates the major themes shared by many high school publications of the time and agrees with Patrick Ryan's findings in his dissertation, "Shaping Modern Youth," 256–327. My interpretation has also been influenced by Glen Elder's work, in which he examined 540 issues of an Oakland high school newspaper in the 1930s; Elder, *Children of the Great Depression*, 142–145. The quotation in the paragraph is from the *June Bug*, Catonsville County, Maryland, Catonsville High School, Class of 1933, 4, 56, housed in the Maryland Department at the Enoch Pratt Library, Baltimore.

49. Bob Oetting, "Our Help Is Needed," and "The Depression," *The Mercury*, Riverside High School, Milwaukee, November 1, 1931; "Popping the Question," *The Scroll*, Washington High School, Milwaukee, February 15, 1933, all articles reprinted in "Children in Urban America," Milwaukee: Marquette University, http://xserver1.its.mu.edu/, accessed May 20, 2004.

50. *June Bug*, June 1932, 106.

51. Fass, *Outside In*, 79–111.

52. *Sidelights*, Towson High School, Towson, Md., 1939, 47, located in the Yearbook Collection, Maryland Department, Enoch Pratt Library, Baltimore.

53. Elder, *Children of the Great Depression*, 129, 144.

54. Letter from an unnamed girl to Eleanor Roosevelt, May 24, 1934, Dows, Iowa, and letter from an unnamed girl in Alliance, Ohio, December 5, 1934, both in Cohen, *Dear Mrs. Roosevelt*, 46, 48–49.

55. For example, see the Mississippi State Code for 1942, Sec. 6486, also listed in the current version of the state code under Sec. 37-11-39: "Any public high school fraternity, sorority, or secret society organization . . . is hereby declared to be inimical to public free schools and therefore unlawful."

56. John D. McKee, *Two Legs to Stand On* (New York: Appleton, 1955), 84–85.

57. Jack W. Berryman, "The Rise of Boys' Sports in the United States, 1900–1970," in Frank L. Smoll and Ronald E. Smith, ed., *Children and Youth*

in Sport: A Biopsychosocial Perspective (Madison, Wisc.: Brown and Benchmark, 1996); Elliott Gorn and Warren Goldstein, *A Brief History of American Sports* (New York: Hill and Wang, 1993); Natalie Guice Adams and Pamela J. Bettis, *Cheerleader! Cheerleader!: An American Icon* (New York: Palgrave Macmillan, 2003), 4; Janice A. Beran, *From Six on Six to Full-Court Press: A Century of Iowa's Girls' Basketball* (Ames: Iowa State University Press, 1993); and H. G. Bissinger, *Friday Night Lights: A Town, a Team, and a Dream* (New York: Da Capo Press, 2000). School yearbooks provide a good indicator of participation in and the importance of team sports.

58. Ryan, "Shaping Modern Youth," 256–327.

59. Ralph G. Marshall, "Wolf at the Door," in Ralph G. Marshall, *Autobiography* [1934] (Bard, Calif.: the author, 1988), section reprinted in Holt, *Model Ts,* 189.

60. Simon Martinez, "Life Outside the Barrio: Simon Martinez Interview [1939–1941]," in Holt, *Model Ts,* 235.

61. Lynd, *Middletown in Transition,* 205–208.

62. Letter from M.L.A. to Eleanor Roosevelt, included in Cohen, *Dear Mrs. Roosevelt,* 99; see also letters on pages 97–107.

63. Interview with Robert Omata, conducted by the author in Millersville, Md., June 25, 2004, audiotape in author's possession. It should be noted that Omata was forced to quit college in 1942 when he and 120,000 other Americans of Japanese descent were ordered to War Relocation Authority camps. Omata was sent to the Gila River Relocation Center and was finally able to complete his doctorate in 1949 at the University of Minnesota. Interview with Agnes Harrell, transcription by Annie Ruth Davis, Federal Writers' Project, 1936–1940, February 24, 1939, included in "American Life Histories," accessed July 19, 2004.

64. "500 Pupils and Teachers Are Killed in Explosion of Gas in Texas School; 100 Injured Taken from the Debris," *New York Times,* March 19, 1937; "Economy Traced as Blast Factor," *New York Times,* March 21, 1937; "Survey Shows Rise of 'Consolidates,'" *New York Times,* March 28, 1937.

65. Ronald D. Cohen, *Children of the Mill: Schooling and Society in Gary, Indiana, 1906–1960* (New York: Routledge Falmer, 2002), 154–155.

66. Howard K. Beale, *A History of the Freedom of Teaching in American Schools* (New York: Octagon Books, 1966), 78–156, 264–276.

67. Sealander, *Failed Century,* 205; U.S. Census Bureau, "School Retention Rates—Fifth Grade Through College Entrance: 1924–1932 to 1962–1970," *Historical Statistics of the United States, Bicentennial Edition* (Washington,

D.C.: Government Printing Office, 1976), 379; and in the same volume, "Kindergarten, Elementary, and Secondary Schools and Enrollment: 1870–1970," 368. On the complexities of expanding public education in the context of race and Progressive reform, see Mary S. Hoffschwelle, *Rebuilding the Rural Southern Community: Reformers, Schools, and Homes in Tennessee, 1900–1930* (Knoxville: University of Tennessee Press, 1998).

Chapter 5. Players and Consumers in Popular Culture

1. John Smith Barney, *Porter Township* (Urbana, Ohio: Rotabar, 1988), 34; Ralph Luedtke, "Childhood Memories," included in "Children in Urban America," accessed December 10, 2004; Gerald Nachman, *Raised on Radio: In Quest of the Lone Ranger . . .* (Berkeley: University of California Press, 2000), 181–194.

2. William H. Young with Nancy K. Young, *The 1930s* (Westport, Conn.: Greenwood Press, 2002), 34; Mintz, *Huck's Raft,* 251.

3. Richard deCordova, "Child-Rearing Advice and the Moral Regulation of Children's Movie Going," *Quarterly Review of Film and Video,* 15 (1995), 99–109; Bruce Lenthall, "Critical Reception: Public Intellectuals Decry Depression-Era Radio, Mass Culture, and Propaganda," 41–62; and Matthew Murray, "The Tendency to Deprave and Corrupt Morals: Regulation and Irregular Sexuality in Golden Age Radio Comedy," both in Michele Hilmes and Jason Loviglio, eds., *Essays in the Cultural History of Radio* (New York: Routledge, 2001), 135–156.

4. Young and Young, *The 1930s,* 236.

5. Spring, *Educating the Consumer-Citizen,* 107–110; Peter N. Stearns, *Anxious Parents: A History of Modern Childrearing in America* (New York: New York University Press, 2003), 179.

6. Interview with John Healey, wife and son, Lynn, Mass., Federal Writers' Project, 1936–1940, February 28, 1939, included in "American Life Histories," accessed May 10, 2004.

7. Letter from Mr. Grant, New York, N.Y., August 8, 1932, included in U.S. Children's Bureau Papers, box 389, file 4-12-7-1-4, RG 102, 1929–1932, National Archives and Records Administration, College Park, Md.

8. Spring, *Educating the Consumer-Citizen,* 119; Clara Savage Littledale, "Better Radio Programs for Children," *Parents Magazine,* vol. 18, no. 13 (May 8, 1933); Sidonie Matsner Gruenberg, "Radio and the Child," *Annals of the American Academy of Political and Social Science,* 177 (January 1935), 123–128.

9. Stearns, *Anxious Parents,* 177–178. William Paley, "Radio as a Cultural Force": these notes on the economic and social philosophy of America's radio industry, as represented by the policies and practices of the Columbia Broadcasting System, were embodied in a talk on October 17, 1934, before the Federal Communications Commission, in its inquiry into proposals to allot fixed percentages of the nation's radio facilities to non-commercial broadcasting; located in CBS Reference Library, New York, N.Y., 8–9, as quoted in Spring, *Educating the Consumer-Citizen,* 116–117, see also pages 118–124.

10. "New Policies: A Statement to the Public, to Advertisers, and to the Advertising Agencies," May 15, 1935, CBS Reference Library, 4, quoted in Spring, *Educating the Consumer-Citizen,* 122–123.

11. Spring, *Educating the Consumer-Citizen,* 107–110; W. W. Charters, *Motion Pictures and Youth: A Summary* (New York: Macmillan, 1933), 12–13; Lary May, *Screening Out the Past: The Birth of Mass Culture and the Motion Picture Industry* (New York: Oxford University Press, 1980), 203.

12. The U.S. Censuses of 1930 and 1940 include information about radio ownership; Steve Craig, "How America Adopted Radio: Differences in Set Ownership Patterns Reported in the 1930, 1940, and 1950 U.S. Censuses," Department of Radio, Television and Film, University of North Texas, 2003, http://www.rtvf.unt.edu/people/craig/pdfs/adopt.pdf, accessed January 20, 2005.

13. Ibid., 7; Christopher H. Sterling and John M. Kittross, *Stay Tuned: A Concise History of American Broadcasting,* 2nd ed. (Belmont, Calif.: Wadsworth, 1990); Young and Young, *The 1930s,* 207–216; T. H. Watkins, *The Hungry Years: America in an Age of Crisis, 1929–1939* (New York: Henry Holt, 1999), 254–255.

14. Davega-City Radio Stores advertisement, published in the *New York Times,* 1932 (image no. R0378) and Westinghouse radio advertisement, published in *Maclean's Magazine,* 1934 (image no. R0603), available online at the John W. Hartman Center for Sales, Advertising and Marketing History, Rare Book and Manuscript Center, Duke University Library, http://scriptorium.lib.duke.edu/hartman/, accessed October 12, 2004.

15. Christopher H. Sterling and Michael Keith, eds., *The Encyclopedia of Radio* (New York: Fitz Roy Dearborn Publishers, Routledge, 2003) 316–323.

16. The RadioLovers.com website includes hundreds of hours of radio programs from the 1930s, Bored.com network, http://www.radiolovers.com/. For a good summary of children's hour shows, see Young and Young, *The 1930s,* 28–31; on *Little Orphan Annie* and other 1930s programs for children, see the

Radio Hall of Fame, 400 N. State St., Chicago, http://www.radiohof.org/adventuredrama/littleannie.html, and the organization's publication. Sterling and Keith, *Encyclopedia of Radio,* see especially 299–300, 678–679, 878–879; and Young and Young, *The 1930s,* 47.

17. Erica Scharrer, "Children's Programs," in Sterling and Keith, *Encyclopedia of Radio*, 318–320.

18. Ibid., *War of the Worlds,* 318–320; Hadley Cantril, *The Invasion from Mars: A Study in the Psychology of Panic, with the Complete Script of the Famous Orson Welles Broadcast* (Princeton: Princeton University Press, 1940).

19. Young and Young, *The 1930s,* xviii, 30–31.

20. Melvin Patrick Ely, *The Adventures of Amos and Andy: A Social History of an American Phenomenon* (Charlottesville: University of Virginia Press, 2001; originally published by Free Press, 1991).

21. Letter from M.N.C., Greary, Okla., to Eleanor Roosevelt, April 20, 1935, reprinted in Cohen, *Dear Mrs. Roosevelt,* 183.

22. Jean Lobe, "Simple as Child's Play: Memories of 1930s Pastimes," May 1, 2001, "Children in Urban America," accessed December 10, 2004; Andrew Bergman, *We're in the Money: Depression America and Its Films* (New York: Harper & Row, 1971).

23. Colin Schindler, *Hollywood in Crisis: Cinema and American Society* (New York: Routledge, 1996), 4–20.

24. Schindler, *Hollywood in Crisis,* 64–65, 105; Spring, *Educating the Consumer-Citizen,* 108–114.

25. McElvaine, "Snow White and the Seven Dwarfs," in McElvaine, *Encyclopedia of the Great Depression*, II, 892–893.

26. Young and Young, *The 1930s,* 187.

27. Ibid.; Billy Graebner, "Date Dope," *The Mercury,* Riverside High School, Milwaukee, December 2, 1938, reprinted in "Children in Urban America," accessed December 21, 2004; interview with Walter Schmitt, Wessels Living History Farm, York, Nebr., http://www.livinghistoryfarm.org/farminginthe30s/life_16.html, accessed January 3, 2005.

28. Letter from W.C., Chicago, to Eleanor Roosevelt, acknowledged November 13, 1935, reprinted in Cohen, *Dear Mrs. Roosevelt,* 188.

29. Young and Young, *The 1930s,* 203–204; Gary Cross, *The Cute and the Cool: Wondrous Innocence and Modern American Children's Culture* (New York: Oxford University Press, 2004), 128–129, 172, 194; National Academy of Motion Picture Arts and Sciences, "Awards Database," Special Award, Shirley Tem-

ple, 1934, http://awardsdatabase.oscars.org/ampas_awards/DisplayMain.jsp?
curTime=1101585939519, accessed October 12, 2004.

30. Cross, *The Cute and the Cool*, 63, 128; Diana Cary, *Jackie Coogan, the World's Boy King: A Biography of Hollywood's Legendary Child Star* (Lanham, Md.: Scarecrow Press, 2002); Rob King, "The Kid from the Kid: Jackie Coogan and the Consolidation of Child Consumerism," *Velvet Light Trap*, 48 (Fall 2001), 4–19; Diana Cary, *Hollywood's Children: An Inside Account of the Child Star* (Fort Worth: Southern Methodist University Press, 1997), 91, 94, 131–134; Paramount Studios' 1930 *Tom Sawyer* was the year's highest-grossing film; information on movie release dates and box office data, Bruce Nash, *The Numbers,* 1997–2004, http://www.the-numbers.com/movies/index.html, accessed December 12, 2004.

31. Mintz, *Huck's Raft,* 250–251; Norman J. Zierold, *The Child Stars* (New York: Coward-McCann, 1965).

32. The *Little Rascals* were also known as *Our Gang;* Leonard Maltin and Richard W. Bann, *Our Gang: The Life and Times of the Little Rascals* (New York: Crown, 1977); Dan Steibel, "Itinerant Filmmakers and Amateur Casts: A Homemade Our Gang, 1926," *Film History* (Australia), 15 (2003), 177–192. The best website on the *Little Rascals* series is Thomas Staedeli, *Little Rascals,* located at http://www.cyranos.ch/ourg-e.htm, accessed November 12, 2004. Coogan also appeared in several *Little Rascals* shorts during the 1920s; Maltin and Bann, *Our Gang*; Steibel, "Itinerant Filmmakers," 177–192. I also gathered information on the *Little Rascals* by watching shorts and from Thomas Staedeli's website, located at http://www.cyranos.ch/ourg-e.htm.

33. Mintz, *Huck's Raft,* 249.

34. Young and Young, *The 1930s,* 202–203; Mintz, *Huck's Raft,* 249.

35. John Baxter, *Hollywood in the Thirties* (New York: A. S. Barnes, 1968), provides a good overview of 1930s film themes; see also Bradford W. Wright, "Hollywood and the Film Industry," in McElvaine, *Encyclopedia of the Great Depression*, I, 448–452.

36. Cary, *Hollywood's Children*, 240–241.

37. Gail Murray, *American Children's Literature and the Construction of Childhood* (New York: Twayne Publishers, 1998), 147; Cross, *The Cute and the Cool,* 134–147.

38. Murray, *American Children's Literature,* 151–152.

39. Marjorie Kinnan Rawlings, *The Yearling* (New York: Scribner's, 1938); Charles Poore, "Books of the Times," *New York Times,* April 1, 1938.

40. Murray, *American Children's Literature*, 160–164; Young and Young, *The 1930s*, 31–32; Nancy Rost Goulden and Susan Stanfield, "Leaving Elsie Dinsmore Behind: 'Plucky Girls' as an Alternative Role Model in Classic Girl's Literature," *Women's Studies*, 32 (March 2003), 183–208.

41. Peter A. Soderbergh, "Bibliographical Essay: The Negro in Juvenile Literature Series Books, 1899–1930," *Journal of Negro History*, 58 (April 1973), 179–186.

42. "American Comic Strips," *Fact Monster* (New York: Pearson Education, 2000), http://www.factmonster.com/ce6/ent/A0857472.html, accessed December 12, 2004; Young and Young, *The 1930s*, 269–274; Cross, *The Cute and the Cool*, 128–134.

43. Hastings, *A Nickel's Worth of Skim Milk*, 100.

44. Bradford W. Wright, *Comic Book Nation: The Transformation of Youth Culture in America* (Baltimore: Johns Hopkins University Press, 2001), 1–29; William M. Tuttle, Jr., "The Homefront in Children's Popular Culture: Radio, Movies, Comics—Adventure, Patriotism, and Sex-typing," in West and Petrik, *Small Worlds*, 143–164.

45. Ibid.; Brian Walker, *The Comics Before 1945* (New York: Harry N. Abrams, 2004). Some critics began to complain about newspaper comic strips as a poor influence on children as early as the first decade of the twentieth century, but 1930s comic books seemed to have escaped the radar of most critics. Stearns, *Anxious Parents*, 169.

46. Hastings, *A Nickel's Worth of Skim Milk*, 83.

47. I wish to thank Doris Lindenmeyer, my stepmother, for reminding me that mothers and grandmothers made most of the clothing for dolls. My mother, Rebecca Lynne, told me about the many paper dolls she and her sister made during the 1930s. Other women I have talked to and read about confirm that they had the same experiences playing with dolls during the Great Depression. On girls and doll play, see Miriam Formanck-Brunell, *Made to Play House: Dolls and the Commercialization of American Girlhood, 1830–1930* (Baltimore: Johns Hopkins University Press, 1998).

48. On children's games, see Kathryn Grover, ed., *Hard at Play: Leisure in America, 1840–1940* (Amherst: University of Massachusetts Press, 1992), 227–250; Gary Soto, ed., *California Childhood, Floyd Salas* (Berkeley, Calif.: Creative Arts, 1988), 10–17.

49. Lisa Jacobson, "Revitalizing the American Home: Children's Leisure and the Revaluation of Play, 1920–1940," *Journal of Social History*, 30 (March 1, 1937), 582–596; Young and Young, *The 1930s*, 124–133.

50. Posluzny was much luckier than the young female performer Gladys Cote who was working on stage with Ruthie. The lion seriously injured Cote's left arm, breast, right thigh, and back; she died three days later from a gangrene infection resulting from her injuries. Frederick N. Rasmussen, "Baltimore's Wild History of Animal Attacks," *Baltimore Sun* (October 11, 2003).

51. Drowning-death statistics from reports written by Robert Moses about the New York City WPA program, quoted on "Everything About a Pool: The McCarren Park Pool," *The Next Big Thing,* radio broadcast aired July 4, 2003, http://www.nextbigthing.org/archive/episode.html?07042003, accessed January 23, 2005.

52. Mark A. McCloskey, "For City Children at Play, Variety Is the Spice of Life," *New York Times,* April 9, 1939.

53. Hastings, *A Nickel's Worth of Skim Milk,* 84–85; interview with Hiroko Kamikawa Omata.

54. Young and Young, *The 1930s,* 169–175; Geoffrey C. Ward and Ken Burns, *Jazz: A History of America's Music* (New York: Alfred A. Knopf, 2000), and the accompanying video series, *Jazz,* episodes 4, 5, and 6, Sony Productions, 2000; David Suisman, "Co-workers in the Kingdom of Culture: Black Swan Records and the Political Economy of African American Music," *Journal of American History,* 90 (March 2004), 1295–1324.

55. Young and Young, *The 1930s,* 169–175.

56. "Coney Island and Moonlight Gardens" in Geoffrey J. Giglierano, et al., *Bicentennial Guide to Cincinnati. A Portrait of Two Hundred Years* (Cincinnati: Cincinnati Historical Society, 1989).

57. Ward and Burns, *Jazz,* and accompanying video series, episodes 5 and 6.

58. Ibid.

59. Molly Knight and Frederick N. Rasmussen, "Hippodrome Kept Them on the Move," *Baltimore Sun,* February 7, 2004, 1D-2D.

60. Letter from Ethel Rush, Elsinore, Calif., August 22, 1931, and response from Ella Oppenheimer, M.D., September 4, 1931, included in U.S. Children's Bureau Papers, box 389, file 4-12-7-1-4, RG 102, 1929–1932, National Archives and Records Administration, College Park, Md.

61. Young and Young, *The 1930s,* 32–33; "Big Camp Houses 2,000 Boy Scouts," *New York Times,* July 12, 1936; Valerie Matsumoto, "Redefining Expectations: Nisei Women in the 1930s," *California History,* 73 (1994), 44–53, and presentation at "Resourceful Women: Researching and Interpreting American Women's History," held at the Library of Congress in Washington, D.C.,

June 19–20, 2003; a recorded version is available at http://www.loc.gov/rr/ women/awprogram.html.

62. Beth L. Bailey, *From Front Porch to Back Seat: Courtship in Twentieth-Century America* (Baltimore: Johns Hopkins University Press, 1988), 31, 60–62.

63. Mary McComb, "Rate Your Date: Young Women and the Commodification of Depression-Era Courtship," in Sherrie Innes, *Delinquents and Debutantes: Twentieth-Century American Girls' Cultures* (New York: New York University Press, 1998), 45.

64. Bailey, *From Front Porch to Back Seat*, 27–28, 34, 42; Palladino, *Teenagers*, 22–30; interview with "Ed and Mary Jackson, Chapel Hill, North Carolina," Federal Writers' Project, 1936–1940, September 27, 1938, included in "American Life Histories," accessed January 26, 2005; Champlin, *Back There Where the Past Was*, 177; Clausen, *American Lives*, 422.

65. Clausen, *American Lives*, 398–399.

66. On the increasing condemnation of homosexuality, see John Donald Gustav-Wrathall, *Take the Young Stranger by the Hand: Same Sex Relations and the YMCA* (Chicago: University of Chicago Press, 1998).

67. Enid Severy Smith, *A Study of Twenty-five Adolescent Unmarried Mothers in New York City* (New York: Salvation Army Women's Home and Hospital, 1935), 47–48, quoted in Palladino, *Teenagers*, 31.

68. Elizabeth Toon and Janet Golden, " 'Live Clean, Think Clean, and Don't Go to Burlesque Shows': Charles Atlas as Health Advisor," *Journal of the History of Medicine and Allied Sciences*, 57 (January 2002), 39–60; Charles Atlas website, http://www.charlesatlas.com/, accessed December 12, 2003.

69. On the development of commercial cosmetics in America, see Kathy Peiss, *Hope in a Jar: The Making of America's Beauty Culture* (New York: Metropolitan Books, 1998); Mimi Minnick, "History/Biography: Break Girls Collection ca. 1936–1995," National Museum of American History Archives, Smithsonian Institution, RG 651, Washington, D.C., 1998, also available online at: http://americanhistory.si.edu/archives/d7651.htm, accessed December 10, 2004.

70. Brumberg, *The Body Project*, 101, 108–109.

71. Ibid., 75.

72. Ibid., 109–110; Jockey Company Corporate History, http://www.jockey.com/ en-US/CorporateInfo/History/ history1935.htm, accessed February 3, 2005.

73. Brumberg, *The Body Project*, 44–48, 108–109; Palladino, *Teenagers*, 31–32.

74. Letter from A.C. to Eleanor Roosevelt, Port Morris, N.J., March 20, 1934, quoted in Cohen, *Dear Mrs. Roosevelt*, 23.

75. McKee, *Two Legs to Stand On,* 84–85.
76. "Author of 'Penrod and Sam' Declares Modern Little Boys Are 'Wise Guys,'" *Milwaukee Sentinel,* November 11, 1937, reprinted in "Children in Urban America," accessed May 20, 2004.

Chapter 6. Uncle Sam's Children

1. Rural Electrification Administration, "Power and the Land," 1940; William and Hazel Parkinson and their five children appear in the 1930 Census, Belmont County, Ohio, April 2, 1930, sheet 2A; Rose Dudley Scearce, "What REA Service Means to Our Farm Home," *Rural Electrification NEWS,* March 1939, Carmody Papers, Franklin D. Roosevelt Library, Hyde Park, N.Y., included in http://newdeal. feri.org/texts/185.htm, accessed December, 12, 2004.
2. *Mr. Smith Goes to Washington,* Frank Capra, director (Columbia Pictures, 1939).
3. Roosevelt, *Public Papers and Addresses,* II, 80.
4. Sealander, *Failed Century,* 156–162.
5. Ibid., 158–161.
6. Joyce L. Kornbluh, "The She-She-She Camps: An Experiment in Living and Learning, 1934–1937," included in Joyce L. Kornbluh and Mary Frederickson, eds., *Sisterhood and Solidarity: Workers' Education for Women, 1914–1984* (Philadelphia: Temple University Press, 1984), 254–274.
7. Stieglitz, "Talking About Youth," 416–418.
8. Sealander, *Failed Century,* 156–158.
9. Luther C. Wandall, "A Negro in the CCC," *Crisis,* August 1935, 244, 253–254, included in New Deal Network, http://newdeal.feri.org/aaccc/aaccc01.htm, accessed November 24, 2004; "CCC Youth Refuses to Fan Flies Off Officer; Is Fired," *Norfolk Journal and Guide,* January 13, 1934, included in New Deal Network, http://newdeal.feri.org/aaccc/aaccc02.htm, accessed February 6, 2005.
10. Wandall, "A Negro in the CCC."
11. Scalander, *Failed Century,* 160–162.
12. "Selection of Enrollees for the Civilian Conservation Corps," First Biennial Report of the Utah State Department of Public Welfare, 1936–1938, Papers of the Civilian Conservation Corps, RG 35, folder, "Division of Selection, State Procedural Records (Utah)," 1938, NARA, Washington, D.C., included in New Deal Network, http://newdeal.feri.org/texts/302.htm, accessed February 10, 2004.

13. David M. Kennedy, *Freedom from Fear: The American People in Depression and War, 1929–1945* (New York: Oxford University Press, 1999), 144–148.

14. National Association of Civilian Conservation Corps Alumni, http://www.cccalumni.org/, accessed February 1, 2004; Helen Walker, *The CCC Through the Eyes of 272 Boys: A Summary of a Group Study of the Reactions of 272 Cleveland Boys to Their Experiences in the Civilian Conservation Corps* (Cleveland, Ohio, 1938), cited by Sealander, *Failed Century*, 159–160.

15. Gilbert Dick was my father-in-law. Minehan, *Boy and Girl Tramps of America*, 166; interview with Agnes Harrell, transcription by Annie Ruth Davis, Federal Writers' Project, 1936–1940, February 24, 1939, included in "American Life Histories," accessed July 19, 2004.

16. Leslie Lacy, *The Soil Soldiers: The Civilian Conservation Corps in the Great Depression* (Radnor, Pa.: Chilton, 1976), 94–138; John A. Salmond, *The Civilian Conservation Corps, 1933–1942: A New Deal Case Study* (Durham, N.C.: Duke University Press, 1967).

17. *Public Papers and Addresses of Franklin D. Roosevelt,* "Executive Order No. 7086, June 26, 1935," reprinted in Bremner, *Children and Youth*, 77.

18. Reiman, *New Deal and American Youth.*

19. Ibid.; Leuchtenburg, *Franklin D. Roosevelt and the New Deal,* 129; Palladino, *Teenagers,* 39–44; Betty and Ernest K. Lindley, *A New Deal for Youth: The Story of the National Youth Administration* (New York: Viking Press, 1938), 7; Palladino, *Teenagers,* 40–43.

20. Quotation included in Fass, *Outside In,* 128–134.

21. Quotation included in Palladino, *Teenagers,* 38; Glen Van Gundy is probably the same "Glen Vangundy" counted in the 1930 Census as a thirteen-year-old living with his parents, two sisters, and three brothers in Des Moines, Iowa, "Fifteenth Census," Polk County, April 21, 1930, sheet 3B.

22. Letter from F.D.H., Pittsburgh, Pa., to Eleanor Roosevelt, December 1, 1937, reprinted in Cohen, *Dear Mrs. Roosevelt,* 158.

23. Sarah Elizabeth Bundy, "A Sidelight on the NYA," *The Survey,* 73 (August 1937), 252.

24. American Youth Congress, "The Declaration of the Rights of Youth," July 4, 1936, Robert Cohen Personal Collection, reprinted on New Deal Network, http://newdeal.feri.org/students/ayc.htm, accessed December 5, 2004.

25. U.S. Census Bureau, "Education Summary—Enrollment, Graduates, and Degrees: 1900 to 1998, and Projections 1999 and 2000," No. 1425 in *Statistical Abstract of the United States, 20th Century Statistics* (Washington, D.C.: Government Printing Office, 1999), 876; *U.S. Census Bureau, Statistical Abstract*

of the United States, 2001–2005, "Education: High School Dropouts by Race and Hispanic Origin, 1975–1999," no. 257, 162, http://www.census.gov/prod/2002pubs/01statab/educ.pdf, accessed February 15, 2005.

26. Sealander, *Failed Century,* 234; Sonya Michel, *Children's Interests/Mother's Rights: The Shaping of America's Child Care Policy* (New Haven, Conn.: Yale University Press, 1999), 57–92.

27. Ann Hulbert, *Raising America: Experts, Parents, and a Century of Advice About Children* (New York: Vintage Books, 2004), 108; M. W. Zapoleon and L. M. Stolz, "Helen Bradford Thompson Wolley," in Paul Boyers, et al., eds., *Notable American Women 1607–1950: A Biographical Dictionary* (Cambridge, Mass.: Belknap Press of Harvard University Press, 1971), 658–659.

28. Edna Ewing Kelley, "Uncle Sam's Nursery Schools," *Parents Magazine,* March 1936, 24–25, 48–49, reprinted in Bremner, *Children and Youth,* III, 679; Michel, *Children's Interests,* 118–119, 127–128; and Rose, *A Mother's Job,* 144–152; and Susan Ware, *Holding Their Own: American Women in the 1930s* (Boston: Twayne Publishers, 1982), 27.

29. J. Christopher Schnell, "Works Progress Administration," in McElvaine, *Encyclopedia of the Great Depression,* II, 1063–1066; Joseph M. Hawes, *Between the Wars: American Childhood 1920–1940* (New York: Twayne Publishers, 1997); New Louisiana Division of the New Orleans Public Library, "Children of the WPA—Education," http://nutrias.org/~nopl/exhibits/wpakids/nursery .htm, accessed January 5, 2005.

30. Rose, *A Mother's Job,* 182–188.

31. Leuchtenburg, *Franklin D. Roosevelt and the New Deal,* 120–123.

32. Ibid., 124–128; Debbie Elliot interview with Kathryn Tucker Windham, web feature related to radio broadcast of "The Women of Gee's Bend," broadcast on NPR "All Things Considered," November 28, 2004, http://www.npr.org/templates/story/story. php?storyId=4184856, accessed November 28, 2004.

33. Fass, *Outside In,* 117–123.

34. Federal Works Agency, *Final Report of the WPA Program, 1935–1943* (Washington, D.C.: Government Printing Office, 1946).

35. Elfenbein, *Making of a Modern City,* 117.

36. Steven A. Riess, "Sports," in McElvaine, *Encyclopedia of the Great Depression,* II, 925–926.

37. Drowning-death statistics from reports written by Robert Moses, New York City Park Department Commissioner, about the New York City WPA program, included in "Everything About a Pool: The McCarren Park Pool," *The Next Big Thing,* radio broadcast aired July 4, 2003; the http://www

.nextbigthing.org/archive/episode.html?07042003, accessed January 23, 2005. Articles in the *New York Times* about the pools include "$1,000,000 City Pool Opens Wednesday," June 21, 1936; "The Swimming Pools," July 11, 1936; "New Swimming Pool Will Open Tomorrow," August 7, 1936.

38. Ibid.; Alan Kniberg changed his name to Alan King when he entered show business as a comedian in his late teens.

39. "700 WPA Men Act as School Police," *New York Times*, June 10, 1937.

40. Grace Abbott, "How Have Children Fared as a Whole? The Chief of the Children's Bureau Deals with These Questions," *New York Times,* December, 1932; Grace Abbott, *From Relief to Social Security* (Chicago: University of Chicago Press, 1941), 161–197; U.S. Children's Bureau, "Effects of the Depression on Child Health and Child Health Services," *Congressional Record,* 72d Cong., 1st sess., 3095–3099.

41. U.S. Children's Bureau, Annual Report of the Chief (1931), 121; Martha M. Eliot, M.D., "Child Health Recovery Program," unpublished report, May 1934, Records of the Committee on Economic Security (CESP), National Archives, RG 47, box 5, file "Misc."

42. Grace Abbott, "What About Mothers' Pensions Now?" *Survey,* 70 (March 1934), 80–81.

43. Letter of resignation, from Grace Abbott to Franklin Roosevelt, June 13, 1934, Franklin Delano Roosevelt Papers, OF15c, box 7, file "a-al, 1934," Franklin and Eleanor Roosevelt Library, Hyde Park, N.Y.

44. For a more thorough discussion of the debate about each provision, see Kriste Lindenmeyer, *"A Right to Childhood,"* 179–195.

45. Linda Gordon, *Pitied But Not Entitled: Single Mothers and the History of Welfare, 1890–1935* (New York: Free Press, 1994), 283–285.

46. Edwin E. Witte, *Development of the Social Security Act* (Madison: University of Wisconsin Press, 1962), 91; House Committee on Ways and Means, Hearings on H.R. 4120, 74th Cong., 1st sess., 650, 1140; LeRoy Ashby, *Endangered Children: Dependency, Neglect, and Abuse in American History* (New York: Twayne Publishers, 1997), 114–116.

47. Social Security Board, Bureau of Assistance, "Effect of Federal Participation in Payments for Aid to Dependent Children in 1940"; Arthur J. Altmeyer, "The Social Security Program," reprinted in Bremner, *Children and Youth,* 536–538; Ashby, *Endangered Children,* 116–117.

48. For examples of Franklin Roosevelt's endorsement of efforts to gain a federal law ending child labor, see transcripts of Roosevelt's Fireside Chats, May 7, 1933; July 24, 1933; June 18, 1934; June 30, 1934; on his claim that the FLSA

ended child labor, see June 24, 1938, all included in New Deal Network, http://www.fdrlibrary.marist.edu/, accessed May 22, 2004.

49. Trattner, *Crusade for the Children,* 197–210; the 1938 Fair Labor Standards Act (52 *U.S. Statutes-At-Large,* Section 13, 1060–1069) exempted "any child under sixteen employed in agriculture outside of school hours or where the child was employed by his parent or a person standing in place of his parent on a farm owned or operated by such parent or person"; reprinted in Bremner, *Children and Youth,* III, 340–343; Lindenmeyer, *"A Right to Childhood,"* 198; Bureau of Labor Statistics, "Youth and Labor," U.S. Department of Labor, http://www.dol.gov/dol/topic/youthlabor/exemptionsFLSA.htm, accessed February 15, 2005.

50. Scalander, *Failed Century,* 138–141.

Chapter 7. Modern Childhood and the New Deal Generation

1. Leuchtenburg, *Franklin D. Roosevelt and the New Deal,* 119–140; letter from H.S. to Eleanor Roosevelt, Moorhead, Minn., March 26, 1934, included in McElvaine, *Down and Out in the Great Depression,* 117; letter from E.B., Double Springs, Ala., December 27, 1934, included in Cohen, *Dear Mrs. Roosevelt,* 49.

2. Letter from Anonymous to Mr. and Mrs. Roosevelt, Chicago, February 1936, included in McElvaine, *Down and Out in the Great Depression,* 117.

3. Letter from N.K. to President Roosevelt, Cleveland, Ohio, November 7, 1934; letter from H.S. to Eleanor Roosevelt, Moorhead, Minn., March 26, 1934, both included in McElvaine, *Down and Out in the Great Depression,* 117–119; Cohen, *Dear Mrs. Roosevelt,* 3–41.

4. Franklin D. Roosevelt, Radio Address to the Young Democrat Clubs of America, August 24, 1935, reprinted in *Public Papers and Addresses of Franklin D. Roosevelt,* IV, 336.

5. Uys, *Riding the Rails,* 255–263.

6. Caliguri interview.

A Note on Sources

MANY OF THE SOURCES for this book are the traditional primary and secondary materials used to uncover the history of America's Great Depression. In consulting them, most historians of the 1930s have overlooked the situation of children and youth during this volatile decade. The items noted in this essay also reflect my interest and enthusiasm for the growing number of high-quality online sources.

The 1930s have an extensive and well-developed historiography. The classic overviews of the Roosevelt administration's New Deal include, along with many others, William E. Leuchtenburg, *Franklin D. Roosevelt and the New Deal* (New York: Harper and Row, 1963); Anthony J. Badger, *The New Deal: The Depression Years, 1933–1940* (Chicago: Ivan R. Dee paperback, 2002); Robert S. McElvaine, *The Great Depression: America, 1929–1941* (Pittsburgh: Three Rivers Press, 1993); and T. H. Watkins, *The Hungry Years: A Narrative History of the Great Depression in America* (New York: Henry Holt, 1999). Other works tell the story of specific New Deal programs and, with nuanced reading, offer insights about such programs and young Americans. For example, see Joseph L. Arnold, *The New Deal in the Suburbs: A History of the Greenbelt Town Program, 1935–1954* (Columbus: Ohio State University Press, 1971). Books such as Francisco E. Balderrama and Raymond Rodríguez, *Decade of Betrayal: Mexican Repatriation in the 1930s* (Albuquerque: University of New Mexico Press, 1995); Harvard Stikoff, *New Deal for Blacks: The Emergence of Civil Rights as a National Issue* (New York: Oxford University Press, 1978); and Lizabeth Cohen, *Making a New Deal: Industrial Workers in Chicago, 1919–1939* (New York: Cambridge University Press, 1990) add the perspectives of race, ethnicity, and class. None of these studies concentrates on children and youth, but together they provide a useful framework for examining the experiences of young Americans in a larger context.

Research in women's history often touches on the experiences of children. Some useful examples include Sarah Deutsch, *Women and the City: Gender, Space, and Power in Boston, 1870–1940* (New York: Oxford University Press, 2000); Estelle B. Freedman, *Maternal Justice: Miriam Van Waters and the Female Reform Tradition* (Chicago: University of Chicago Press, 1996); Linda Gordon, *Pitied But Not Entitled: Single Mothers and the History of Welfare, 1890–1935* (New York: Free Press, 1994); *Heroes of Their Own Lives: The Politics and History of Family Violence, Boston, 1880–1960* (Urbana: University of Illinois Press, 2002); and Robyn Muncy, *Creating a Female Dominion in American Reform* (New York: Oxford University Press, 1991). The same attention to children may be found in works examining family history, such as Carl N. Degler, *At Odds: Women and the Family in America from the Revolution to the Present* (New York: Oxford University Press, 1980); Tamara K. Hareven, *Themes in the History of the Family* (Worcester, Mass.: American Antiquarian Society, 1978); and Steven Mintz and Susan Kellogg, *Domestic Revolutions: A Social History of the American Family* (New York: Free Press, 1988).

Several authors have written general overviews of the history of American childhood and adolescence that include helpful information on the 1930s. For example, see Joseph M. Hawes, *Children Between the Wars: American Childhood from 1920 to 1940* (New York: Twayne Publishers, 1997); Joseph Illick, *American Childhoods* (Philadelphia: University of Pennsylvania Press, 2002), Joseph Kett, *Rites of Passage: Adolescence in America, 1790 to the Present* (New York: Basic Books, 1977); Grace Palladino, *Teenagers: An American History* (New York: Basic Books, 1996); Steven Mintz, *Huck's Raft: A History of American Childhood* (Cambridge, Mass.: Belknap Press of Harvard University Press, 2004); Elliott West and Paula Petrik, eds., *Small Worlds: Children and Adolescents in America, 1850–1950* (Lawrence: University of Kansas Press, 1992); and Viviana Zelizer, *Pricing the Priceless Child: The Changing Social Value of Children* (Princeton: Princeton University Press, 1994).

Only a few writers concern themselves exclusively with America's children and youth in the 1930s. These include Leroy Ashby, "Partial Promises and Semi-Visible Youths: The Depression and World War II," in Joseph M. Hawes and N. Ray Hiner, eds., *American Childhood: A Research Guide and Historical Handbook* (Westport, Conn.: Greenwood Press, 1985), 489–531; John A. Clausen, *American Lives: Looking Back at the Children of the Great Depression* (New York: Free Press, 1993); Robert Cohen, *When*

A Note on Sources

the Old Left Was Young: Student Radicals and America's First Mass Student Protest Movement (New York: Oxford University Press, 1993); Glen Elder, Jr., *Children of the Great Depression,* 25th anniversary edition (Boulder, Colo.: Westview Press, 1999); and Richard A. Reiman, *The New Deal and American Youth: Ideas and Ideals in a Depression Decade* (Athens: University of Georgia Press, 1993). The Civilian Conservation Corps is covered in Leslie Lacy, *The Soil Soldiers: The Civilian Conservation Corps in the Great Depression* (Radnor, Pa.: Chilton, 1976), and John A. Salmond, *The Civilian Conservation Corps, 1933–1942: A New Deal Case Study* (Durham, N.C.: Duke University Press, 1967).

Books that examine the history of American social welfare generally do not concentrate on children, but exceptions include Leroy Ashby, *Endangered Children: Dependency, Neglect, and Abuse in American History* (New York: Twayne, 1997); Judith Sealander, *The Failed Century of the Child: Governing America's Young in the Twentieth Century* (New York: Cambridge University Press, 2003); and my own *A Right to Childhood: The U.S. Children's Bureau and Child Welfare, 1912–1946* (Urbana: University of Illinois Press, 1997). Documentary collections centered on children's welfare are also helpful. Volume 3 of Robert H. Bremner, et al., *Children and Youth in America: A Documentary History* (Cambridge, Mass.: Harvard University Press, 1973) remains a seminal work; Paula S. Fass and Mary Ann Mason, eds., *Childhood in America* (New York: New York University Press, 2000) is an important contribution.

In the 1930s, public acceptance of adoption rose at the same time the nation's birthrate fell to the lowest level in history to that time. Julie Berebitsky, *Like Our Very Own: Adoption and the Changing Culture of Motherhood, 1851–1950* (Lawrence: University of Kansas Press, 2000); E. Wayne Carp, *Family Matters: Secrecy and Disclosure in the History of the Adoption* (Cambridge, Mass.: Harvard University Press, 1998); and Barbara Melosh, *Strangers and Kin: The American Way of Adoption* (Cambridge, Mass.: Harvard University Press, 2002) point to significant shifts in this history for the early to mid-twentieth century. Linda Tollett Austin tells of the dangers of the growing value of children for adoption in *Babies for Sale: The Tennessee Children's Home Adoption Scandal* (Westport, Conn.: Praeger, 1993). Ellen Herman, *The Adoption History Project,* http://darkwing.uoregon.edu/~adoption/, includes a timeline, bibliography, archival documents, and other materials on the history of adoption.

Evidence left by adopted children and those who lived in institutions is rare. Patrick Joseph Ryan gained access to juvenile and family court files on dependent children in Cleveland for his unpublished Ph.D. dissertation, "Shaping Modern Youth: Shaping Policies and Growing Up Working Class in Industrial America, 1890–1945" (Case Western Reserve University, 1998). The recollections of adults about their experiences as children can also be helpful. For example, see Ira A. Greenberg, et al., *The Hebrew National Orphan Home: Memories of Orphanage Life* (Westport, Conn.: Bergin and Garvey, 2001), and Art Buchwald, *Leaving Home: A Memoir* (New York: Putnam, 1993).

School was an important part of children's lives. Joel Spring's *Educating the Consumer-Citizen: A History of the Marriage of Schools, Advertising, and Media* (Mahwah, N.J.: Lawrence Erlbaum Associates, 2003) emphasizes the importance of the depression years in making education a commodity. Paula Fass provides an excellent overview of important shifts in school-based education for minorities during the 1930s in *Outside In: Minorities and the Transformation of American Education* (New York: Oxford University Press, 1989). Franklin Odo, *No Sword to Bury: Japanese Americans in Hawaii During World War II* (Philadelphia: Temple University Press, 2004) is a good example of a book centered on the World War II generation that also describes his subjects' high school experiences. School yearbooks and other student publications, though ultimately overseen by adults, offer a glimpse into the perspectives of young people at the time. Local history societies and public libraries house such materials. James Marten's *Children in Urban America* website, http://xserver1.its.mu.edu/, is also a good source for such materials in Milwaukee, Wisconsin. The website also includes newspaper articles, photographs, and personal testimonies.

Personal narratives and autobiographies are important sources for any historian of childhood. It is not difficult to find such materials describing the lives of celebrities, but the stories of more ordinary Americans as children and adolescents are also available. A few examples of both include Russell Baker, *Growing Up* (New York: Congdon & Weed, 1982); Charles Champlin, *Back There Where the Past Was* (Syracuse: Syracuse University Press, 1989); Robert J. Hastings, *A Nickel's Worth of Skim Milk: A Boys View of the Great Depression* (Carbondale: Southern Illinois University Press, 1972); Frank F. Mathias, *The GI Generation: A Memoir* (Lexington: University of Kentucky Press, 2000); and Virginia van der Veer, *Looking for Clark Gable and Other 20th-Century Pursuits: Collected Writings* (Tuscaloosa: University of Alabama Press, 1996).

A wealth of archival papers and documents provide evidence of childhood experiences in the 1930s. Most, however, are not easily identified because they are not catalogued as childhood or adolescent materials. The papers of the U.S. Children's Bureau, housed at the National Archives and Records Administration (NARA) in College Park, Maryland, are an exception. The files contain letters from the public, including some from children and adolescents, and correspondence and memos generated by bureau staff. The CB papers are organized by topic and year, and include a few sub-categories filed by state. The agency also published annual reports and numerous topical pamphlets. The papers of the U.S. Public Health Service are a good source of information about general health trends, but most of the federal efforts to improve children's physical well-being were accomplished through the Children's Bureau.

Private organizations interested in children's issues are a good source of information. Two that complement the federal perspective are the Child Welfare League of America collection, housed at the University of Minnesota's Social Welfare History Archives, and the National Child Labor Committee Papers in the Manuscript Division at the Library of Congress. Walter I. Trattner, *Crusade for the Children: A History of the National Child Labor Committee and Child Labor Reform in America* (Chicago: Quadrangle Books, 1970) remains an excellent analysis of child labor reform. Shelley Sallee's *The Whiteness of Child Labor Reform in the New South* (Athens: University of Georgia Press, 2004) is newer scholarship that incorporates issues of race, class, gender, and region into an analysis of this important issue.

The papers of New Deal agencies that dealt with topics concerning young Americans are housed at the NARA. These include the Civilian Conservation Corps (CCC), the Farm Security Administration (FSA), the National Youth Administration (NYA), the Works Progress Administration (WPA), and the Resettlement Administration. The NARA also houses the papers of the Committee on Economic Security, which wrote the 1935 Social Security Act. In addition, the Social Security Administration Archive in Baltimore, Maryland, has some of these materials and other unique sources. The agency's historian and archivist, Larry DeWitt, has compiled an extensive website with analytical essays, images, and primary documents at http://www.ssa.gov/history/.

The Bureau of Indian Affairs was created long before the New Deal, but many changes took place under John Collier's directorship that affected children and youth living on reservations. This collection is maintained by the NARA. Kenneth R. Philip offers an overview of Collier's policies in *John Collier's Crusade for Indian Reform, 1920–1954* (Tucson: University of Arizona Press, 1977). Marilyn Holt's *Indian Orphanages* (Lawrence: University of Kansas Press, 2001) summarizes the history of Indian education policy.

The NARA and the Library of Congress house extensive collections of photographs and documentary films produced by New Deal agencies. Many of the Library of Congress images are available online through the Prints and Photographs Division website at http://www.loc.gov/rr/print/. In addition, the Library's online *American Memory Project* includes a number of collections important to the study of 1930s childhood. Two of the most useful image collections are the *Depression Era to World War II—Farm Security Administration/Office of War Information 1935–1945*, available at http://memory.loc.gov/ammcm/fsowhome.html, and *WPA Posters, 1936–1943*, http://memory.loc.gov/ammem/wpaposters/wpahome.html. The University of Maryland, Baltimore County has created an online database that includes more than 4,700 photographs taken by Lewis Hine for the National Child Labor Committee. The collection is keyword searchable, and most images may be viewed online at (http://aok.lib.umbc.edu/reference/catalogs.php3).

Unfortunately, letters and diaries written by children and adolescents during the 1930s are still difficult to find in America's archives—except for the thousands of letters that young Americans sent to the president and first lady. These are housed at the Franklin D. Roosevelt Presidential Library in Hyde Park, New York. Robert Cohen has skillfully edited a representative sampling of these letters in *Dear Mrs. Roosevelt: Letters from Children of the Great Depression* (Chapel Hill: University of North Carolina Press, 2002). Robert S. McElvaine's *Down and Out in the Great Depression: Letters from the Forgotten Man* (Chapel Hill: University of North Carolina Press, 1983) also contains the voices of youngsters as well as parents' concerns about their children. The FDR library's website, http://www.fdrlibrary.marist.edu/online14.html, includes transcripts of the president's famous fireside chats and several of his speeches that are keyword searchable for topics on children and youth.

Oral history is another important tool for historians of childhood, though it can also be problematic. Historians must always consider questions of accuracy and the effects of distance, experience, and time on recalled memories. The New Deal's WPA Federal Writers' Project and Folklore Project include oral histories conducted during the 1930s. These collections provide wonderful information about rural family life, but it is important to remember that the interviews were conducted with adults, not children. In addition, federal employees of varying skill levels transcribed the interviews and certainly allowed the final product to be colored by their own attitudes and experiences. Nonetheless, these documents offer a window into the lives of Americans that is not usually available. The Library of Congress has the printed transcripts from these projects and has put 2,900 of them online in a keyword searchable database at http://memory.loc.gov/ammem/wpaintro/wpahome.html. Another oral history collection, though much smaller, was put together by Studs Terkel, with audio clips available through the Chicago Historical Society's online exhibition at http://www.studsterkel.org/. These excerpts are the voices of individuals featured in Terkel's 1970 book *Hard Times: An Oral History of the Great Depression* (New York: New Press reprint, 2000). Published collections of oral history interviews, such as Marilyn Holt's *Model Ts, Pep Chapels, and a Wolf at the Door: Kansas Teenagers, 1900–1941* (Lawrence: University of Kansas Press, 1994) and Jeane Westin's *Making Do: How Women Survived the '30s* (Chicago: Follett, 1976) offer the perspectives of adolescents and youth. CCC alumni have a large presence on the Internet and have gathered some important personal narratives. CCC alumni are also a source of information about the depression years. One good source is the website at Civilian Conservation Corps Alumni, http://www.cccalumni.org/.

The U.S. Census includes much useful information about children and their families. The entire 1930 Census, including the individual schedule sheets, is now available. The Census Bureau maintains a website at http://www.census.gov/. A commercial source, Ancestry.com, http://ancestry.com, provides the Census as a searchable database. Jack Fox's free website, http://www.facster.com/, makes the statistical abstracts easier to use. The University of Virginia Library's Geostat Center database, http://fisher.lib.virginia.edu/collections/stats/histcensus/, permits the compilation of sorted information within several categories.

Numerous sources in print and online concern popular culture in 1930s America. Nostalgia drives many of the hundreds of websites featuring images and recordings. I point to a few of these sites in my chapter on popular culture. The Library of Congress maintains an extensive collection of magazines, newspapers, and films. The Special Collections Department at the University of Maryland, Baltimore County, has a good selection of comic books. William H. Young and Nancy K. Young, *The 1930s* (2002), pay special attention to children and youth culture in an entertaining and well-researched book.

The New Deal Network, http://newdeal.feri.org, features a growing collection of images and documents on the 1930s. Some of this material touches on childhood and youth. More such work needs to be done for both virtual and traditional archives. It is important to collect the letters, diaries, material culture, and personal memories of the generation that grew up during America's Great Depression. Their stories are essential to understanding the history of this decade as well as the important shifts in the nature of American childhood that occurred in these years.

Index

Abbott, Grace, 94, 232–233, 234

Abortion, 36–37, 197

Abuse of children, 42, 43, 47, 101, 235

Actors, child actors, 174–177, 179–180

ADC (Aid to Dependent Children), 235–238, 246

Adoption, 43–44

Adventure books, 182–183

African American communities: execution rate among, 86; feminine ideals, 200; Gee's Bend, 9–12, *11*, 44–45, 229; income levels, 28, 52, 78; orphanages, 43; radio portrayals, 169; schooling levels, 51, 135–139, 219–221, 225; schooling quality, 111; unemployment rates, 28, 61; work, 21, 58, 61; work-relief programs, 211, 212–213

Age- and grade-level schools, 114–115, 151–155

Agriculture. *See* Farm work; Land ownership; Rural areas

Aid to Dependent Children (ADC), 235–238, 246

Air Cadets, 195

Alabama: Carbon Hill, *20*, 35, 39, 230; Gee's Bend, 9–12, *11*, 44–45, 229; Paint Rock, 89; Scottsboro, 89–92

Alliance (Ohio), 145–146

Alvarez, Mary Smith, 133

Alvarez, Roberto, 133, 134

American Indians: health care, 38–39; incomes, 28; radio portrayals, 169;

schools, 131, 139–141; work-relief programs, 141, 211

American Legion, 119, 195

American Student Union (ASU), 106

American Youth Congress (AYC), 106–108, 217

America's Youth Problem. *See* Youth problem

Andy Hardy movie series, 177

Anti-Semitism, 170

Arcus, Sam George, 42

Arizona, transients in, 92

ASU (American Student Union), 106

Atlas, Charles, 199–200

AYC (American Youth Congress), 106–108, 217

Baker family, 23–24

Baker, Russell, 23–24, 127–129

Baletti, Arthur, 104

Baltimore (Maryland), 128–129, 135–139, 143, 193–194

Banks, mortgage debt collection, 17–18, 28, 29, 47

Barney, John Smith, 156–157

Barr family, 12–13

Bates, Ruby, 89–92

Beer and Wine Revenue Act, 98

Benson, Harriet Wirt, 182

Berkeley (California), 12

Bethune, Mary McCleod, 107, 218, 220

Birth, 33–36; government acts concerning, 25–26, 34; home birth, 33, 34–35; infant mortality rate, 34; premature, 33. *See also* Birth control; Birth rates.
Birth control, 36–37, 197
Birth rates, 14, 29
Boarding schools, 139–141
Bodies: improvement of, 198–202. *See also* Health care; Hygiene.
Bodybuilding, 199–200
Books, 180–183; comic books, 183–185, 199–200
Bootblacks, 54, 59–61, *60*
Bootlegging, 23
Boscobel (Wisconsin), *160*
Bossier City (Louisiana), 81
Boulder City (Nevada), 34–35
Boy and Girl Tramps of America (Minehan), 99–104
Boy Scouts, 194–195
Brady, Alfred, 23
Brady Gang, 23
Brain clot, 37
Brink, Carol Ryrie, 181
Brinkley, A.C., 133
Bronx (New York), 63–64
Brooklyn (New York), 19–22
Brumbaugh, Martin, 68
Buchwald, Art, 41, 42
Bundy, Sarah Elizabeth, 221–222
Burglary, 23, 85, 86

Caddie Woodlawn (Brink), 181
California: adoptions in, 43; Berkeley, 12; Fresno, 113, 114, 116–117; Lemon Grove, 130–135; Los Angeles, 28, 232; Oakland, 12, 14–15, 50, 144–145, 196–197; schools, 131–135; transients in, 92
California Child Actors Law, 179–180
Caliguri, Mary, 16, 19–22, 246
Campbell, Stuart, 24–25
Capitalism, criticism of, 118–119, 162
Capra, Frank, 208–209
Captain Midnight, 167
Carbon Hill (Alabama), *20*, 35, 39, 230

Carr, Charlotte E., 73
Cars, selling of, 16, 18
Carstens, C.C., 93–94
Cartoons, 171–172. *See also* Comic books.
Case Western Reserve University CCC study, 216
Catholic schools, 121, 139, 143
Catonsville (Maryland), 135–139, 142, 143
CBS censorship codes, 162–163
CCC (Civilian Conservation Corps), 104–106, *105*, 126–127, 210–217, 223–224, 225, 244–245; education, 124, 215, 225, 244; exclusive aspects, 211–214, 223–224; income, relief programs, 126–127, 212, 216–217, 244–245; pay, 126–127, 212, 216–217, 244–245; projects completed by, 215–216; success of, 108, 223–224, 244–245
Censorship codes, 162–163, 170–172, 179
Cerebral palsy, 33, 146
Cermak, Anton, 103
Chambers, Claude, 134
Champlin, Charles, 196
Charitable health care, 29, 37–41, 45, 221, 233–234, 236
Chavez, Cesar, 56
Chicago, 28, 41, 122–123, 191–192, 242–243
Chicanos. *See* Mexican Americans
Child actors, 174–177, 179–180
Child labor laws, 47–51, 76–77, 206, 222, 238–240; conditions mandated, 238–239; factory work, 67–68, 74–75; farm work, 47, 48, 56, 76; piecework and, 69–70; street trades, 59–61, 65; unemployment rates and, 49, 51, 52, 64, 68–69, 75, 77, 124; World War II and, 240; youth movements, 107–108
Children: ideals of, 14, 15, 75–76, 80–81, 175–178, 206, 209, 238, 240, 245–246; movie portrayals, of, *173*, 174–176; percentage of population, 14
Child's Health and Recovery Program (CHRP), 233–234
Chinese Americans, schools, 113, 120–121, 131

Chronic illness, 30–33
CHRP (Child's Health and Recovery
    Program), 233–234
Church, reduced attendance, 18
City College (Baltimore), 128–129
City life: Baltimore (Maryland), 128–129,
    135–139, 143, 193–194; Bossier City
    (Louisiana), 81; Bronx (New York),
    63–64; Brooklyn (New York), 19–22;
    Chicago, 28, 41, 122–123, 191–192,
    242–243; Cleveland (Ohio), 54–55;
    entertainment, 21–22, *186*, 188–189;
    Gary (Indiana), 153–155; Milwaukee
    (Wisconsin), 142–143; Muncie
    (Indiana), 150; New York City, 67,
    188–189, 192, 230–232; Oakland
    (California), 12, 14–15, 50, 144–145,
    196–197; Pittsburgh (Pennsylvania), *189*;
    relief expenditures in cities, 27;
    schooling levels, 51; schools, 114–115,
    128–130, *129*; starvation, 27; street
    trades, 54, 59–65, *60*, *63*; Washington,
    D.C., *186. See also* Factory work; Town
    life.
Civic works, 241; health care related to, 39.
    See also CCC; PWA; WPA.
Civil rights: NYA goals, 218–225. *See also*
    Prejudice; Racism.
Class ideals, 218, 219
Class prejudice, 144–146, 218
Cleveland (Ohio), 54–55
Cloe, Delmar, 95
Cloe, J. Newton, 95
Clothes: inability to buy, 127, 143, 145–146,
    202, 203; money-saving techniques, 202
Cochrane family, 32–33
College preparatory schools, 116–117,
    128–130
Colleges: attendance rates, 18; hardships of
    attending, 128; scholarships, 128–129;
    segregation, 135; youth movements,
    106–108. *See also* NYA.
Collier, John, 140
Collier, Slim, 46–48, 50–51
Colorado, ranching life, 24

Comic books, 183–185, 199–200
Comic strips, 183–184
Commercialization, 156–163, 167, 199–200,
    202–205
Communism, criticized, 119
Consumerism, 156–159, 162, 167, 198–205
Contagious illnesses, 39–40. *See also*
    Health care; Illness.
Contraception, 36–37, 197
Coogan, Jackie, 174–175, 179–180
Coonan, Dorothy, 96–97
Cosmetics, 201
Cotton prices, rural life affected by, 10, 58
Coughlin, Charles, 118
Country life. *See* Farm work; Ranching;
    Rural areas
Crash. *See* Stock market crash
Crime: adoption black market, 43–44;
    bootlegging, 23; increase in, 86; media
    portrayals, 86, 178–179; murder, 86;
    punishments, 86–87, 140; rape, 84,
    89–92, 103; robbery, 23, 85, 86; youth
    problem and, 84–92, 93, 97, 104, 212
Curriculums in public schools, 113,
    115–120, 139–140
Cutting, Bronson Murray, 93

D. & D. Shirt Company, 66, 72–73, 74
Dalhover, Rhuel James, 23
Dance marathons, 193
Dancing, 192–194
Darro, Frankie, 96
Dashefsky brothers, 72–73, 74
Dating, 195–198
Davis, Kingsley, 92–93
Day-care facilities, 225–226, 228. *See also*
    Nursery schools.
D.C. Comics, 184
Dead End Kids, 176
Death penalty, 86–87, 90
Deaths: drownings, 188–189, 230–231;
    executions, 86–87; freight train
    accidents, 84, 85, 94, 97; of
    grandparents, 22; infant mortality rate,
    34; murder, 86, 103; New London

Deaths (*continued*)
    school explosion, 151–153; of parents, 23–25, 42, 101, 184; poverty related to, 30–31, 39–40; suicide rates, 27
Debt: attitudes toward, 16; mortgage debt collection, 17–18, 28, 29, 47
DeMarco, Frank, 62
Deodorant, 201
Deportation, Mexican Americans, 28, 132
Dermatology, 201–202
Derring, Doris, 152
Desertion of children by fathers, 29. *See also* Foster care; Orphanages.
Diabetes, 30–32
Dick, Gilbert, 216
Diphtheria, 41
Discrimination. *See* Prejudice; Racism
Divorce, 29, 42
Dixon, Franklin W., 182
Doak, William K., 69
Domanski, John, 104
Donenfield, Harry, 184
Dows (Iowa), 145
Duncan, Frank I., 138–139
Dust Bowl, 24
Duval family, 32

Earhart, Amelia, 195
Economics: capitalism criticized, 118–119, 162; cotton prices, 10, 58; education and, 110–111; mortgage debt collection, 17–18, 28, 29, 47; relief expenditures, 27, 28; schools affected by, 18, 122–124, 154; unemployment rates, 27. *See also* Income; Jobs; Money; Relief services; Stock market crash.
EDN (Emergency Day Nurseries), 225–228
Education, 110–155; CCC camps, 124, 215, 225, 244; age- and grade-level, 114–115, 151–155; citizenship and, 117–118; economic advantages of, 110–111, 117, 124–130, 144–145, 151; ideals, 144–145, 148, 226–227, 229; importance attached to, 110, 117, 124–130, 137, 144–145, 151; levels, 18, 52–53, 81, 101, 108–109, 111,
112, 124–141, 148–151, 211, 219–221, 224–225. *See also* Colleges; High Schools; Schools.
Edwards, Clyde, 32
Edwards, Duval, 32, 81, 85
Elder, Glen, 16
Electricity, 15, 164, 206–207
Ellington, Duke, 191
Embarrassment due to poverty, 17, 29, 54. *See also* Respectability.
Emergency Banking Act, 98
Emergency Day Nurseries (EDN), 225–228
Employment rates: children, 67, 76–77; teenagers, 52, 66, 67, 76–77; teenagers and adults compared, 52. *See also* Unemployment rates.
Emporia (Kansas), 146
Entertainment, *147*, 156–205, *186*, 204–205; CCC camps, 214; autonomy of children, 187–188, 190; cities, 21–22, *186*, 188–189; dancing, 192–194; dangers of, 188–190; hobbies, 188, 195; money-saving techniques, 183–184, 185–190; recreation programs, 188–189, 230–232, *231*; rural areas, 18, 147–149, *147*, 156–158, 172, 196, 230. *See also* Popular culture; Social life; Sports; Youth organizations.
Erector sets, *13*
Executions, 86–87
Exploitation on the job, 48, 51, 52, 56–58, 62–64, 69–75, 222. *See also* Child labor laws; Strikes.
Explosion in New London school, 151–153
Extracurricular school activities, 117–118, 141–148, *147*, 195, 203–204

Factory work, 65–75, *72*, 74–75
Fair Labor Standards Act, 49, 65, 77, 238–240
Families: adoption, 43–44; birth rates, 14, 29; deaths in, 22, 23–25; divorce rates, 29; generational differences, 194–198, 202–203, 244; ideals of, 44, 187; marriage rates, 28–29; as migrant farm

workers, 57, *59*; respectability's importance to, 13–14, 17, 19, 29, 43, 44, 54, 203; splitting of, 23–24, 35–36, 79, 216; statistics, 13–14; wealthy families, 12–13, *13*. *See also* Children; Fathers; Foster care; Households; Mothers; Orphanages; Parents.

Famous Funnies, 184

Farm Security Administration, 38, 45

Farm work, 47–48, 55–58, *59*; child labor laws, 47, 48, 56, 76; conditions, 56–58; family farms, 47–48, 58, 78–79, 206–207; migrant farm workers, *38*, 55–58, *59*, 239; sharecropping, 57

Farmers: finances, 28, 98, 207. *See also* Farm work; Land ownership; Rural areas.

Farms. *See* Farm work; Farmers; Land ownership; Rural areas

Fathers: children deserted by, 25, 29, 150, 193, 234. *See also* Mothers; Parents; Splitting of families.

FCC (Federal Communications Commission) radio hearings, 162

Fechner, Robert, 212, 213

Federal Communications Commission (FCC) radio hearings, 162

Federal Emergency Relief Administration (FERA), 37, 38, 123, 155, 210, 228–229. *See also* CCC; EDN; NYA.

Federal Writers' Project: CCC experiences, 216–217; educational aims recorded by, 110; health problems recorded by, 35, 36, 37; media influence opinions recorded by, 161

Felderman, Leon, 64

FERA (Federal Emergency Relief Administration), 37, 38, 123, 155, 210, 228–229. *See also* CCC; EDN; NYA.

Fights, 89, 187

Fletcher, Edward, 136

Flood relief services, 27, 215–216

Food: CCC camps, 214; milk for children, 16, 35; money-saving techniques, 16, 17, 221; relief services, *154, 220*, 221, 229, 233. *See also* Hunger; Starvation.

Football, 147–148, *147*

Ford, Henry, 170

Foreclosure. *See* Land ownership; Mortgage debt collection

Forman, Henry James, 159

Foster care, 41–42. *See also* Orphanages.

Fox, Charles, 69

Freight train riding, 80, *80*, 83–85, 88–92, 94, 96–97, 99

French, Paul Comly, 71

Fresno (California), 113, 114, 116–117

Gaines, M.C., 184

Gakuen, 120–121

Games, 185–190

Gang crime, 86, 179

Garland, Judy, *178*

Gary (Indiana), 153–155

Gee's Bend (Alabama), 9–12, *11*, 44–45, 229

Gender prejudice: popular culture, 166, 181–183, 201–202; schools, 129, 136, 145; work-relief programs, 106, 211, 224

Girl Scouts, 194–195

Girls. *See* Women

Goodman, Benny, 191–192, 193

Government role in child welfare, 14, 25–29, 37–41, 44–45, 206, 208–209, 228–229, 241–246; adoption laws, 43–44; child labor laws, 47–51, 56, 59–61, 65, 67–68, 74–77, 206, 222, 238–240; Farm Security Administration, 38, 45; Federal Emergency Relief Administration, 37, 38, 123, 155, 210; foster care, 41–42; Office of Indian Affairs, 38–39; Resettlement Administration, 37, 44–45; school attendance laws, 47, 49, 50–51, 53, 68, 73–74, 75, 81, 239; school support, 112, 121–122, 123–124, 140, 141, 151, 153–155, 210, 215, 217–229; Sheppard-Towner Maternity and Infancy Act, 25–26; Social Security, 206; U.S. Children's Bureau, 25, 27, 51–53, 56–58, 75, 92, 194, 227, 232–236; White House Conference on Child Health and Protection, 26–27,

Government role in child welfare (*continued*)
  87, 121–122; young transients, 80–81, 87, 104–109. *See also* Health care; New Deal.
Grandparents, 22
Green, Jerome T., 132–133
Greenbelt neighborhood, 230
Grocery clerking, 54
Gundy, Glen Van, 221
Gura, Benjamin, 64
Guss, Hale A., 73
Guy, Tilda, 125–126

Hair care, 200–201
Hampton, Lionel, 193
Hardison family, 126–127
Hardy Boys books (Dixon), 182
Harrell, Agnes, 216–217
Harrell, Charlie, 216–217
Harrell, Jasper, 150–151
Hart, Fred, 69
Hastings family, 16–19, 30–31
Hastings, LaVerne, 30–31
Hastings, Robert, 16–19, 30–31, 183–184, 185
Hawes, Frances W., 93
Hays Production Code, 171–172, 179
Hays, Will, 171
Health care, 29–41; birth control, 36–37, 197; charitable, 29, 37; civic works contributing to, 39; cost hardships, 31–37, 40–41; dermatology, 201–202; government agencies, 37–41, 45, 221, 233–234, 236; home remedies, 29–30; hospitals, 31; hygiene, 119–120, 201–203, 219; immunization, 41; infant health care, 35–36; mastoid surgery, 40; mental health care, 32–33; national health insurance, 236; schools and, 39–40, 119–120. *See also* Birth; Illness; Injuries.
Helmi, Mavis, 202
Henderson, Fletcher (Skitch), 191
High schools: attendance rates, 18, 51, 81, 111, 112, 116, 124–141, 218, 224–225; college preparatory schools, 116–117, 128–130; curriculums, 115–120, 139–140; extracurricular activities, 117–118, 141–148, *147*, 195, 203–204; hardships in attending, 125–128, 142–146, 149–151, 221, 242; hierarchies within, 144–146; ideals, 144–145, 148, 198–199; tracking, 116

Historical settings of children's books, 180–181
Hobbies, 188, 195
Holt, Marilyn, 141
Home birth, 33, 34–35
Home remedies, 29–30
Homelessness, 27, 54. *See also* Mortgage debt collection; Transients.
Hoopes, Harold, 83–84
Hoover Dam, construction of, 34
Hoover, Herbert, 26–27, 28, 95, 123, 229
Hoovervilles, 27
Hopkins, Harry, 210, 226–227, 233
Hospitals, 31, 32–33
Households: jobs for children within, 21, 47, 58; modern conveniences, 15, 16–17, 18–19, 24, 47, 164, 206–208; mortgage debt collection, 17–18, 28, 29, 47. *See also* Families; Income; Money-saving techniques.
Houston, Charles, 135
Hunger, 16, 27, 92. *See also* Food; Starvation.
Hygiene, 119–120, 201–203, 219. *See also* Health care.

Ideals: childhood, 14, 15, 75–76, 80–81, 175–178, 206, 209, 238, 240, 245–246; class, 218, 219; education, 144–145, 148, 226–227, 229; families, 44, 187; feminine, 200–202; government, 207–209; popular culture portrayals, 158–159, 162–163, 166, 167, 168, 171–172, 175–178, 180–184, 198–204, 207–209; self-improvement, 198–204; sex, 198; wandering youth, 92–93, 212
Illinois: Chicago, 28, 41, 122–123, 191–192, 242–243; Marion, 16–19

Illness, 29–41; abortion-induced, 37; brain clot, 37; cerebral palsy, 33, 146; chronic, 30–33; contagious illnesses, 39–40; diabetes, 30–32; diphtheria, 41; farm work contributing to, 57; Federal Writers' Project records, 35, 36, 37; foster care due to, 42; infections, 40; malaria, 39; measles, 40; multiple children contributing to, 35–37; pellagra, 39; polio, 41; poverty related to, 29, 35, 39, 54; relief distribution and, 29; rural areas, 10–11, 30–31; whooping cough, 40. *See also* Health care; Injuries.

Immigration limits, 132

Immunization, 41

Income: African American vs. white families, 28, 52; American Indian families, 28; child labor, 49–50, 52, 54–55, 62, 64, 65, 126–127, 149–151, 239; Depression averages, 15; farmers, 28; piecework, 70; relief programs, 126–127, 212, 216–217, 234–238, 244–245. *See also* Economics; Jobs; Money; Money-saving techniques; Strikes.

Indiana: Gary, 153–155; Muncie, 150

Infections, 40

Injuries, 32–33, 57, 188–190. *See also* Deaths.

Integration: music, 192–193; schools, 113, 114, 228. *See also* Segregation.

International Labor Defense, 90

Iowa: child labor laws, 47–48; Dows, 145; school attendance rates, 50–51, 81; Waterloo, 46–48

Jack Armstrong, The All American Boy, 166

Jackson, Sally, 196

James, William, 211

Japanese Americans: education, 113, 114, 116–117, 120; radio portrayals, 169; social life, 120–121

Jews, prejudice against, 170

Jimmie Allen Club, 195

Jobs, 46–77; acting, 174–177; bootlegging, 23; child labor laws, 47–51, 56, 59–61, 65, 67–68, 74–75, 206, 222, 238–240; competition for, 48, 81; dancing, 193–194; education's importance for, 110, 117, 124–130, 144–145, 151; exploitation, 48, 51, 52, 56–58, 62–64, 69–75; factory work, 51–52, 65–75, 72; farm work, 47–48, 55–58, 78–79, 206–207, 239; gender differences, 21, 50; grocery clerking, 54; household jobs for children, 21, 47; layoffs, 46–47, 96, 216; migrant farm workers, 38, 55–58, 59, 239; mothers, 21, 227; part-time work, 27–28, 46–47; starvation rates and, 27; street trades, 54, 59–65, 60, 63, 76; vocational training, 115–116, 139–140, 215, 221, 223; wage cuts, 27–28; wealthy children, 12; women in the work force, 21, 24, 66–75, 72; WPA, 16, 19. *See also* Employment; Income; Strikes; Unemployment; Work-relief programs.

Jones, Mary Harris ("Mother"), 66–67

Junior Birdmen of America, 195

Juvenile literature, 180–183

Kamikawa, Hiroko, 113, 114, 116–117

Kansas: Emporia, 146; Paradise, 83; Patowatomi Prairie band reservation, 140

Kentucky, 208

Key, Ellen, 25

Kine, Mildred, 34–35

Kniberg, Alan, 231–232

Land ownership: mortgage debt collection, 17–18, 28, 29, 47; Resettlement Administration, 44–45

Lane, Rose Wilder, 181

Layoffs, 46–47, 96, 216, 242–243

Lee, Clarence, 78–80, 88

Lee County (South Carolina), 58

Lee, James E., 137

Legion of Decency, 163

Lemon Grove (California), 130–135

Lipsic (Ohio), 216

Literature. *See* Books; Media; Newspapers
Little House books (Wilder), 180–181
Little League Baseball, 195
Little Orphan Annie Show, 157, 165
Little Rascals, 175–176
Lobe, Jean, 170
Long, Huey, 118
Los Angeles (California), 28, 232
Louis, Joe, 168
Louisiana: Bossier City, 81; rural life, 78–79
Loyalty oaths, 119
Luedtke, Ralph, 157–158
Lunch programs, *154,* 229

McCloskey, Mark A., 189
McKee, John D., 33, 146, 203–204
McMahon, Jane, 24
Makeup, 201
Máki, Ina, 84
Malaria, 39
Malnutrition. *See* Hunger; Starvation
"March of the Mill Children, The," 67
Marion (Illinois), 16–19
Marketing: children as consumers, 156–159, 162, 198–205; movie strategies, 172; newspaper strategies, 62–63, 65, 173–174; radio strategies, 164–165
Marriage rates, 28–29
Marshall, Ralph G., 148–149
Marshall, Thurgood, 135, 137–139
Martinez, Simon, 149
Maryland: Baltimore, 128–129, 135–139, 143, 193–194; Catonsville, 135–139, 142, 143; Greenbelt neighborhood, 230
Massachusetts, Northampton, 66, 72–73, 74
Mastoid surgery, 40
Masumoto, Valerie, 121
Mattwaoshshe, Lorenzo, 140–141
Measles, 40
Media: crime portrayals, 86, 178–179; criticism of, 161–162, 170; influence of, 159–163, 204–205; sex portrayed in, 159, 161, 178, 179; stereotypes in, 169, 183;

student publications, 141–144; youth problem coverage, 87–88, 93, 95–104. *See also* Books; Movies; Newspapers; Radio.
Menstruation, 202–203
Mental health care, 32–33
Mexican Americans: deportation of, 28, 132; farm work, 56–57; prejudice against, 132; schooling levels, 225; segregation and, 130–135
Migrant farm workers, *38,* 55–58, *59,* 239
Military service, job opportunities and, 48
Milk for children, 16, 35
Milwaukee (Wisconsin), 142–143
Minehan, Thomas Patrick, 99–104
Mintz, Steven, 177
Mitchell, Jim, 244–245
Modern conveniences, 15; economies practiced, 16–17, 24; improvements made, 18–19, 47, 164, 206–208
Money: attitudes toward, 15–16. *See also* Debt; Economics; Income; Jobs; Money-saving techniques.
Money-saving techniques: clothes, 202; cosmetics, 201; dating, 195–198; entertainment, 183–184, 185–190; food, 16, 17, 221; health care, 29–30, 31–37, 40–41; modern conveniences, 16–17, 24; shared housing, 19–20
Montgomery, Olen, 89–92
Mortgage debt collection, 17–18, 28, 47; illness and, 29
Mothers, *20;* pension programs, 234–238; Sheppard-Towner Maternity and Infancy Act, 25–26, 233; work outside the home, 21, 227, 228, 234, 236–237. *See also* Birth; Families; Fathers; Parents.
Motion Picture Producers and Directors Association of America (MPPDA), 170–171
Movies, 159–163, 170–180, *173;* censorship codes, 162–163, 170–172, 179; child actors, 174–177, 179–180; educational, 202–203; government portrayed in,

207–209; influence on children, 159–161, 170, 204–205; marketing strategies, 172; popularity of, 170; transients portrayed in, 95–99
Mr. Smith Goes to Washington, 208–209
Muncie (Indiana), 150
Murder, 86, 103
Murray, Donald, 135
Murray, Gail, 180
Music, 190–194
Mystery books, 182–183

NAACP (National Association for the Advancement of Colored People), 90, 213–214
NAM (National Association of Manufacturers), 119
Nancy Drew books (Keene), 182–183
National Association for the Advancement of Colored People (NAACP), 90, 213–214
National Association of Manufacturers (NAM), 119
National Child Labor Committee, 64, 75
National Recovery Administration (NRA), 238
National Repatriation Program, 132
National Youth Administration (NYA), 106, 107, 108, 217–225, *223*
Native Americans. *See* American Indians
Nebraska, rural life, 114, 147–148, 172
Neighborhoods: child-raising role, 21–22; social life, 22, 185–190. *See also* Recreation programs.
Nevada, Boulder City, 34–35
New Deal, 13–15, 80–81, 241–246; Aid to Dependent Children, 235–238, 246; Beer and Wine Revenue Act, 98; childhood ideals and, 14, 15, 80–81, 206, 238, 240, 245–246; Children's Bureau programs, 232–236; criticism of, 242–243, 246; electrification programs, 165, 206–208; Emergency Banking Act, 98; Fair Labor Standards Act, 49, 65, 77, 238–240; health care, 37–39; movie

portrayals, 206–209; school and training programs, 112, 206, 210–229; work-relief programs, 15, 106, 210–220; World War I veteran bonus grant, 98. *See also* CCC; FERA; NYA; PWA; Relief services; WPA.
New London (Texas), 151–153
New York City, 67, 188–189, 192–193, 230–232; Bronx, 63–64; Brooklyn, 19–22; music, 192–193; recreation programs, 188–189, 230–232; strike marches, 67
New York (state): Rochester, 60–61; teen and youth study, 94–95. *See also* New York City.
Newspaper selling, 59–65, *63*; income, 62, 64, 65; job conditions, 62–64. *See also* Newspapers.
Newspapers: comics, 183–184; crime coverage, 86; immigration coverage, 132; marketing strategies, 62–63, 65, 173–174; Scottsboro case coverage, 90–91; selling, 59–65, *63*; strike coverage, 67, 69–71; student newspapers, 141–143, 148; youth problem coverage, 87–88, 93, 98, 103, 104
Newton family, 124–125
Nickel's Worth of Skim Milk, A (Hastings), 185
Noon, Fred C., 133
Norris, Charles, 89–92
North Carolina, 196
Northampton (Massachusetts), 66, 72–73, 74
NRA (National Recovery Administration), 238
Nursery schools, 124, 225–228. *See also* Day-care facilities.
NYA (National Youth Administration), 106, 107, 108, 217–225, *223*; criticism of, 221–222, 224; success of, 220–224

Oakland (California), 12, 14–15, 50, 144–145, 196–197

"Oakland Growth Study" (University of California at Berkeley), 12, 14–15

Oetting, Bob, 142–143

Office of Indian Affairs, health care, 38–39

Ohio: Alliance, 145–146; Cleveland, 54–55; Lipsic, 216; orphanages, 43; St. Clairsville, 207

Ohio State University commercial culture study, 159–160

Omata, Robert, 150

Oppenheimer, Ella, 194

Oregon, 30

Orphanages, 42–43

Our Movie-Made Children (Forman), 159

Paint Rock (Alabama), 89

Paley, William, 162

Paradise (Kansas), 83

Parents: abuse of children, 42, 47, 101, 235; childraising training for, 228; death of, 23–25, 42, 101, 184; generational difference, 194–198, 202–203, 244; importance of children's education to, 110, 117, 124–130, 137, 144–145, 151. *See also* Families; Fathers; Foster care; Mothers; Orphanages.

Park facilities, CCC construction, 215–216

Parkinson family, 206–207

Part-time work, 27–28, 46–47

Patowatomi Prairie band reservation (Kansas), 140

Patterson, Haywood, 89–92

Payne Center commercial culture study, 159–160

Pellagra, 39

Penn-Allen Shirt Company, 66, 74

Penniger, Joe, 110

Pennsylvania: child labor laws, 67–68; Pittsburgh, *189*; textile industry, 66–75

Perkins, Frances, 94–95, 228, 233

Pettway, Jennie, 10–11

Pimples, 201–202

Pinchot, Cornelia Bryce, 73–74

Pinchot, Gifford, 69

Pittsburgh (Pennsylvania), *189*

Polio, 41

Popular culture, 156–205; books, 180–185; comic books, 193–195, 199–200; commercialization, 156–163, 167, 199–200, 202–205; dancing, 192–194; generational differences, 194–198, 202–203, 244; ideals portrayed in, 158, 162–163, 166, 167, 168, 171–172, 175–178, 180–184, 207–209; influence of, 159–163, *160*; movies, 95–99, 159–163, 170–180, 202–205, 207–208; music, 190–194; radio, 157–158, 161, 162–163, 164–170, 190–192, 193; self-improvement, 198–204; studies of, 159–161. *See also* Entertainment; Media; Social life; Sports; Youth organizations.

Population, children's percentage of, 14

Posluzny, Edward, 188

Powell, Ozzie, 89–92

Pregnancy rates (teens), 197–198

Prejudice: class prejudice, 144–146, 218; gender prejudice, 106, 129, 136, 145, 166, 181–183; media portrayals, 169, 183; Mexican Americans and, 132; religious prejudice, 121, 170. *See also* Civil rights; Racism.

Premature birth, 33

Preschools, 124, 225–228

Price, Victoria, 89–92

Prince family, 42

Prince, Samuel, 42, 113

Progressive Era, childhood ideals, 75–76

Prosser, Charles, 115

Prostitution among transients, 102–103

Public Works Administration (PWA), 123–124

Punishments in schools, 114, 140

PWA (Public Works Administration), 123–124

Racism: employment, 28; government goals to reduce, 122, 219–220; immigration limits, 132; income levels, 28, 52; media portrayals, 169, 183; music venues, 193; orphanage conditions, 43;

relief programs, 107, 211, 212–214, 224–225, 237–238; schools, 52–53, 111, 113, 129–141, 219–221; street trades, 61; transients and, 79, 88–92. *See also* Civil rights; Prejudice.

Radio, 164–170; censorship issues, 162–163; children's programs, 157–158, 161, 162–163, 165–169; consumerism promoted by, 157–159, 162, 167, 204–205; music, 190–192, 193; racist stereotypes, 169

Ranching, 24

Rape, 84, 89, 103

Raushenbush, Stephen, 69–70

Rawlings, Marjorie, 181

Recreation programs, 188–189, 230–232, *231*. *See also* Entertainment; Social life; Youth organizations.

Red Cross, rural areas helped by, 11, 44

Refrigeration, 15

Relief services, 27, 28, 228–229; disasters, 27, 215–216; failures of, 242–243; farmers, 98, 207; food, *154*, *220*, 221, 229, 233; health care, 29, 37–41, 45, 221, 233–234, 236; illness and the need for, 29; increase in need for, 27, 28; racism, 107, 211, 212–213, 224–225, 237–238; refusal of, 54; strikes and, 69. *See also* CCC; EDN; FERA; NYA; PWA; Work-relief programs; WPA.

Religion-based organizations, 116, 120–121, 163, 194

Religious prejudice, 121, 170

Resettlement Administration, 37, 44–45

Respectability: importance to families, 13–14, 17, 19, 29, 43, 44, 54, 203. *See also* Embarrassment.

Rice, Janice, 197

Riis, Jacob, 75

Roach, Hal, 175

Road conditions, 22

Robbery, 23, 85, 86

Robertson, Willie, 89–92

Roman, Charles R., 199–200

Rooney, Mickey, 176–177, *178*

Roosevelt, Eleanor: education stance, 117–118, 217; public response to, 31, 54–55, 145–146, 173–174, 203, 221, 242–243, 246; student movements and, 107

Roosevelt, Franklin D., 92, 104–106, 123–124, 194–195; child labor laws, 238–240; public response to, 242–246; school programs, 226; work-relief programs, 210, 212, 213, 217, 218. *See also* New Deal.

Roosevelt, Theodore, 25, 67

Ruiz, David, 131, 133

Runaways, 47–48, 53–54, 81, 82–83, 101–102. *See also* Transients.

Rural areas: Alabama, 9–12, *11*, 44–45, 229; Colorado, 24; electrification programs, 164, 206–208; entertainment, 18, 147–149, *147*, 156–158, 169–170, 172, 188–189, 196, 230; Illinois, 16–19; illness, 10–11, 30–31; Iowa, 46–48; Kansas, 83, 140; Kentucky, 208; land ownership, 17–18, 28, 29, 44–45; Louisiana, 78–79; Nebraska, 114, *147–148*, 172; North Carolina, 196; Ohio, 207; ranching, 24; schools, 114–115, 117, 125–126, 153; social life, 18, 83; South Carolina, 58; starvation, 10–11, *11*, 24; stock market crash effects, 9–12; vacations in the country, 22. *See also* Farm work; Farmers; Land ownership.

Rural Electrification Administration, 206–208

Russian-Germans, farm work, 57

Safety. *See* Child labor laws; Health care; Illness; Injuries; Strikes

St. Clairsville (Ohio), 207

Salas, Floyd, 187

Salt Lake City (Utah), 27

Sanitary napkins, 202–203

Scearce, Rose Dudley, 208

Schmeling, Max, 168

Schmitt, Walter, 114, 172

Scholarships, 128–129

Schools, *129*; age- and grade-level, 114–115, 151–155; attendance laws, 47, 49, 50–51, 53, 68, 73–74, 75, 81, 239; attendance rates, 50–51, 77, 81, 111, 112, 124–141, 148–151, 218; boarding schools, 139–141; Catholic schools, 121, 139, 143; contagious illnesses, 39–40; curriculums, 113, 115–120, 139–140; dangers of buildings, 151–153; economic difficulties of, 18, 122–124, 154; education levels, 18, 51, 52–53, 81, 101, 108–109, 111, 112, 124–141, 148–151, 211, 219–221, 224–225; *Gakuen*, 120–121; gender prejudice, 129–130, 136, 145; government support, 112, 121–122, 123–124, 140, 141, 151, 153–155, 206, 210, 215, 217–229; health care and, 39–40, 119–120; integrated, 113, 114, 228; loyalty oaths, 119; lunch programs, *154*, 229; migrant farm worker children, 56; nursery schools, 124, 225–228; punishments, 114, 140; quality of, 111–112, 114–115, 116–117, 125–126, 227–228; racism, 52–53, 111, 113, 129–141, 219–221; vocational, 115, 139–140, 215, 221, *223*. *See also* Colleges; Education; High schools.

Schulz, Bill, 172

Scott, Lucille, 136–139

Scottsboro (Alabama), 89–92

Scottsboro Boys case, 88–92

Security, fears about, 25

Segregation: music audiences, 193; schools, 111, 113, 131–141; work-relief programs, 212–214. *See also* Integration; Racism.

Self-improvement, 198–204

Series literature, 182–183

Sex: abortion, 197; adolescent changes, 200–203; birth control, 36–37, 197; dating, 195–198; education on, 119; ideals, 198; media portrayals, 159, 161, 178, 179; pimples related to, 201; pregnancy rates, 197–198; prostitution, 102–103; transients' sex lives, 102–103

Sexual harassment, 73

Shadow, The, 167–168

Sheppard-Towner Maternity and Infancy Act, 25–26, 233

Shoe shining, 54, 59–61, *60*

Simmons, Eddie, 213

Skin care, 201–202

Skinner, Dorothy, 58

Skinner, Virginia, 58

Smith, Lusette, 127

Snow White and the Seven Dwarfs, 171–172

Social life: dating, 195–198; ethnic and religious organizations, 116, 120–121, 163, 194; extracurricular school activities, 117–118, 141–148, *147*, 195, 203–204; neighborhoods, 22, 185–190; rural areas, 18, 83; transients, 102–103. *See also* Entertainment; Popular culture; Youth organizations.

Social Security, 206, 235–238, 246; ADC, 235–238, 246; national health insurance, 236

Soup kitchens, 27, 92

South Carolina, Lee County, 58

Spargo, Jonathan, 75

Splitting of families, 23–24, 35–36, 79, 216

Sports: bodybuilding, 199–200; high school, 147–148, *147*, 203–204; neighborhood, 186, 188–189; organized, 195; radio broadcasts, 168; recreation programs, 230; self-improvement from, 198–199; swimming, *189*, 204, 230–231

Starvation: cities, 27; illness related to, 29, 35, 39; infants and pregnant women, 35; rural areas, 10–11, *11*, 24; unemployment's relationship to, 27. *See also* Food; Hunger.

Stereotypes: in the media, 169, 183. *See also* Prejudice; Racism.

Stewart, Jimmy, 208–209

Stock market crash: child labor and, 50, 68–69; relief expenditures and, 27; rural life affected by, 9–12. *See also* Economics.

Stone, Irving F., 91

Stoop labor, 57

Storck, Frances, 201

Stortz, Carl E., 195

Stratemeyer, Edward, 182–183

Street trades, 54, 59–65, *60*, *63*, 76

Strikes: child labor laws affected by, 67–68, 72–73, 74–75; legality of, 73–74; media coverage, 67, 69–71; newsies, 62–64; strikebreaking tactics, 64, 74; teachers, 123; textile workers, 66–67, 68–75. *See also* Youth movements.

Stuart family, 24–25

Sugar-beet workers, 56–58, 239

Suicide, 27, 42

Sunday, Billy, 170

Superman, 184

Sweeney, Mildred, 70

Swimming, *189*, 204, 230–231

Swing bands, 190–194

Symmonds, Robert, 98–99

Tampons, 202–203

Tann, Georgia, 43

Tarkington, Booth, 204

Teachers' strikes, 123

Teenagers. *See* Youth; Youth movements; Youth organizations; Youth problem

Temple, Shirley, 173–174, *173*

Tennessee, adoption practices, 43

Texas: New London, 151–153; Waco, 42

Textile mills, 51–52, 66–75, *72*

Thurner, Hazel, 143

Town life: Boscobel (Wisconsin), *160*; Boulder City, 34–35; Catonsville (Maryland), 135–139, 142, 143; Fresno (California), 113, 114, 116–117; Lemon Grove (California), 130–135; New London (Texas), 151–153; Oakland, 12, 14–15, 50, 144–145, 196–197; schools, 116–117; Scottsboro (Alabama), 89–92. *See also* City life; Factory work.

Toys, *13*, 187, 227

Transients, 78–109, *80*; education levels, 101, 108–109; freight train riding, 80, *80*, 83–85, 88–92, 94, 96–97, 99; girls, 82, 96–97, 98, 102–103, 106; government rejected by, 216, 245; hardships of, 79–80, 83–86, 88–92, 94, 102–104; movie portrayals, 95–99; numbers of, 93–94; pleasures of, 84, 99; prostitution among, 102–103; public views of, 85–104, 212; racism and, 79, 88–92; relief services, 104–109; runaways, 47–48, 53–54, 81, 82–83, 101–102; social life, 102–103; studies on, 92–95, 99–104; unemployment rates and, 47–48, 53–54, 80–82, 87–88, 94–95, 101, 103–104, 108. *See also* Homelessness.

Travel, road conditions, 22

Travis, Dempsey, 61

Trials: Coogan earnings, 179–180; Domanski pickpocket charge, 104; Scottsboro case, 88–92; segregation, 131, 133–139; Simmons CCC discharge, 213–214

Underwear, 202

Unemployment rates, 27, 28; African Americans, 28, 61; child labor laws and, 49, 51, 52, 64, 68–69, 75, 77, 124; health care and, 30; military service and, 48; teens and youth, 28, 53, 55, 81, 109; World War II's effect on, 108–109; youth problem, 47–48, 53–54, 80–82, 87–88, 92–95, 101, 103–104, 108, 212. *See also* Employment rates; Layoffs.

University of California at Berkeley, "Oakland Growth Study," 12, 14–15

U.S. Children's Bureau, 25, 27, 51–53, 55–58, 75, 92, 194, 227, 232–236

U.S. government. *See* Government role in child welfare

Utah, Salt Lake City, 27

Vacations in the country, 22

VandeGraaf, Adrian Sebastian, 10, 45

Violence in the media, *160*, 161–162, 178–179

Vocational training, 115, 139–140, 215, 221, *223*

Wabaunsee, James, 140
Waco (Texas), orphanages, 42
Wadsworth, Gene, 85
Wage cuts, 27–28
Wallace, George, 91
Wandall, Luther C., 212–213, 214
Washington, D.C.: entertainment, *186. See also* Government.
Waskins, Richard, 40
Water, running water in households, 16, 18–19, 24, 47
Waterloo (Iowa), 46–48
Wealthy families, 12–13, *13*
Weems, Charles, 89–92
Welles, Orson, 167–168
Wellman, William, A., 96, 176
West Virginia, 27
Whalen, Lillian, 35
Wheeler-Nicholson, Malcolm, 184
White House Conference on Child Health and Protection, 26–27, 87, 121–122
Whooping cough, 40
Wicker, Ireene, 167
Wilbur, Ray Lyman, 28
Wild Boys of the Road (Warner Brothers), 95–99, 176
Wilder, Laura Ingalls, 180–181
Williams, Aubrey, 218, 219–220
Williams, Eugene, 89–92
Williams, Joshua, 137
Williams, Margaret, 135–139
Wilson, Irvin A., 122–123
Wilson, Woodrow, 25–26
Wisconsin: Boscobel, *160*; Milwaukee, 142–143
Witt, Ann (Susie), 193–194
Women: gender prejudice, 106, 129, 136, 145, 166, 181–183, 201–202, 211, 224; ideals of, 200–202; menstruation, 202–203; on the road, 84, 86, 89, 96–97, 98, 102–103; sexual harassment, 73; sexual mores, 195–198; in the work force, 21, 24, 66–75, *72. See also* Factory work; Mothers.
Woolley, Helen, 226

Work. *See* Employment; Jobs; Unemployment; Work-relief programs; *types of work by name*
Work-relief programs, 15, 106, 210–229; gender prejudice, 106, 211, 224; racism, 211, 212–213, 224–225. *See also* CCC; NYA; PWA; WPA.
Works Progress Administration. *See* WPA
World War I veteran bonus grant, 98
World War II: child labor and, 240; unemployment rates and, 108–109
WPA (Works Progress Administration), 16, 19, *20*, 123–124, 141, 227, 230; EDN, 227–228; hot lunch program, *154*, 229; NYA, 106, 217–225; recreation programs, 230–232, *231*
Wright, Andy, 89–92
Wright, Roy, 89–92

Yearbooks, 142–144, 148
Yearling, The (Rawlings), 181
YMCA (Young Men's Christian Association), 116, 121, 195
YMHA (Young Men's Hebrew Association), 121
Young, Bill, 196
Youth: ideals about, 92–93, 212; movie portrayals of, 95–99, 177–178, *178. See also* Youth movements; Youth organizations; Youth problem.
Youth movements, 106–108
Youth organizations, 120–121, 194–195, 230; federal organizations, 230; religion-based organizations, 116, 120–121, 163, 194; YMCA, 116, 121, 195; YWCA, 116, 121, 195. *See also* CCC; NYA.
Youth problem, 78–109; crime and, 84–92, 93, 97, 104, 212; media coverage, 87–88, 93, 95–104; relief programs, 104–109; studies on, 92–95, 99–104; youth movements, 106–108
YWCA (Young Women's Christian Association), 116, 121, 195

Zimmerman, David, 137–138
Zorsch, George W., 60–61

A NOTE ON THE AUTHOR

Kriste Lindenmeyer was born in Cincinnati, Ohio, and grew up there. She worked as a department store buyer and became a wife and mother before studying at the University of Cincinnati, where she received B.A., M.A., and Ph.D. degrees in American history. She has taught at Tennessee Technological University and at Vanderbilt University, and is now associate professor of history at the University of Maryland, Baltimore County. She has concentrated on American social history with an emphasis on public policy, the history of childhood, and women and gender in the nineteenth and twentieth centuries. Her other books include *A Right to Childhood* and, as editor, *Ordinary Women, Extraordinary Lives* and *Politics of Progress*. She lives in Owings Mills, Maryland.